BIBLICAL ELDERSHIP

ABOUT THE AUTHOR:

———◆———

Alexander Strauch resides with his wife and two teenage daughters in Littleton, Colorado, and also has two married daughters in the area. Mr. Strauch is a gifted Bible teacher and an elder in a church in Littleton, Colorado, where he has served for the past twenty-seven years. Other works by Mr. Strauch include:

Study Guide to Biblical Eldership:
Twelve Lessons for Mentoring Men for Eldership

The Mentor's Guide to Biblical Eldership:
Twelve Lessons for Mentoring Men for Eldership
(co-authored with Richard Swartley)

Biblical Eldership:
Restoring the Eldership to its Rightful Place in the Church

The New Testament Deacon:
The Church's Minister of Mercy

The New Testament Deacon: Study Guide

The Hospitality Commands:
Building Loving Christian Community;
Building Bridges to Friends and Neighbors

Agape Leadership:
Lessons in Spiritual Leadership from the Life of R.C. Chapman
(co-authored with Robert Peterson)

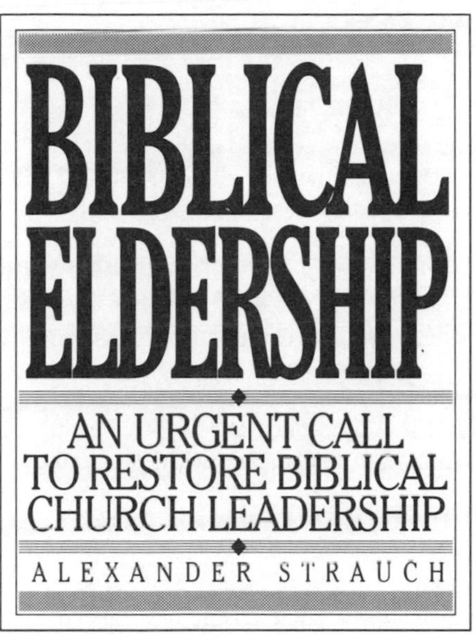

BIBLICAL ELDERSHIP

AN URGENT CALL TO RESTORE BIBLICAL CHURCH LEADERSHIP

ALEXANDER STRAUCH

REVISED AND EXPANDED

LEWIS AND ROTH PUBLISHERS
P.O. Box 569, Littleton, Colorado 80160 U.S.A.

Cover Design: Stephen T. Eames

Editors: Stephen and Amanda Sorenson

Library of Congress Cataloging-in-Publication Data

Strauch, Alexander, 1944-
Biblical eldership: an urgent call to restore biblical church leadership / Alexander Strauch. — 3rd ed.
p. cm.
Includes bibliographical references and index.
ISBN 0-936083-11-5
1. Elders (Church officers)—Biblical teaching. 2. Christian leadership—Biblical teaching. 3. Bible—Criticism, interpretation, etc. I. Title.
BS680. L4S77 1995 94-42210
262'.15—dc20 CIP

Printed in the United States of America

01 00 9

ISBN 0-936083-11-5

Table of Contents

Acknowledgments

I gratefully acknowledge the help of many dear Christian friends in writing this book. Special thanks is due to my editors, Stephen and Amanda Sorenson, and proofreaders, Barbara Peek and Maggie K. Crossett. Five special friends who have consistently encouraged me in this project through the years are Doyle Roth, Barney Visser, Craig Van Schooneveld, David J. MacLeod, and Paul B. Sapp. Above all, I thank my wife, Marilyn, whose personal sacrifice and support cannot be measured or duly praised.

Abbreviations

BOOKS OF THE BIBLE

1. Old Testament

Gen.	Genesis	2 Chron.	2 Chronicles	Dan.	Daniel
Ex.	Exodus	Ezra	Ezra	Hos.	Hosea
Lev.	Leviticus	Neh.	Nehemiah	Joel	Joel
Num.	Numbers	Est.	Esther	Amos	Amos
Deut.	Deuteronomy	Job	Job	Obad.	Obadiah
Josh.	Joshua	Ps. (Pss.)	Psalm(s)	Jonah	Jonah
Judg.	Judges	Prov.	Proverbs	Mic.	Micah
Ruth	Ruth	Eccl.	Ecclesiastes	Nah.	Nahum
1 Sam.	1 Samuel	Song	Song of Solomon	Hab.	Habakkuk
2 Sam.	2 Samuel	Isa.	Isaiah	Zeph.	Zephaniah
1 Kings	1 Kings	Jer.	Jeremiah	Hag.	Haggai
2 Kings	2 Kings	Lam.	Lamentations	Zech.	Zechariah
1 Chron.	1 Chronicles	Ezek.	Ezekiel	Mal.	Malachi

2. New Testament

Matt.	Matthew	Phil.	Philippians	James	James
Mark	Mark	Col.	Colossians	1 Peter	1 Peter
Luke	Luke	1 Thess.	1 Thessalonians	2 Peter	2 Peter
John	John	2 Thess.	2 Thessalonians	1 John	1 John
Acts	Acts of the Apostles	1 Tim.	1 Timothy	2 John	2 John
Rom.	Romans	2 Tim.	2 Timothy	3 John	3 John
1 Cor.	1 Corinthians	Titus	Titus	Jude	Jude
2 Cor.	2 Corinthians	Philem.	Philemon	Rev.	The Revelation to John (Apocalypse)
Gal.	Galatians	Heb.	Hebrews		
Eph.	Ephesians				

Why This Book Is Needed

In his magisterial epistle to the Hebrews, the inspired writer concludes with the exhortation, "Obey your leaders, and submit to them; for they keep watch over your souls..." (Heb. 13:17). This book is about those who keep watch over the souls of the Lord's people, those whom both Paul and Peter commanded to pastor the flock of God (Acts 20:28; 1 Peter 5:2). This book is about the church elders.

My first encounter with church elders occurred when I was a young teenager preparing for confirmation. During confirmation classes I told the minister about my conversion to Christ, which had taken place the previous summer at a Bible camp. He was so intrigued by my youthful, exuberant testimony of Christ that he asked me to share my story with the church elders. So I met with the elders and told them about my new relationship with Jesus Christ. They sat speechless, looking totally puzzled. I was saddened by their response because I realized that they didn't understand what I was saying. That experience left me with little confidence in the elders or the church.

My next encounter with church elders, however, was altogether different. While attending college away from home, I was invited to a church that taught and practiced authentic biblical eldership. The elders of this church took seriously the New Testament commands for elders to be biblically qualified and to actively shepherd the flock of God. They provided strong leadership, loving pastoral care and discipline, sound Bible teaching, and humble, sacrificial examples of Christian living. As a result, they were highly esteemed by the church. The inspiring example of these men first awakened in me a positive interest in the subject of church eldership.

Later, while attending seminary, my growing interest in eldership was vigorously challenged. During a class on church polity, which stubbornly resisted any notion of an elder-led church, I asked the professor, "But what do you do with all the Scripture texts on elders?"

His quick response was, "Numbers of texts on elders mean nothing!"

I thought to myself, but didn't have the nerve to say publicly, *Well, what does mean something? Your nonexistent texts on clerics?* This and other similar experiences, however, served only to stir my increasing conviction that eldership was a biblically sound doctrine that most churches either ignored or misinterpreted.

Several years later I was preparing a series of sermons on the doctrine of the Church. When I came to the subject of eldership, I was shocked to discover that there was no full-length book on the subject. There were small booklets, journal articles, and chapters within books, but no thorough treatment of the subject from an expository viewpoint. This lack of exposition was hardly believable, especially when I considered the elders' primary role as leaders in the first churches and the number of Scripture texts devoted to elders. It finally ignited my desire to write on the subject of biblical eldership.

I don't believe any doctrine of Holy Scripture should be neglected or defined out of existence. Yet this is precisely what many churches have done to the doctrine of eldership. Even among churches that claim to practice eldership, the elders have been reduced to temporary church board members, which is quite contrary to the New Testament, apostolic model of pastoral eldership. Although such churches may have an eldership, it is not a biblical eldership.

Literally tens of thousands of churches worldwide practice some form of eldership because they believe it to be a biblical teaching.[1] Unfortunately, because the advocates of eldership have been so terribly delinquent in adequately articulating this doctrine, there is a great deal of confusion and unbiblical thinking surrounding the topic among most elder-led churches. There are persistent, crippling misconceptions about eldership that hinder churches from practicing authentic biblical eldership. This subject is too important to the local church to be bogged down in such confusion. Thus this book is aimed primarily at churches that practice eldership but misunderstand its true biblical character and mandate. Its purpose is to define, as accurately as possible from Scripture, what biblical eldership is.

In order to define biblical eldership, we must go back to the only God-given, authoritative source of authentic Christianity, the text of Holy Scripture. Church history amply demonstrates the disastrous consequences of drifting from the light of Scripture. Merle d' Aubigne

(1794-1872), a noted Reformation historian, states the problem with remarkable precision: "As we advance through the centuries, light and life begin to decrease in the Church. Why? Because the torch of the Scripture begins to grow dim and because the deceitful light of human authorities begins to replace it."[2]

Due to the "deceitful light of human authorities," which replaced the New Testament's teaching on eldership, the Christian doctrine of eldership was lost for nearly fourteen centuries. The doctrine was ignored until the time of the Reformation when John Calvin (1509-1564), the influential French Reformer, decried the loss of the church eldership and promoted its restoration.[3] The sixteenth-century efforts, however, were only partially successful because the Reformers could not break free from the hardened soil of long-standing, clerical traditions.[4] In the nineteenth century, George Müller, the famous orphanage director and man of faith, and other participants in the Brethren Movement in England restored the eldership to its rightful place in the church.[5] At the same time, the Restoration Movement in America made noble attempts to restore church eldership.[6] But because of insufficient systematic exposition and teaching, these efforts were short-lived and limited to a small body of churches. Thus the New Testament model of church eldership remains largely unknown to most Christians.

The burden God has placed upon my heart is twofold: first, to help clarify the biblical doctrine of eldership and second, to help church elderships function effectively. This book is intended to fulfill the first purpose, so it is primarily doctrinal and exegetical in nature. To fulfill the second purpose, I have developed additional written and audio materials that will promote effective leadership and help train future elders. It is not enough merely to have an eldership; the eldership must be actively functioning, competent, and spiritually alive.

Part One of this book (chapters 1 to 5) presents the five major features of biblical eldership: pastoral leadership, shared leadership, male leadership, qualified leadership, and servant leadership. These five principles are absolutely essential to biblical church leadership. Unfortunately, these principles are being attacked both by secular society and from within the Christian community. There are horrendous pressures on churches today to conform to the world-wide, feminist spirit and its ruthless eradication of all male-female distinctions in the church. Part of the church growth movement, in its obsession with bigness and numbers, preaches giving as much power and authority as possible to one person. Multitudes of churches are oblivious to the moral and spiritual qualifications outlined in the New Testament for church shepherds. Worldly attitudes of bigness, power, self-promotion, and success in "the ministry" are deeply ingrained in the minds of too many church leaders. This is why I have subtitled the book "An Urgent Call to Restore Biblical Church Leadership." Biblical eldership requires a biblical church leadership structure and a biblical leadership style, both of which desperately need fresh clarification and Spirit-empowered restoration.

Part Two (chapter 6) is a biblical defense of the doctrine of eldership. Part Three (chapters 7 to 13) provides fresh, in-depth exposition of all the biblical texts on church eldership. It is the heart and soul of this book, and the solid-rock foundation upon which the five major features of biblical eldership are built. I am fully convinced that if reverent, accurate exposition of God's Word will not convince Christian people of the nature and importance of biblical eldership, then nothing will. I hope that this book will not only fulfill a need for an in-depth, biblical study, but will inspire many others to search the vast treasure of God's Word. Precious truths, no doubt, still await discovery.

Part One

BIBLICAL ELDERSHIP

CHAPTER 1

Pastoral Leadership

"Therefore, I exhort the elders among you...shepherd [pastor] the flock of God."

1 Peter 5:1*a*,2*a*

While attending a music concert, I received an insightful lesson in ecclesiology. As I walked into the main foyer of the church where the concert was held, I immediately noticed the pictures and names of the senior pastor and his staff. The pictures were arranged in a pyramid with the senior pastor at the top, his three associate pastors below, and the rest of the church staff completing the base of the pyramid. As I walked further into the building and down a side hall, I saw another glass encasement with the pictures and names of the church elders. I immediately thought, *What a superb illustration of how the church elders have been pushed aside to a scarcely visible position in the church!* This is quite different from the New Testament model of eldership.

When most Christians hear of church elders, they think of an official church board, lay officials, influential people within the local church, or advisers to the pastor. They think of elders as policymakers, financial officers, fund raisers, or administrators. They don't expect church elders to teach the Word or be involved pastorally in the lives of people. Victor A. Constien, a Lutheran official and author of *The Caring Elder,* explains this common view of the elders' role: "Members of a congregation's board of elders are not assistant pastors. They *assist* their pastor.... Through the senior pastor, elders establish a caring link with each person on the professional staff, whether assistant pastor; director of Christian education, evangelism.... But, even more important, elders help facilitate and strengthen the working relationship of the church staff."[1]

Such a view, however, not only lacks scriptural support but flatly contradicts the New Testament Scriptures. One doesn't need to read Greek or be professionally trained in theology to understand that the contemporary, church-board concept of eldership is irreconcilably at odds with the New Testament definition of eldership. According to the New Testament concept of eldership, elders lead the church, teach and preach the Word, protect the church from false teachers, exhort and admonish the saints in sound doctrine, visit the sick and pray, and judge doctrinal issues. In biblical terminology, elders shepherd, oversee, lead, and care for the local church. Let us now consider the New Testament model for pastoral care by shepherd elders.

SHEPHERD ELDERS

The biblical image of a shepherd caring for his flock—standing long hours ensuring its safety, leading it to fresh pasture and clear water, carrying the weak, seeking the lost, healing the wounded and sick—is precious. The whole image of the Palestinian shepherd is characterized by intimacy, tenderness, concern, skill, hard work, suffering, and love. It is, as former London Bible College professor Derek J. Tidball remarks in his book, *Skillful Shepherds*, "a subtle blend of authority and care," and "as much toughness as tenderness, as much courage as comfort."[2]

The shepherd-sheep relationship is so incredibly rich that the Bible uses it repeatedly to describe God and His loving care for His people. In one of the most beloved of all the Psalms, David, the shepherd turned king, wrote: "The Lord is my shepherd, I shall not want. He makes me lie down in green pastures: He leads me beside quiet waters" (Ps. 23:1,2). The Bible also uses shepherd imagery to describe the work of those who lead God's people (Ezek. 34).

Thus when Paul and Peter directly exhorted the elders to do their duty, they both employed shepherding imagery. It should be observed that these two giant apostles assign the task of shepherding the local church to no other group or single person but the elders. Paul reminds the Asian elders that God the Holy Spirit placed them in the flock as overseers for the purpose of shepherding the church of God (Acts 20:28). Peter exhorts the elders to be all that shepherds should be to the flock (1 Peter 5:2). We, then, must also view apostolic, Christianized elders to be primarily pastors of a flock, not corporate executives, CEOs, or advisers to the pastor.

If we want to understand Christian elders and their work, we must understand the biblical imagery of shepherding. As keepers of sheep, New Testament elders are to protect, feed, lead, and care for the flock's many practical needs. Using these four, broad, pastoral categories, let us consider the examples, exhortations, and teachings of the New Testament regarding shepherd elders.

PROTECTING THE FLOCK

A major part of the New Testament elders' work is to protect the local church from false teachers. As Paul was leaving Asia Minor, he summoned the elders of the church in Ephesus for a farewell exhortation. The essence of Paul's charge is this: *guard the flock—wolves are coming*:

> And from Miletus he sent to Ephesus and called to him the elders of the church…. "*Be on guard for yourselves and for all the flock*, among which the Holy Spirit has made you overseers, to shepherd the church of God which He purchased with His own blood. I know that after my departure *savage wolves will come in among you*, not sparing the flock; and from among your own selves men will arise, speaking perverse things, to draw away the disciples after them. *Therefore be on the alert….*" (Acts 20:17,28-31*a*; italics added).

According to Paul's required qualifications for eldership, a prospective elder must have enough knowledge of the Bible to be able to refute false teachers:

> For this reason I left you in Crete, that you might set in order what remains, and appoint elders in every city as I directed you, namely, if any man be above reproach...holding fast the faithful word which is in accordance with the teaching, *that he may be*

> *able...to refute those who contradict* [sound doctrine] (Titus 1:5,6,9; italics added).

The Jerusalem elders, for example, met with the apostles to judge doctrinal error: "And the apostles and the elders came together to look into this [doctrinal] matter" (Acts 15:6ff). Like the apostles, the Jerusalem elders had to be knowledgeable in the Word so that they could protect the flock from false teachers.

Protecting the flock also includes seeking lost, straying sheep—a critical aspect of shepherding that many church shepherds totally neglect. Moreover, protecting the flock involves disciplining sin, admonishing improper behavior and attitudes (1 Thess. 5:12), and stopping bitter infighting. Although the New Testament emphasizes the elders' role in protecting against doctrinal error, the elders cannot neglect seeking the lost and correcting sinful behavior.

Protecting the flock is vitally important because sheep are defenseless animals. They are utterly helpless in the face of wolves, bears, lions, jackals, or robbers. Phillip Keller, writing from his wealth of experience as a shepherd and agricultural researcher in East Africa and Canada, explains how unaware and vulnerable sheep are to danger, even inevitable death:

> It reminds me of the behavior of a band of sheep under attack from dogs, cougars, bears, or even wolves. Often in blind fear or stupid unawareness they will stand rooted to the spot watching their companions being cut to shreds. The predator will pounce upon one then another of the flock raking and tearing them with tooth and claw. Meanwhile, the other sheep may act as if they did not even hear or recognize the carnage going on around them. It is as though they were totally oblivious to the peril of their own precarious position.[3]

Guarding sheep from danger is clearly a significant aspect of the shepherding task. The same is true for church shepherds. They must continually guard the congregation from false teachers. Although the guarding ministry is a negative aspect of shepherding, it is indispensable to the flock's survival. Charles E. Jefferson (1860-1937), pastor and author of *The Minister as Shepherd*, underscores this vital point: "The journey from the cradle to the grave is hazardous....if every man is surrounded by perils, if the universe is alive with forces hostile to the soul, then watchfulness becomes one of the most critical of all the pastor's responsibilities."[4] Elders, then, are to be protectors, watchmen, defenders, and guardians of God's people. In order to accomplish this, shepherd elders need to be spiritually alert and must be men of courage.

Spiritually Alert

A good shepherd is always on the alert to danger. He knows the predator well and understands the importance of acting wisely and quickly. So too, shepherd elders must be spiritually awake and highly sensitive to the subtle dangers of Satan's attacks. It's hard, however, to be alert and ready to act at all times. That is why Paul exhorts the Asian elders "be on the alert" (Acts 20:31). He knows the natural tendency of shepherds to become spiritually lazy, undisciplined, prayerless, and weary. The Old Testament proves that. The Old Testament prophets cried out against Israel's shepherds because they failed to keep watch and be alert to protect the people from savage wolves. Israel's leaders are vividly depicted by Isaiah as blind city watchmen and dumb dogs:

> All you beasts of the field,
> All you beasts in the forest,
> Come to eat.
> His watchmen are blind,
> All of them know nothing.
> All of them are dumb dogs unable to bark,
> Dreamers lying down, who love to slumber;
> And the dogs are greedy, they are not satisfied,
> And they are shepherds who have no understanding;
> They have all turned to their own way,
> Each one to his unjust gain, to the last one.
> "Come," they say, "let us get wine, and let us drink
> heavily of strong drink;
> And tomorrow will be like today, only more so"
> (Isa. 56:9-12).

Shepherd elders must be watchful and prayerful. They must be aware of changing issues both in society and the church. They must continuously educate themselves, especially in Holy Scripture, diligently guard their own spiritual walk with the Lord, and always pray for the flock and its individual members.

Who can calculate the damage done during the past two thousand years to the churches of Jesus Christ because of inattentive, naive, and prayerless shepherds? Many churches and denominations that once stood for sound, orthodox doctrine and life now reject every major tenet of the Christian faith and condone the most deplorable moral practices conceivable. How did this happen? The local church leaders were naive, untaught, and prayerless and became inattentive to Satan's deceptive strategies. They were blind watchmen and dumb dogs, preoccupied with their own self-interests and comforts. When their seminaries jettisoned the truths of the gospel and the divine inspiration of the Bible, they were asleep. They naively invited young wolves in sheep's clothing into their flocks to be their spiritual shepherds. Hence they and their flocks have been devoured by wolves.

Courageous

Shepherds must also have courage to fight fierce predators. King David was a model shepherd of outstanding courage. First Samuel records David's experiences as a shepherd protecting his flock from the lion and the bear:

> Then Saul said to David, "You are not able to go against this Philistine to fight with him; for you are but a youth while he has been a warrior from his youth."
>
> But David said to Saul, "Your servant was tending his father's sheep. When a lion or a bear came and took a lamb from the flock,
>
> I went out after him and attacked him, and rescued it from his mouth; and when he rose up against me, I seized him by his beard and struck him and killed him.
>
> Your servant has killed both the lion and the bear; and this uncircumcised Philistine will be like one of them, since he has taunted the armies of the living God."
>
> And David said, "The Lord who delivered me from the paw of the lion and from the paw of the bear, He will deliver me from the hand of this Philistine." And Saul said to David, "Go, and may the Lord be with you" (1 Sam. 17:33-37).

“We have somehow
got hold of the idea
that error is only that
which is outrageously wrong;
and we do not seem
to understand that
the most dangerous person of all
is the one
who does not emphasize
the right things.”

(D. Martyn Lloyd-Jones, *Sermon on the Mount,* 2: 244)

Courage such as David possessed is an essential leadership quality. An internationally known statesman was once asked by reporters, "What is the most important quality for a national leader to possess?" His answer: "Courage." This is true not only for political leaders, but for church elders as well. To discipline sin in the church (especially the sin of prominent members or leaders), to confront internal strife, and to stand up to powerful teachers and theological luminaries who expound high-sounding false doctrines requires courage. Without courage to fight for the truth and the lives of God's people, the local church would be washed away by every new doctrinal storm or internal conflict.

There are many weak, immature, and unstable believers, so the elders must act as a wall of safety around the people, protecting them from the fearsome danger of savage wolves and other destructive influences. The hireling, on the other hand, " 'beholds the wolf coming, and leaves the sheep, and flees, and the wolf snatches them, and scatters them. He flees because he is a hireling, and is not concerned about the sheep' " (John 10:12*b*). A good shepherd elder, like the "Chief Shepherd," however, is ready to lay down his life for the local flock. He will die before he allows wolves to devour the flock.

FEEDING THE FLOCK

Throughout the New Testament, extraordinary emphasis is placed on the centrality of teaching God's Word. Jesus, the Good Shepherd, was preeminently a teacher, and He commissioned others to teach all that He had taught (Matt. 28:20). To Peter He said, " 'Feed [teach] my sheep' " (John 21:17, NIV). The apostles were teachers, and the early Christians steadfastly devoted themselves to teaching (Acts 2:42). Barnabas sought Paul to come to Antioch to help teach (Acts 11:25,26). Paul exhorted Timothy to give attention to "the public reading of Scripture, to exhortation, and teaching" (1 Tim. 4:13). In the order of gifts in 1 Corinthians 12:28, the teaching gift is listed third, after apostle and prophet. So, teaching is one of the greater gifts a congregation should desire (1 Cor. 12:31).

James Orr (1844-1913), a Scottish theologian and apologist, is best known as general editor of the enduring, multi-volume Bible encyclopedia, *The International Standard Bible Encyclopedia.* He readily observed the preeminence of teaching in the early Christian Church. He wrote, "If there is a religion in the world which exalts the office of teaching, it is safe to say that it is the religion of Jesus Christ."[5]

Unlike modern board elders, all New Testament elders were required to be "able to teach" (1 Tim. 3:2). In the list of elder qualifications in his letter to Titus, Paul states, "[the elder must hold] fast the faithful word which is in accordance with the teaching, *that he may be able both to exhort in sound doctrine* and to refute those who contradict" (Titus 1:9; italics added). In an extremely significant passage on elders, Paul speaks of some elders who labor at preaching and teaching and who thus deserve financial support from the local church:

> Let the elders who rule well be considered worthy of double honor, especially *those who work hard at preaching and teaching*. For the Scripture says, "You shall not muzzle the ox while he is threshing," and "The laborer is worthy of his wages" (1 Tim. 5:17,18; italics added).

Paul reminded the Ephesian elders that he had taught them and the church the full plan and purpose of God: "For I did not shrink from declaring to you the whole purpose of God" (Acts 20:27). Now it was time for the elders to do the same. Since elders are commanded to shepherd the flock of God (Acts 20:28; 1 Peter 5:2), part of their shepherding task is to see that the flock is fed God's Word.

The importance of feeding sheep is evidenced by the fact that sheep are nearly incapable of feeding and watering themselves properly. Without a shepherd, sheep would quickly be without pasture and water, and would soon waste away. So, as Charles Jefferson aptly reminds us, "everything depends on the proper feeding of the sheep. Unless wisely fed they become emaciated and sick, and the wealth invested in them is squandered. When Ezekiel presents a picture of the bad shepherd, the first stroke of his brush is—'he does not feed the flock.'"[6]

The Christian community is created by the Spirit's use of God's Word (1 Peter 1:23; James 1:18). The community also matures, grows, and is protected by the Word. Therefore, it is a scriptural requirement that an elder "be able both to exhort in sound doctrine and to refute those who contradict" (Titus 1:9). The elders protect, guide, lead, nourish, comfort, educate, and heal the flock by teaching and preaching the Word. Indeed, many pastoral needs of the people are met through teaching of the Word. The failure of church elders to know and teach the Bible is one of the chief reasons doctrinal error floods churches today and drowns the power and life of the church.

Commenting on the biblical requirement for elders to know the Bible and to be able to teach and defend the Word, Neil Summerton, church elder and author of *A Noble Task: Eldership and Ministry in the Local Church,* remarks:

> Hence to both Timothy and Titus, Paul is crystal clear that the indispensable quality, which incidentally distinguishes the elder from the deacon, is the ability to master Christian doctrine, to evaluate it in others, to teach it, and to debate it with those who teach falsehood (*1 Timothy* 3:2; *Titus* 1:9-16).
>
> The pastor-teacher ministry is also one of the principle means by which the elders' leadership and vision is communicated to the congregation, and the ability to communicate is one of the key requirements of effective leadership.
>
> There may well be those who are inclined to rebel against this emphasis and to argue that elders need more practical gifts in order to ensure that their administration is smooth and efficient. In answer, it may be said, first, that this mistakes the emphasis which both Old and New Testaments place on the need for the flock of God to be led by shepherds who will ensure that it is fed spiritually. For this purpose soundness of character needs to be brought together with the reception and transmission of the word of the Lord as the means of feeding, protecting and restoring individual members of the flock. This ministry does not necessarily have to be exercised from the platform and the centre of gravity of the gifts of one elder may be towards teaching while that of another may be towards pastoring. But all need a sound grasp of the Faith and the ability to teach and instruct in small groups and one-to-one in the pastoral situation.
>
> Secondly, if elders lack practical skill in such administration as is necessary in the flock, let them appoint a person or persons (perhaps as deacons if they have the high spiritual qualities also demanded for that office) to assist them. Moreover, in an eldership of any size one or more of the body may be able to discharge these tasks so long as they do not prevent them from giving priority

to the overseeing tasks. But at all costs the error of appointing those who lack either the character and spiritual qualities, or eldership gifts, or both, should be avoided.[7]

LEADING THE FLOCK

In biblical language, to shepherd a nation or any group of people means to lead or to govern (2 Sam. 5:2; Ps. 78:71,72). According to Acts 20 and 1 Peter 5, elders shepherd the church of God. So to shepherd a local church means, among other things, to lead the church. To the church in Ephesus Paul states: "Let the elders who rule [*lead, direct, manage*] well be considered worthy of double honor" (1 Tim. 5:17*a*). Elders, then, lead, direct, govern, manage, and care for the flock of God.

In Titus 1:7, Paul insists that a prospective elder be morally and spiritually above reproach because he is "God's steward." A steward is a "household manager," someone with official responsibility over the master's servants, property, and even finances. Elders are stewards of God's household, the local church.

Elders are also called "overseers," which signifies that they supervise and manage the church. Peter uses the verb form of *overseer* when he exhorts the elders: "Therefore, I exhort the elders among you...shepherd the flock of God among you, exercising oversight" (1 Peter 5:1*a*,2*a*). In this instance, Peter combines the concepts of shepherding and overseeing when he exhorts the elders to do their duty. Hence we can speak of the elders' overall function as the pastoral oversight of the local church.

Leading and managing a flock is important because, as Jefferson remarks, sheep are born followers:

> Sheep are not independent travelers. They must have a human conductor. They cannot go to predetermined places by themselves. They cannot start out in the morning in search of pasture and then come home at evening time. They have, apparently, no sense of direction. The greenest pasture may be only a few miles away, but the sheep left to themselves cannot find it. What animal is more incapable than a sheep? He realizes his impotence, for no animal is more docile. Where the shepherd leads, the sheep will

go. He knows that the shepherd is a guide and that it is safe to follow him.[8]

Sheep must be led to fresh water, new pasture, and relief from dangerous summer heat. This often means traveling rugged roads and narrow paths through dangerous ravines. The sheep must also be made to rest. At evening, they must be brought into the fold. Thus shepherds must know how and where to lead their flock. They must use land and water supplies wisely, constantly planning for future needs and anticipating problems.

Management Skill

The same leading and managing principles involved in shepherding sheep also apply to shepherding the local church. A congregation needs leadership, management, governance, guidance, counsel, and vision. Hence all elders must be, to some measure, leaders and managers.[9] The eldership must clarify direction and beliefs for the flock. It must set goals, make decisions, give direction, correct failures, affect change, and motivate people. It must evaluate, plan, and govern. Elders, then, must be problem solvers, managers of people, planners, and thinkers.

A healthy, growing flock of sheep doesn't just appear; it is the result of the shepherd's skillful management of sheep and resources. He knows sheep and is skillful in caring for them. A good shepherd elder knows people. He knows how sensitive they are. He knows their needs, troubles, weaknesses, and sins. He knows how they can hurt one another. He knows how stubborn they can be. He knows how to deal with people. He knows that they must be slowly and patiently led. He knows when to be tough and when to be gentle. He knows peoples' needs and what must be done to meet those needs. He knows how to accurately assess the health and direction of the congregation. And when he doesn't know these things, he is quick to find answers. He loves to learn better skills and methods for managing the flock.

Since shepherd elders must lead and manage a congregation of people, the New Testament requires that all elder candidates evidence management ability by the proper management of their own households: "He [the prospective elder] must be one who manages his own household well...but if a man does not know how to manage his own household, how will he take care of the church of God?" (1 Tim. 3:4,5).

The Scripture also says that "the elders who rule [manage, lead, direct] well be considered worthy of double honor" (1 Tim. 5:17). So elders who manage the church well desire to be recognized for their leadership and management ability and service.

Hard Work

Not only does leading and managing a flock demand skill and knowledge, it requires lots of hard work. Shepherding is hard and often uncomfortable work. Sheep don't take vacations from eating and drinking, nor do their predators vanish. Observe Jacob's description of his life as a shepherd: "Thus I was: by day the heat consumed me, and the frost by night, and my sleep fled from my eyes" (Gen. 31: 40). Because a good shepherd must work hard, a self-seeking shepherd is, according to the biblical writers, a bad shepherd (Ezek. 34: 2, 8). An idle, lazy shepherd is a disgrace and danger to the flock (Nah. 3:18; Zech. 11:17).

Pastoring God's flock requires a life of devoted work. That is why Paul exhorts believers to highly honor and love those who work hard at caring for the flock (1 Thess. 5:12; 1 Tim. 5:17). What J. Hudson Taylor (1832-1905), founder of the China Inland Mission, said of missionary service can also be said of shepherding a flock of God's people: "The work of a true missionary is *work* indeed, often very monotonous, apparently not very successful, and carried on through great and varied but unceasing difficulties."[10] When the church eldership is viewed as a status or board position in the church there will be plenty of volunteers, but when it is viewed as a demanding, pastoral work, few will rush to volunteer.

One reason there are so few shepherd elders or good church elderships is that, generally speaking, men are spiritually lazy. Spiritual laziness is an enormous problem in the Christian community. Spiritual laziness is a major reason why most churches never establish a biblical eldership. Men are more than willing to let someone else fulfill their spiritual responsibilities, whether it be their wives, the clergy, or church professionals.

Biblical eldership, however, cannot exist in an atmosphere of nominal Christianity. There can be no biblical eldership in a church where there is no biblical Christianity. If a biblical eldership is to function effectively, it requires men who are firmly committed to our Lord's principles of discipleship. Biblical eldership is dependent on men who seek first the kingdom of God and His righteousness (Matt. 6:33), men who have presented themselves as living sacrifices to God and slaves of the Lord Jesus Christ (Rom. 12:1,2), men who love Jesus Christ above all else and willingly sacrifice self for the sake of others, men who love as Christ loved, men who are self-disciplined and self-sacrificing, and men who have taken up the cross and are willing to suffer for Christ.

Some people say, "You can't expect laymen to raise their families, work all day, and shepherd a local church." But that is simply not true. Many people raise families, work, and give substantial hours of time to community service, clubs, athletic activities, and/or religious institutions. The cults have built up large lay movements that survive primarily because of the volunteer time of their members. We Bible-believing Christians are becoming a lazy, soft, pay-for-it-to-be-done group of Christians. It is positively amazing how much people can accomplish when they are motivated to work for something they love. I've seen people build and remodel houses in their spare time. I've also seen men discipline themselves to gain a phenomenal knowledge of the Scriptures.

The real problem, then, lies not in men's limited time and energy but in false ideas about work, Christian living, life's priorities, and—especially—Christian ministry. To the Ephesian elders Paul said, "You yourselves know that these hands ministered to my own needs and to the men who were with me. In everything I showed you that by working hard in this manner you must help the weak and remember the words of the Lord Jesus, that He Himself said, 'It is more blessed to give than to receive'" (Acts 20:34,35). How do working men shepherd the church yet maintain family life and employment? They do it by self-sacrifice, self-discipline, faith, perseverance, hard work, and the power of the Holy Spirit. R. Paul Stevens, author and instructor at Regent College, Vancouver, British Columbia, sets us on the right track when he writes:

> And for tentmakers to survive three full-time jobs (work, family and ministry), they must also adopt a sacrificial lifestyle. Tentmakers must live a pruned life and literally find leisure and rest in the rhythm of serving Christ (Matt. 11:28). They must be willing to forego a measure of career achievement and private leisure for the privilege of gaining the prize (Phil. 3:14). Many

would like to be tentmakers if they could be wealthy and live a leisurely and cultured lifestyle. But the truth is that a significant ministry in the church and the community can only come by sacrifice.[11]

Caring For Practical Needs

In addition to the familiar, broad categories of protecting, feeding, and leading the flock, elders also bear responsibility for the practical care of the flock's many diverse needs. For example, James instructs sick members of the flock to call for the elders of the church: "Is anyone among you sick? Let him call for the elders of the church, and let them pray over him, anointing him with oil in the name of the Lord" (James. 5:14). Paul exhorts the Ephesian elders to care for the weak and needy of the flock: "In everything I showed you that by working hard in this manner *you must help the weak* and remember the words of the Lord Jesus, that He Himself said, 'It is more blessed to give than to receive'" (Acts 20:35; italics added).

As shepherds of the flock, the elders must be available to meet whatever needs the sheep have. This means visiting the sick, comforting the bereaved; strengthening the weak; praying for *all* the sheep, even those who are difficult; visiting new members; providing counsel for couples who are engaged, married, or divorcing; and managing the many day-to-day details of the inner life of the congregation.

We must, however, balance what we have been saying about the elders' ministry with the parallel truth of every-member ministry. Although the elders lead and are officially responsible for the spiritual oversight of the *whole* church, they are not the total ministry of the church. They are not *the* ministers. Ministry is the work of the whole church. Ministry is not the work of one person or even one group of people.

The local church is not only a flock; it is also a body of Spirit-gifted, royal priests who minister to the Lord and His people. Thus, the care of the local body is not the sole responsibility of the elders, but of all the members. Each member of Christ's body is equipped by the Spirit to minister to the needs of others. The elders are dependent upon the gifts and skills of others (some of whom may be more gifted than any of the elders in certain areas of ministry) for the overall care of the local church. Biblical elders do not want to control a passive congregation. They desire to lead an active, alive, every-member-ministering church.

Furthermore, the deacons are the church's ministers of mercy. Like the elders, they are to attend to the people's many practical care needs (Acts 6:1-6). So the elders need to delegate to the deacons many of the practical mercy needs of the congregation. Like the apostles, the church elders must remember that although they are involved in ministering to practical care needs, their priorities must always be "prayer, and...the ministry of the word" (Acts 6:4).

Love for the Lord's People

The secret to caring for sheep is love. A good shepherd loves sheep and loves to be with them (2 Sam. 12:3). The best elders, likewise, are those who love people, love to be with them, and are fervently involved with them. Charles Jefferson admirably summarizes this quality when he writes, "This was the crowning virtue of the shepherd—his self-sacrificing love."[12]

The shepherd's love for his sheep is widely recognized by those who know sheep and shepherds. Old Testament professor John J. Davis discovered this truth while doing research on shepherds. He questioned a modern Palestinian shepherd named Mohammad Yaseen about the attitudes required of a good shepherd and reports that the shepherd "constantly mentioned the fact that the best shepherds are those who genuinely love their sheep."[13] Phillip Keller, in his delightful book on Psalm 23 (which should be required reading for every elder), also takes note of the shepherd's love: "All the care, all the work, all the alert watchfulness, all the skill, all the concern, all the self-sacrifice are born of His Love—the love of One who loves His sheep, loves His work, loves His role as a Shepherd."[14]

The loving heart of a true pastor is dramatically displayed in the life of Paul. Reminding the troublesome Corinthians of his deepest motives and feelings, Paul writes: "For out of much affliction and anguish of heart I wrote to you with many tears; not that you should be made sorrowful, but that you might know the love which I have especially for you" (2 Cor. 2:4). D. A. Carson, professor of New Testament at Trinity Evangelical Divinity School, describes Paul's life and prayers as "a passion for people." Detailing Paul's passionate love for the new Christians in Thessalonica, Carson writes:

> Here is a Christian so committed to the well-being of other Christians, especially new Christians, that he is simply burning up inside to be with them, to help them, to nurture them, to feed them, to stabilize them, to establish an adequate foundation for them. Small wonder, then, that he devotes himself to praying for them when he finds he cannot visit them personally.[15]

If you were to ask the average Christian what he or she most wants from spiritual leaders, the answer in most cases would be, "To be loved and cared for!" Nothing ministers to people's deepest needs more than genuine Christian love. There is an old saying that should be inscribed and placed on the wall of every elder's home: "Man before business, because man is your business."[16]

The elders' work is people-oriented work. If a body of elders lacks certain gifts or dynamic personalities, the elders' love for the people can compensate for such deficiencies. There is, however, no compensation for a lack of love and compassion on the part of the elders. Without love the eldership is an empty shell. Without love an elder is "a noisy gong," "a clanging cymbal," a spiritual zero (1 Cor. 13:1,2). So, like the Lord Jesus Christ, a good shepherd elder loves people.

CLARIFYING OUR TERMINOLOGY

Before ending this chapter we must return to a tough, deeply rooted problem that we raised at the beginning of the chapter—the definition of the term *elder*. Although the term *elder* is the predominate New Testament term used to describe local church leaders and is especially suited to the nature of the New Testament churches, it conveys to the overwhelming majority of Christians and non-Christians today ideas that are different from those found in the New Testament. People today think of church elders as lay, church-board members who are separate and distinct from the professional, ordained pastor (or clergyman). I refer to these elders as "board elders;" they are not true New Testament, Christian elders. They are advisers, committee men, executives, and directors.

A true biblical eldership is not a businesslike committee. It's a biblically qualified council of men that jointly pastors the local church.

So to communicate the New Testament idea of eldership, we need to reeducate ourselves as to the New Testament usage of the term *elder,* and in some cases choose a different term.

The New Testament uses a term other than *elder* to describe local church leaders. That term is *overseer*, and it comes from the Greek word *episkopos*.[17] The term *overseer* was a common designation used by Greeks for a variety of officials. In contrast to all priestly or lordly titles, nothing in the title *overseer* (or *elder*) violated the local church's family character, humble-servant nature, or priestly and holy status. The fact that the apostles and first Christians used the term *overseer* as a synonym for *elder* demonstrates flexibility in the use of leadership terminology and the desire to communicate effectively among Greek-speaking people.

The New Testament apostles, led by the Holy Spirit, were extremely careful in choosing the vocabulary they used to describe the person and work of Jesus Christ, His "new creation" the Church (Gal. 6:15), and those who provided leadership for the people of God. It is critically important for Christians today to understand that the language we use to describe our church leaders has the power to accurately reflect biblical thinking and practice or, conversely, to lead us far away from the true Church of Jesus Christ and into the false church. The term *episkopos* (*overseer*), for example, developed a meaning that was quite different from the New Testament usage. It became one of the most significant ecclesiastical titles of the hierarchical church. We know the term in English as *bishop*, meaning a church official who presides over many churches and the lower clergy. Thus the original sense of the term *episkopos,* which was synonymous with elder and indicated a local church official, was lost.

If we choose to use the term *elder*, which many Protestant churches do because it is a key biblical term for church leaders, it is necessary to explain that the term *elder* means "pastor elders," "shepherd elders," or "pastors." I use these terms interchangeably depending on the audience to which I am speaking. Throughout this book I use these descriptions in order to distinguish between "board elders," which is a misleading concept, and "shepherd elders," which is the biblical concept. In some churches the term *elder* is used in its full New Testament sense, thus no need to search for another term exists. The people in these churches know that the elders are their spiritual leaders, but this is true of very few churches.

I know some churches that sought to implement a biblical eldership but weren't able to make it work effectively until they dropped the term *elder* and called their elders "pastors." In these churches the term *elder* was so deeply entangled with temporary, committee-board connotations that the term was a hindrance to the practice of biblical eldership. Even the elders were helped by the language change. They started thinking of themselves as pastors who were responsible for the spiritual care of the flock and began to function as pastors. Despite the clerical and professional connotations of the term *pastor*, it best communicated what the church wanted to say about their elders' function and position.

Many times I use the word *shepherd* because it does not carry all the unbiblical connotations that people usually associate with the terms *pastor* or *elder*. However, even the term *shepherd*, like all the other terms, has its own problems: it is a word devoid of religious meaning for most people outside the church, and some inside as well. Some people might think you are referring to a literal shepherd and may want to know where your farm is located!

Whatever terminology you choose to describe local church leaders will have advantages and disadvantages. In the end, every local church is responsible to teach its people the meaning of the terms it uses to describe its spiritual leaders, whether it be elders, overseers, ministers, preachers, or pastors. Biblically sensitive church leaders will insist that the terminology they use represents, as accurately as possible, the original biblical terms and concepts of a New Testament eldership. False teachers have had their greatest triumphs when they redefine biblical words in a way that is contrary to the original meaning. Listen to the judicious counsel of Nigel Turner, one of the world's foremost Greek grammarians:

> The Church today is concerned about communicating with the contemporary world and especially about the need to speak in a new idiom. The language of the Church had better be the language of the NT. To proclaim the Gospel with new terminology is hazardous when much of the message and valuable overtones that are implicit in the NT might be lost forever. "Most of the distortions and dissensions that have vexed the Church," observed the late Dean of York, "where these have touched theological understanding, have arisen through the insistence of sects or

> sections of the Christian community upon words which are not found in the NT."[18]

Nowhere is this definition problem more evident than with the vocabulary Christians use to describe their church officials. Much of our church vocabulary is unscriptural and terribly misleading. Words such as *clergyman*, *layman*, *reverend*, *minister*, *priest*, *bishop*, *ordained*, and *ministerial* convey ideas contrary to what Jesus Christ and His apostles taught. Such terminology misrepresents the true nature of apostolic Christianity and makes it difficult, if not impossible, to recapture it. As a result, most of our churches are in desperate need of language reform. I hope that this book will challenge church leaders to more faithfully adhere to the true meaning of biblical terms and concepts.

CHAPTER 2

Shared Leadership

"Let the elders who rule well be considered worthy of double honor, especially those who work hard at preaching and teaching."

1 Timothy 5:17

One of the deep joys of my life has been to share with a team of dedicated pastor elders the pastoral leadership of a church. During the more than twenty years we have served together, we have experienced many problems and frustrations, but we have also experienced growth, joy, laughter, and deep friendship and love for one another. As partners in the work of shepherding God's precious, blood-bought people, we have sharpened, balanced, comforted, protected, and strengthened one another through nearly every conceivable life situation. I do not hesitate to say that the relationship with my fellow elders has been the most important tool God has used, outside of my marriage relationship, for the spiritual development of my Christian character, leadership abilities, and teaching ministry. As a result, I believe, we have been able to provide stable, long-term, pastoral care for the people of God.

Vastly more important than my experience (or that of anyone else) as a member of an eldership team, however, is what God's Word says about the leadership structure (or government) of the local church. As we will discover in this chapter, the New Testament provides conclusive evidence that the pastoral oversight of the apostolic churches was a team effort—not the sole responsibility of one person.

THE NEW TESTAMENT MODEL OF SHARED PASTORAL LEADERSHIP

Shared leadership should not be a new concept to a Bible-reading Christian. Shared leadership is rooted in the Old Testament institution of the elders of Israel and in Jesus' founding of the apostolate. It is a highly significant and often overlooked fact that our Lord did not appoint one man to lead His Church. He personally appointed and trained twelve men. *Jesus Christ gave the Church plurality of leadership.* The Twelve comprised the first leadership council of the Church and, in the most exemplary way, jointly led and taught the first Christian community. The Twelve provide a marvelous example of unity, humble brotherly love, and shared leadership structure.

Shared leadership is also evidenced by the Seven who were appointed to relieve the twelve apostles of the responsibility of dispensing funds to the church's widows (Acts 6:3-6). The Seven were the prototype of the later deacons.[1] There is no indication that one of the Seven was chief and the others were his assistants. As a body of servants, they did their work on behalf of the church in Jerusalem. Based on all the evidence we have, the deacons, like the elders, formed a collective leadership council.

The New Testament reveals that the pastoral oversight of many of the first churches was committed to a plurality of elders. This was true of the earliest Jewish Christian churches in Jerusalem, Judea, and neighboring countries, as well as many of the first Gentile churches. Note the following evidence:

- The elders of the church in Jerusalem united with the twelve apostles to deliberate over doctrinal controversy (Acts 15). Like the apostolate, the elders comprised a collective leadership body.

- James instructed the sick believer to "call for the elders [plural] of the church [singular]" (James 5:14).

- At the end of Paul's first missionary journey, he appointed a council of elders for each newly founded church: "And when they had appointed elders [plural] for them in every church [singular], having prayed with fasting, they commended them to the Lord in whom they had believed" (Acts 14:23). Note that here, as in James 5:14, the term *elder* is plural and the word *church* is singular. Thus each church had elders.

- When passing near the city of Ephesus during a hurried trip to Jerusalem, Paul summoned the "elders of the church," not the pastor, to meet for a final farewell exhortation (Acts 20:17,28). The church in Ephesus was under the pastoral care of a council of elders. First Timothy 5:17 demonstrates beyond question that a plurality of elders led and taught the church in Ephesus: "Let the elders who rule well be considered worthy of double honor, especially those who work hard at preaching and teaching."

- When Paul wrote to the Christians at Philippi, he greeted "the overseers [plural] and deacons" (Phil. 1:1).

- At both the beginning and end of Paul's ministry, he appointed (or instructed others to appoint) a plurality of elders to care for the churches he founded or established (Acts 14:23; Titus 1:5). According to the Titus 1:5 passage, Paul did not consider a church to be fully developed until it had functioning, qualified elders: "For this reason I left you in Crete, that you might set in order what remains, and appoint elders in every city as I directed you" (Titus 1:5).

- When writing to churches scattered throughout the five Roman provinces of Pontus, Galatia, Cappadocia, Asia, and Bithynia in northwestern Asia Minor (1 Peter 1:1), Peter exhorted the elders to pastor the flock (1 Peter 5:1). This indicates that Peter knew that the elder structure of government was standard practice in these churches.

In addition to explicit statements regarding a plurality of elders, other examples of shared leadership exist throughout the New Testament (Acts 13:1; 15:35; 1 Cor. 16:15,16; 1 Thess. 5:12,13; Heb. 13:7,17,24). On the local church level, the New Testament plainly witnesses to a consistent pattern of shared pastoral leadership. Therefore, leadership by a plurality of elders is a sound biblical practice.

After methodically examining every passage in the New Testament that addresses local church leadership, Bruce Stabbert, author of the book *The Team Concept: Paul's Church Leadership Patterns or Ours?*, summarizes by stating:

> It is concluded after examining all the passages which mention local church leadership on the pastoral level, that the New Testament presents a united teaching on this subject and that it is on the side of plurality. This is based on the evidence of the seven clear passages which teach the existence of plural elders in single local assemblies. These passages should be allowed to carry hermeneutical weight over the eight other plural passages which teach neither singularity or plurality. This is a case where the clear passages must be permitted to set the interpretation for the obscure. Thus, of the eighteen passages which speak of church leadership, fifteen of them are plural. Of these fifteen, seven of them most definitely speak of a single congregation. Only three passages talk about church leadership in singular terms, and in each passage the singular may be seen as fully compatible with plurality. In all these passages, there is not one passage which describes a church being governed by one pastor.[2]

Interestingly enough, Protestants don't challenge the plurality of deacons in an effort to create a singular deacon, yet many challenge the plurality of elders. It is strange that Christians have no problem accepting a plurality of deacons, but are almost irrationally frightened by a plurality of elders that is far more evident in the New Testament. Despite our fears, a plurality of leadership through a council of elders needs to be preserved just as much as a plurality of deacons.

DEFINITION AND BENEFITS OF SHARED LEADERSHIP

I am convinced that the underlying reason many Christians fear the plurality of elders is that they don't really understand the New Testament concept or its rich benefits to the local church. New Testament eldership is not, as many think, a high-status, board position that is open to any and all who desire membership. On the contrary, an eldership patterned on the New Testament model requires qualified elders who must meet specific moral and spiritual qualifications before they serve (1 Tim. 3:1-7). Such elders must be publicly examined by the church as to their qualifications (1 Tim. 3:10). They must be publicly installed into office (1 Tim. 5:22; Acts 14:23). They must be motivated and empowered by the Holy Spirit to do their work (Acts 20:28). Finally, they must be acknowledged, loved, and honored by the whole congregation. This honor given by the congregation includes the giving of financial support to elders who are uniquely gifted at preaching and teaching, which allows some elders to serve the church full or part time (1 Tim. 5:17,18). Thus a team of qualified, dedicated, Spirit-placed elders is not a passive, ineffective committee; it is an effective form of leadership structure that greatly benefits the church family.

A Council of Equals

Leadership by a council of elders is a form of government found in nearly every society of the ancient Near East. It was the fundamental government structure of the nation of Israel throughout its Old Testament history (Ex. 3:16; Ezra 10:8). For Israel, a tribal, patriarchal society, the eldership was as basic as the family. So when the New Testament records that Paul, a Jew who was thoroughly immersed in the Old Testament and Jewish culture, appointed elders for his newly founded churches (Acts 14:23), it means that he established a council of elders in each local church.

By definition, the elder structure of government is a collective form of leadership in which each elder shares equally the position, authority, and responsibility of the office. There are different names for this type of leadership structure. More formally it is called collective, corporate, or collegiate leadership. In contemporary terms it is referred to as multiple church leadership, plurality, shared leadership, or team leadership. I use these terms synonymously throughout this book. The opposite of collective leadership is unitary leadership, monarchical rule, or one-man leadership.

The Benefits of a Council of Equals

In chapter 6, we will explore biblical and theological reasons for the plurality of elders. For our purposes in this chapter we need only mention some of the practical benefits of shared leadership to the church family and its spiritual leaders.

Balancing people's weaknesses

Collective leadership can provide a church leader with critically needed recognition of and balance for his faults and deficiencies. We all have our blind spots, eccentricities, and deficiencies. We all have what C. S. Lewis (1898-1963) called "a fatal flaw." We can see these fatal flaws so clearly in others, but not in ourselves. Hence, Lewis says, real wisdom is to realize that you, too, have a fatal flaw that has hurt and frustrated others:

> And you see, looking back, how all the plans you have ever made always have shipwrecked on that fatal flaw—on "X's" incurable jealousy, or laziness, or touchiness, or muddle-headedness, or bossiness, or ill temper, or changeableness....
>
> This is the next great step in wisdom—to realize that you also are just that sort of person. You also have a fatal flaw in your character. All the hopes and plans of others have again and again shipwrecked on your character just as your hopes and plans have shipwrecked on theirs.
>
> It is no good passing this over with some vague, general admission such as "Of course, I know I have my faults." It is important to realize that there is some really fatal flaw in you: something which gives the others just that same feeling of despair which their flaws give you. And it is almost certainly something you don't know about—like what the advertisements call "halitosis" which everyone notices except the person who has it.
>
> But why, you ask, don't the others tell me? Believe me, they have tried to tell you over and over again, and you just couldn't "take it." Perhaps a good deal of what you call their "nagging" or "bad temper" or "queerness" are just their attempts to make you see the truth. And even the faults you do know you don't know fully.[3]

These fatal flaws or blind spots distort our judgment. They deceive us. They can even destroy us. This is particularly true of multitalented, charismatic leaders. Blind to their own flaws and extreme views, some talented leaders have destroyed themselves because they had no peers to confront and balance them and, in fact, wanted none.

For the single leader atop a pyramidal structure of organization the important balancing of one another's weaknesses and strengths normally does not occur. Note the strong language Robert Greenleaf, author of the book *Servant Leadership*, uses to convey his observations:

> To be a lone chief atop a pyramid is *abnormal and corrupting*. None of us are perfect by ourselves, and all of us need the help and correcting influence of close colleagues. When someone is moved atop a pyramid, that person no longer has colleagues, only subordinates. Even the frankest and bravest of subordinates do not talk with their boss in the same way that they talk with colleagues who are equals, and normal communication patterns become warped.[4]

In a team leadership structure, however, different members complement one another and balance one another's weaknesses. If one elder has a tendency to act too harshly with people, the others can temper his harshness. If some members fear confrontation with people, others can press for action. Elders who are more doctrinally oriented can sharpen those who are more outreach- or service-oriented, and the outreach- or service-minded elders can ignite the intellectually oriented members to more evangelism and service.

Erroll Hulse, editor of the magazine *Reformation Today*, expresses the matter this way: "Within an eldership extreme ideas are tempered, harsh judgments moderated and doctrinal imbalances corrected. If one elder shows prejudice toward, or personal dislike for any person, in or outside the church, the others can correct that and insist on fair play and justice. If one elder is in a fierce mood over some offender, that offender has others to whom he can appeal."[5]

I believe that traditional, single-church pastors would improve their character and ministry if they had genuine peers to whom they were regularly accountable and with whom they worked jointly. Most pastors are not multitalented leaders, nor are they well suited to singularly lead a congregation effectively. They have personality flaws and talent deficiencies that cause them and the congregation considerable vexation. When placed in a council of qualified pastors, however, a pastor's strengths make important contributions to the church and his weaknesses are covered by the strengths of others.

Lightening the work load

Shared pastoral leadership also helps to lighten a very heavy work load. If the long hours, weighty responsibilities, and problems of shepherding a congregation of people are not enough to overwhelm a person, then dealing with people's sins and listening to seemingly endless complaints and bitter conflicts can crush a person. Even the mighty Moses wilted to near death under the pressures of leading the people of Israel (Num. 11). Certainly every shepherd who has sought to do his duty according to Scripture has felt, at one time or another, like Moses.

To make matters worse, the single-pastor system of leadership is often ruthlessly cruel and unfair to pastors. Many overworked pastors are alone and isolated, with the church board and congregation serving as a multitude of ringside critics. This is one reason why there are so many "short-term" pastors in churches. Many other pastors stay in the same church but are ineffective because they suffer from severe battle fatigue. In a multiple-elder system of leadership, however, the heavy burdens of pastoral life are shared by a number of qualified, functioning, shepherd elders. As Bruce Stabbert masterfully states, "a team ministry provides pastors for each pastor, men from whom one can expect full encouragement and help."[6] Expressing the same idea in more poetic terms, King Solomon wrote, "Two are better than one because they have a good return for their labor. For if either of them falls, the one will lift up his companion. But woe to the one who falls when there is not another to lift him up. Furthermore, if two lie down together they keep warm, but how can one be warm alone? And if one can overpower him who is alone, two can resist him. A cord of three strands is not quickly torn apart" (Eccl. 4:9-12).

Finally, plurality of leadership allows each shepherd elder to function primarily according to personal giftedness rather than being forced to do everything and then being criticized for not being multigifted.

Providing accountability

English historian Lord Acton (1834-1902) said, "power tends to corrupt, and absolute power corrupts absolutely." Because of our Christian beliefs in the reality of sin, Satan, and human depravity, we should understand well why people in positions of power are easily corrupted. In fact, the better we understand the biblical doctrine of sin, the stronger our commitment to accountability will be. The collective leadership of a biblical eldership provides a formal structure for genuine accountability. Only when there is genuine accountability between equals in leadership is there any hope for breaking down the horrible abuse of pastoral authority that plagues many churches.

Shared, brotherly leadership provides needed restraint on pride, greed, and "playing God," to quote Earl D. Radmacher, chancellor of a Baptist seminary in America: "Human leaders, even Christian ones, are sinners and they only accomplish God's will imperfectly. Multiple leaders, therefore, will serve as a 'check and balance' on each other and serve as a safeguard against the very human tendency to play God over other people."[7]

It was never our Lord's will for the local church to be controlled by one individual. The concept of the pastor as the lonely, trained professional—the sacred person over the church who can never really become a part of the congregation—is utterly unscriptural. Not only is this concept unscriptural, it is psychologically and spiritually unhealthy. Radmacher goes on to contrast the deficiencies of a church leadership that is placed primarily in the hands of one pastor to the wholesomeness of leadership shared by multiple pastors:

> Laymen...are indifferent because they are so busy. They have no time to bother with church affairs. Church administration is left, therefore, largely in the hands of the pastor. This is bad for him, and it is bad also for the church. It makes it easier for the minister to build up in himself a dictatorial disposition and to nourish in his heart the love of autocratic power.
>
> It is my conviction that God has provided a hedge against these powerful temptations by the concept of multiple elders. The check and balance that is provided by men of equal authority is most wholesome and helps to bring about the desired attitude expressed by Peter to the plurality of elders: "...shepherd the flock of God among you, not under compulsion, but voluntarily, according to the will of God; and not for sordid gain, but with eagerness; nor yet as lording it over those allotted to your charge, but proving to be examples to the flock" (1 Peter 5:2,3).[8]

Shared leadership provides close accountability, genuine partnership, and peer relationships—the very things imperial pastors shrink from at all costs.

Shared leadership also provides the local church shepherd with accountability for his work. Church leaders (like all of us) can be lazy, forgetful, fearful, or too busy to fulfill their responsibilities. Thus they need colleagues in ministry to whom they are answerable for their work. Coaches know that athletes who train together push one another to greater achievement. When someone else is running alongside, a runner will push a little harder and go a little faster. The same is true in the Lord's work. That is one reason the Lord sent His disciples out in twos.

Left to ourselves, we do mainly what we want to do, not what we should do or what is best for others. This is especially true if we face tense, confrontational situations with erring members. Most people will avoid unpleasant confrontation at all costs. Thus church leaders need the loving encouragement and close accountability that team leadership provides so that they will accomplish their duties promptly and responsibly.

The Hazards of Leadership by a Council of Elders

All this is not to suggest that shared leadership is problem free. Certainly not! Team leadership in a church family can be painfully slow and terribly aggravating. D. E. Hoste (1861-1946), an extraordinarily skilled people manager who succeeded Hudson Taylor of the China Inland Mission, reminds us that "colleagueship calls for an orientation and method different from the direct rule over juniors and subordinates."[9] The orientation of shared leadership requires a great deal of patience, persevering prayer, wisdom, self-control, humility, trust, love, and genuine respect for the gifts and perspectives of others in the body of Christ. Because colleagueship is slower and more difficult than unitary leadership, most pastors prefer to work alone or with a staff under them.

Team leadership can also be an organizational sand trap of inaction if good principles of management, communication, and clear delineation of responsibilities are not implemented. Since the eldership itself is a group, just as the congregation is, it requires organization or it will flounder in disorganization, undiscipline, and aimlessness. The size of the eldership affects how the eldership will organize itself for most effective service. An eldership comprising twenty-five men or more will, by necessity, need more structure and leadership than an eldership of two men. Despite these potential problems, the long-term benefits of shared leadership to the local church and the personal satisfaction of working for the Lord with a team of godly shepherds far outweigh the difficulties and weaknesses.

First Among a Council of Equals: Leaders Among Leaders

An extremely important but terribly misunderstood aspect of biblical eldership is the principle of "first among equals." Failure to understand the concept of "first among equals" (or 1 Tim. 5:17) has caused some elderships to be tragically ineffective in their pastoral care and leadership. Although elders act jointly as a council and share equal authority and responsibility for the leadership of the church, all are not equal in their giftedness, biblical knowledge, leadership ability, experience, or dedication. Therefore, those among the elders who are particularly gifted leaders and/or teachers will naturally stand out among the other elders as leaders and teachers within the leadership body. This is what the Romans called *primus inter pares*, meaning "first among equals," or *primi inter pares*, meaning "first ones among equals."

The principle of "first among equals" is observed first in our Lord's dealings with the twelve apostles. Jesus chose twelve apostles, all of whom He empowered to preach and heal, but He singled out three for special attention—Peter, James, and John ("first ones among equals"). Among the three, as well as among the Twelve, Peter stood out as the most prominent ("first among equals"). Consider the following facts:

- Among the twelve apostles, Peter, James, John, and sometimes Andrew are "first ones among equals." On key occasions Jesus chose only Peter, James, and John to accompany Him to witness His power, glory, and agony (Luke 8:51; 9:28; Mark 14:33).

- Among the three, as well as the Twelve, Peter is unquestionably first among his equals. In all four lists of the apostles' names, Peter's name is first (Matt. 10:2-4; Mark 3:16-19; Luke 6:14-16; Acts 1:13). Matthew actually refers to Peter as "the first"

(Matt. 10:2). By calling Peter "the first," Matthew means "first among his equals." We must not, in reaction to Roman Catholicism's mistaken elevation of Peter, underestimate Peter's outstanding leadership among the Twelve. The Gospel writers don't.

- In all four Gospels, Peter is indisputably the prominent figure among the Twelve. Outside of Jesus, Peter is mentioned most often as speaking and acting. If you doubt this, look up the name Peter in a Bible concordance, then look up the names of the other apostles. You will immediately see Peter's prominence among the Twelve in the four Gospels and in Acts.

- Jesus charged Peter to "strengthen your brothers" (Luke 22:32). Jesus acknowledged Peter as first among his brothers, the natural leader and motivator. He knew that they would need Peter's leadership to help them through the dark days immediately following their Lord's departure.

- The book of Acts richly demonstrates Peter's leadership. Among the Twelve who jointly shared the leadership of the first church (Acts 2:14,42; 4:33,35; 5:12,18,25,29,42; 6:2-6; 8:14; 9:27; 15:2-29), Peter is the chief spokesman and natural leader throughout the first twelve chapters of Acts (Acts 1:15; 2:14; 3:1 ff; 4:8 ff; 5:3 ff; 5:15,29; 8:14-24; 9:32-11:18; 12:3 ff; 15:7-11; Gal. 2:7-14). Some scholars even divide the book of Acts according to its two central figures: the acts of Peter (Acts 1-12) and the acts of Paul (Acts 13-28). Many sound, evangelical Bible commentators interpret Christ's statement in Matthew 16:18 to mean that Peter is the rock and that upon him Christ would build His Church (but not exclusively upon him according to other passages such as Ephesians 2:20). They view the book of Acts as the record of that promise fulfilled (especially Acts 10:1-11:18).

- In Paul's letter to the Galatians, Paul speaks of James, Peter, and John as the acknowledged "pillars" of the church in Jerusalem (Gal. 2:9; see also Gal. 2:7,8).

As the natural leader, the chief speaker, the man of action, Peter challenged, energized, strengthened, and ignited the group. Without

Peter, the group would have been less effective. When surrounded by eleven other apostles who were his equals, Peter became stronger, more balanced, and was protected from his impetuous nature and his fears. In spite of his outstanding leadership and speaking ability, *Peter possessed no legal or official rank or title above the other eleven. They were not his subordinates. They were not his staff or team of assistants. He wasn't the apostles' "senior pastor."* Peter was simply first among his equals, and that by our Lord's own approval.

The "first among equals" leadership relationship can also be observed among the Seven who were chosen to relieve the apostles in Acts 6. Philip and Stephen stood out as prominent figures among the five other brothers (Acts 6:8-7:60; 8:4-40; 21:8). Yet, as far as the account records, the two held no special title or status above the others.

The concept of "first among equals" is further evidenced by the relationship of Paul and Barnabas on their first missionary journey. Paul and Barnabas were both apostles (Acts 13:1-3; 14:4; 15:36-39; 1 Cor. 9:1-6), yet Paul was first between the two because he was "the chief speaker" and dynamic leader (Acts 13:13; 14:12). Although Paul was plainly the more gifted of the two apostles, he held no formal ranking over Barnabas; they labored as partners in the work of the gospel. A similar relationship seems to have existed between Paul and Silas, who was also an apostle (1 Thess. 2:6).

Finally, the "first among equals" concept is evidenced by the way in which congregations are to honor their elders. Paul wrote specific instructions concerning elders to the church in Ephesus: "Let the elders who rule well be considered worthy of double honor, especially those who work hard at preaching and teaching. For the Scripture says, 'You shall not muzzle the ox while he is threshing,' and 'The laborer is worthy of his wages'" (1 Tim. 5:17,18). All elders must be able to teach the Word, but not all desire to work fully at preaching and teaching. Those who are gifted in teaching and spend the time to do so should be properly acknowledged by the local church. They should receive double honor (see chapter 9, page 211).

This doesn't mean, however, that elders who are first among their equals do all the thinking and decision-making for the group, or that they are the pastors while the others are merely elders. To call one elder "pastor" and the rest "elders" or one elder "the clergyman" and the rest "lay elders" is to act without biblical precedence. To do so will not result in a biblical eldership. It will, at least in practice, *create a separate, superior office over the eldership, just as was done in the early second century when the division between "the overseer" and "elders" occurred.*

The advantage of the principle of "first among equals" is that *it allows for functional, gift-based diversity within the eldership team without creating an official, superior office over fellow elders.* Just as the leading apostles, such as Peter and John, bore no special title or formal distinctions from the other apostles, elders who receive double honor form no official class or receive no special title. The differences among the elders are functional, not formal.

Benefits of the Principle of First Among Equals

The principle of "first among equals" allows within the elders' council a highly gifted leader(s) and/or teacher(s) to use his God-given gift to its full potential. In many cases, but not all, this will require the congregation to provide financial support so that the gifted brother can give more time to the service of the local church. When a man has to support himself through daily employment, there is little time left for serious study, outreach, or administrative duties. I'm not suggesting for a moment that self-supporting, or what are sometimes called "tentmaking elders," are not effective teachers or leaders. They most assuredly are, but they have limited time and energy to devote to the task. The church of which I am a member was started by several tentmaking elders and built up to more than two hundred people before anyone became a full-time, church-supported elder. Full- and/or part-time elders significantly enhance the effectiveness and work output of the eldership. In turn, the entire flock prospers.

According to the 1 Timothy 5:17 passage, double honor is due especially to "those who work hard at preaching and teaching." The reason for this is that God has ordained the local church to grow, be strengthened, and be protected from false doctrine through the preaching and teaching of the Word. So we must not neglect to care for those who labor in the Word. They, as Scripture says, are truly "worthy of double honor."

Furthermore, "first among equals" provides desperately needed protection from the all-too-common pitfalls of egoism, greed, personality imbalance, and unholy ambition to which highly gifted leaders and teachers may succumb. An exceptionally gifted leader or teacher can lead and teach with all his zeal and might, as the Scripture commands a leader and teacher to do (Rom. 12:7,8), and yet be held accountable to fellow leaders and teachers. The Christian leader or teacher who refuses brotherly accountability is self-deceived and is headed for self-destruction. The Christian leader who really knows his Bible and has an honest view of his sinfulness and weaknesses understands his undeniable need for the checks and balances provided by fellow colleagues. Only dictators fear accountability from godly colleagues.

Solutions to Common Pitfalls of "First Among Equals"

There are dangers in every form of government or leadership structure administered by sinful humans, and the principle of "first among equals" is no exception. There is the very real danger that the elders will relinquish their God-given responsibilities for the spiritual care of the church to one or two exceptionally gifted men. This danger will always exist because people are selfish and lazy by nature, particularly when it comes to spiritual matters, and are more than eager to pay others to do their work. But once that happens, the elders are reduced to adviser status and the "first among equals" concept becomes "first without equals." Biblical eldership then vanishes.

Another danger is that the principle of "first among equals" will be abused by a dominating, controlling leader. Such a leader may monopolize the church's key ministries, seek his own way, and force out all dissent and disagreement. Controlling leaders don't want colleagues; they want "yes men," "rubber stamps," and loyal subjects.

Such dangers can be avoided, however. Here are several suggestions:

- The local church and its leaders must be serious about the biblical requirements for elders. A "self-willed" man, "lording it over" others, does not qualify to be a church leader according to the New Testament and should be removed from office (Titus 1:7; 1 Peter 5:3). Also, nonfunctioning elders, mere figureheads, are not qualified to serve as elders and should be removed from office (1 Peter 5:2). If the local church is not solidly committed to having biblically qualified elders, it will find itself powerless to act against tyrants or idle shepherds.

- Elders need to work closely together as a united team, building trust and growing together. The elders' meetings, therefore, are an extremely important time for ministering to one another as

well as for doing business. One of the secrets to a successful eldership is regular, effective meetings that include a major portion of time devoted to laboring together in prayer (Acts 6:4). Board elders don't labor in prayer together, but spiritual shepherds cannot do otherwise. To adapt an old cliché, "elders who pray together stay together." In addition to the elders' work, times of relaxed fellowship are also necessary for building friendship, teamwork, and trust. Summerton comments: "It is important that elders (and, I would recommend, their spouses) should give time, despite the press of other things, to prayer, fellowship and relaxation together, without the impediment of any agenda. The purpose is to build the bonds of love which should be evident to the congregation and which will survive the inevitable strains which responsibility imposes in an imperfect world."[10]

- Elders need to be in the business of building up one another's lives. Older, more experienced elders need to mentor younger elders. Elders need to recommend times of sabbatical rest for weary colleagues. Elders need to set up ongoing educational programs for themselves. Elders need to take practical steps toward building an effective, spiritually minded eldership that involves all the elders who share the responsibility of shepherding God's flock.

CHAPTER 3

Male Leadership

"If the foundations are destroyed, what can the righteous do?"
Psalms 11:3

There is much about biblical eldership that offends church-going people today: the concept of elders who provide pastoral care, a plurality of pastors, and the idea of so-called "lay" or nonclerical pastor elders. Yet nothing is more objectionable in the minds of contemporary people than the biblical concept of an all-male eldership. A biblical eldership, however, must be an all-male eldership.

In the minds of most contemporary people, excluding women from church eldership is sexist, discriminatory, and one more example of male dominance. But this need not be the case. No one who truly loves people, who is sensitive to God's Word, and who is aware of the painful dehumanization that women have suffered (and still suffer) worldwide would want to discriminate against women. Women have suffered enough under cruel and irresponsible males, and they have every right to demand justice and change. Discrimination against women is a grievous sin and a dishonor to God in whose image women are created. Yet in our zeal to right the wrongs committed against women, we must not forget that God designed male-female distinctions in order for the sexes to beautifully complement each other and to exercise different functions in society. To deny those distinctions is as destructive and dishonorable as it is to discriminate against women.

We need to be perfectly clear about the biblical teaching regarding women and men as fully equal in personhood, dignity, and value, but distinct in gender roles. These differences are something to be enjoyed, explored more fully, and developed throughout life—not eradicated or hated. Pastor and author John Piper, who is one of the editors of the landmark work *Recovering Biblical Manhood and Womanhood*, clearly expresses his wonder over the marvelous, God-created differences of manhood and womanhood. He writes: "Over the years I have come to see from Scripture and from life that manhood and womanhood are the beautiful handiwork of a good and loving God. He designed our differences and they are profound. They are not mere physiological prerequisites for sexual union. They go to the root of our personhood."[1]

Yet untold numbers of women today are unaware of these marvelous differences. They have no clue what it means to be a woman as distinct from a man. In the name of justice and fairness for women, goals we all would gladly work together to accomplish, women are being deceived about their female identity and God's holy Word. Women are again being exploited, but this time it is by false, feminist philosophers who demean godly femininity and motherhood and who are anti-child, anti-family, and ultimately anti-woman.

To restrict women from the church eldership would be unjust and discriminatory if it were done arbitrarily by males for their own selfish ends, but if such restriction was part of the Creator's wise plan, then it is not discrimination—it is just and good for the welfare of the family, the local church, and the whole human race. As Christians, we would not accuse Jesus Christ of discrimination. He alone is perfect; we are imperfect. Yet Jesus Christ appointed only males to the foundational office of the Church, the apostolate. Although the feminist spirit of the age recoils at such a thought, Jesus is Founder and Lord of the Church, and we must follow His example and teaching.

The Model of Male Leadership Within the Apostolate

For the Bible-believing Christian, the primary example of male leadership is found in the person of Jesus Christ. The most obvious point is that Christ came into the world as the Son of God, not the daughter of God. His maleness was not an arbitrary matter. It was a theological necessity, absolutely essential to his person and work. Jesus was and had to be a first-born male, "holy to the Lord" (Luke 2:23). As the "last Adam" and "the second man," He was the antitype of Adam, not

Eve. Therefore, he had to be male (1 Cor. 15:45,47; Rom. 5:14). He had to be a first-born son of David and Abraham, the true son of promise—the King, not the queen, of Israel and the Lord, not the lady, of the universe. According to the creation order, Jesus could not be a woman because in the male-female relationship the male partner alone is invested with the headship-authority role (Gen. 2:20, 22,23; 1 Cor. 11:3; 1 Tim. 2:12), and Jesus Christ alone is Head of the Church and King of kings. He is the model for every male leader.

During His earthly ministry, Jesus personally trained and appointed twelve men whom He called "apostles" (Luke 6:13). Jesus' choice of male leadership was an affirmation of the creation order as presented in Genesis 2:18-25. Before choosing the Twelve, Luke informs us that Jesus spent the entire night in prayer with His Father (Luke 6:12). As the perfect Son, in complete obedience and submission to His Father's will, Jesus chose twelve males to be His apostles. Thus these men were God the Father's choice. Jesus' choice of male apostles was based on divine principles and guidance.

Despite His divinely inspired choice of a male apostolate, some critics claim that Jesus was merely accommodating to His culture. But how could anyone read the life of Christ and think that Jesus accommodated His choices of male apostles to the spirit of His age? He was hated and finally crucified because He consistently, on the basis of divine principle, violated the false rabbinic traditions. Even His fiercest enemies had to admit that Jesus spoke the truth of God, fearing and showing partiality to no one (Matt. 22:16).

Other critics contend that Jesus' work of redemption abolished all male-female role distinctions. Yet if Jesus intended to abolish all male-female role differences through His work of redemption, the choosing of the Twelve was the crucial moment in history to act and appoint women to the apostolate. As the hailed liberator of women, should Jesus not have chosen six women and six men apostles? At the very least, should He not have chosen *one* woman apostle? If Jesus is the supreme egalitarian that some would like Him to be, He surely failed women at a crucial moment. (I speak foolishly to make an obvious point. Of course Jesus never fails!) Instead, by appointing twelve male apostles, Jesus ratified the Old Testament creation order of male headship, a practice that both Paul and Peter subsequently maintained.

His appointment of a male apostolate does not deny the fact that Jesus honored the dignity of women, ministered to women, traveled with them, and encouraged their service for God and Himself in a way that was quite different from the manner of the religious leaders of His day. Despite His deep affection and close relationship with a number of women (such as Mary and Martha), the fact remains that Jesus Christ established an all-male apostolic office as the enduring foundation of His Church (Eph. 2:20; 3:5; Rev. 21:14). Even when a replacement for Judas, one of the Twelve, became necessary, only "men" (Greek, *andrōn*, Acts 1:21) were considered. One man was chosen for that position by the Lord Himself (Acts 1:24). There is no clear example of a woman apostle in the entire New Testament.

The Twelve followed the example of their Lord and Master by appointing seven men, not seven men and women, when they needed to establish an official body of servants to care for the church's widows and funds (Acts 6:1-6). Even thirty years after Christ's ascension into heaven, Peter wrote to the churches of northwestern Asia Minor and exhorted his Christian sisters to submit to their husbands in the same way the "holy women" of the Old Testament age did. He also exhorted husbands to care for their wives and reminded them that their wives were fellow heirs "of the grace of life." Thus Peter continued to follow His Lord's example and taught both role distinctions and male-female equality:

> In the same way, you wives, be submissive to your own husbands.... Let not your adornment be merely external...but let it be the hidden person of the heart, with the imperishable quality of a gentle and quiet spirit, which is precious in the sight of God. For in this way in former times the holy women also, who hoped in God, used to adorn themselves, being submissive to their own husbands. Thus Sarah obeyed Abraham, calling him lord, and you have become her children if you do what is right without being frightened by any fear (1 Peter 3:1-6).

> You husbands likewise, live with your wives in an understanding way, as with a weaker vessel, since she is a woman; and grant her honor as a fellow heir of the grace of life, so that your prayers may not be hindered (1 Peter 3:7).

Note that Peter supports his teaching on submission with the Old Testament Scriptures and his understanding of God's divine pleasure and will. Those who try to justify women elders find little help from the examples and teachings of Jesus and the Twelve.

THE MODEL OF MALE LEADERSHIP IN THE NEW TESTAMENT CHURCHES

The biblical tradition of male leadership continued throughout the New Testament era. Even a cursory examination of Scripture reveals this to be true. Nearly 70 percent of the New Testament was written by Paul, the great apostle to the Gentiles and the most dominant New Testament figure outside of Christ, or one of his intimate associates. In fact, all the Old and New Testament writers were males, as were the predominate characters in the Bible. For this reason, secular feminists find the Bible to be hopelessly patriarchal. Describing the patriarchal character of the Bible and the liberal religious feminists' frustration with it, Cullen Murphy, a writer for *The Atlantic Monthly,* writes:

> With respect to issues of gender the Bible is also, of course, highly problematic, to use a word that no feminist scholar I've spoken with can help uttering in a tone of ironic politeness.... It is an androcentric [man-centered] document in the extreme. It was written mostly if not entirely by men.... In the Hebrew Bible as a whole, only 111 of the 1,426 people who are given names are women. The proportion of women in the New Testament is about twice as great, which still leaves them a small minority.
>
> ...There is no getting around the disturbing character, for women, of much of the Bible, short of an interpretive reading...that may represent, something of a stretch—short of what one biblical scholar has called an act of "hermeneutical ventriloquism."[2]

So it comes as a mind-jolting shock, after nearly two thousand years of agreeing that Paul (and Jesus) restricted women from eldership, that many Bible-believing Christians and scholars today claim the New Testament and Paul to be egalitarian. This viewpoint is often called Biblical Feminism or Egalitarianism, meaning that men and women are fully equal and that the New Testament does not teach traditional male-female role distinctions involving headship and submission. This viewpoint, however, is supported by the Bible only by means of "hermeneutical ventriloquism." If the Bible is allowed *to speak for itself*, it teaches both the equality of the sexes and gender role distinctions.

It cannot be my purpose in this short chapter to present a full-scale discussion of male and female roles. That has been done by many others and is presented exhaustively in the massive volume, *Recovering Biblical Manhood and Womanhood: A Response to Evangelical Feminism*, edited by John Piper and Wayne Grudem. My specific purpose is to show that Scripture excludes women from the church eldership. Let us now turn to Paul's teaching on the subject, which he delivered to the New Testament churches and their leaders.

HEADSHIP AND SUBMISSION ROLES IN THE MARRIAGE RELATIONSHIP

Regarding the marriage relationship, Paul could not have stated more pointedly the divine order or hierarchy of the husband-wife relationship. In complete agreement with Peter's instruction on the wife's marital submission, Paul teaches that the husband is empowered and commanded to lead in the marriage relationship and that the wife is instructed to submit "as to the Lord." The following texts speak for themselves:

- "Wives be subject to your own husbands, as to the Lord" (Eph. 5:22).

- "But as the church is subject to Christ, so also the wives ought to be to their husbands in everything" (Eph. 5:24).

- "For the husband is the head of the wife, as Christ also is the head of the church" (Eph. 5:23).

- "Wives, be subject to your husbands, as is fitting in the Lord" (Col. 3:18).

- "But as for you, speak the things which are fitting for sound

> doctrine.... That they may encourage the young women to love their husbands, to love their children, to be sensible, pure, workers at home, kind, being subject to their own husbands, that the word of God may not be dishonored" (Titus 2:1,4,5).

Paul exhorted Christian wives to submit to their husbands. The basis for his exhortation is given most compellingly in Ephesians 5:23: "For the husband is the head of the wife." If there is any question as to what is intended by the phrase, "the head of the wife," Paul adds the analogy of Christ's headship over the Church, "as Christ also is the head of the church." The word "head" (Greek, *kephalē*) is used figuratively to mean, as is its constant use, "authority over" and "leadership," not "source" or "origin," as biblical feminists assert.[3]

Colossians 3:18 also states the principle found in Ephesians 5: "Wives, be subject to your husbands, as is fitting in the Lord." Commenting on the Ephesians 5 and Colossians 3 passages, George Knight, III, biblical commentator and New Testament professor at Knox Theological Seminary, observes: "this particular exhortation to the wife to submit to her husband is the universal teaching of the New Testament. Every passage that deals with the relationship of the wife to her husband tells her to 'submit to' him, using this same verb (*hupotassō*): Ephesians 5:22; Colossians 3:18; 1 Peter 3:1; Titus 2:4f."[4]

According to Ephesians 5, the manner in which the wife is to submit to her husband is, "as to the Lord," and in Colossians 3, "as is fitting in the Lord." This means that the wife is to submit to her husband as she would submit to the Lord Jesus Christ (cf. 1 Peter 3:6). Using the analogy of Christ and the Church, the wife is to submit to her husband "as the church is subject to Christ." Knight adds: "She should submit to her husband as she submits to the Lord. The comparative 'as to the Lord' conjures up what should and does characterize the godly submission a Christian renders to the Lord Jesus. This one qualification says it all."[5]

Paul teaches that the marriage relationship is a living picture of the relationship between Christ and the Church: "This mystery is great; but I am speaking with reference to Christ and the church" (Eph. 5:32). The husband and wife relationship thus mirrors the relationship between Christ and His Church. Christ, the Bridegroom, is the Head, and the Church, the bride, is subject to Him in everything. Likewise, the husband is the head of the marriage relationship and the wife submits herself to him in everything.[6] Thus headship-submission in the marriage relationship is not culturally conditioned. On the contrary, "it is part of the *essence of marriage*."[7]

HEADSHIP AND SUBMISSION ROLES IN THE LOCAL CHURCH

Paul loves to use the household analogy when speaking of the nature and order of the local church (1 Tim. 3:15). Just as he teaches male headship in the family, he teaches male headship in the household of God (1 Tim. 2:8-3:7). Since the family is the basic social unit and the man is the established family leader, we should not be surprised that men would be the elders or fathers of the larger, local church family. In his mammoth study, *Man and Woman in Christ*, Catholic scholar Stephen B. Clark cogently highlights this principle:

> There is a further consideration which points toward the desirability of having the men be the elders of the Christian community...the structure of leadership has to be set up in a way that supports the entire social structure of the community. If the men are supposed to be the heads of the family, they must also be the heads of the community. The community must be structured in a way that supports the pattern of the family, and the family must be structured in a way that supports the pattern of the community. It is in the family that they learn their community roles as well. Conversely, what they see in the community reinforces what they learn in the family. Thus, to adopt different principles on the community level weakens the family, and vice versa.[8]

The principle of male headship, however, does not in any way diminish the significance and necessity of active female involvement in the home or church. First-century Christian women played an indispensable role in the Lord's work, and many passages give evidence of women working diligently in the Lord's service. Some of Paul's colaborers in the gospel were women (Rom. 16:1-15; Phil. 4:2,3). Yet their active role in advancing the gospel and caring for the Lord's people was accomplished in ways that did not violate male leadership in the home and church.[9] Consider the following passages that directly provide instruction on the dual roles of male headship and female subordination in the household of God.

First Timothy 2:9-15

In the same way that every individual family is governed by certain standards of conduct, so too, the local church family is governed by certain principles of conduct and social arrangement. The letter of 1 Timothy addresses specifically the issue of proper order and behavior of men, women, and elders in the local church family. To his representative in Ephesus, Paul writes: "I am writing these things to you, hoping to come to you before long; but in case I am delayed, *I write so that you may know how one ought to conduct himself in the household of God*, which is the church of the living God, the pillar and support of the truth" (1 Tim. 3:14,15; italics added).

A major aspect of the church's social arrangement concerns the behavior of women in the congregation. In the church at Ephesus, as a result of false teaching which may have challenged the validity of traditional gender roles, Christian women were acting contrary to acceptable Christian behavior. In order to counter improper female conduct in the church, Paul restates Christian principles of women's conduct:

- Modest dress: "Likewise, I want women to adorn themselves with proper clothing, modestly and discreetly, not with braided hair and gold or pearls or costly garments; but rather by means of good works, as befits women making a claim to godliness" (1 Tim. 2:9,10).

- Submission in the church: "Let a woman quietly receive instruction with entire submissiveness. But I do not allow a woman to teach or exercise authority over a man, but to remain quiet. For it was Adam who was first created and then Eve. And it was not Adam who was deceived, but the woman being quite deceived, fell into transgression" (1 Tim. 2:11-14).

First Timothy 2:11-14 should alone settle the question of women elders. Paul prohibits women from doing two things in reference to the men of the church: (1) teaching and (2) exercising authority over them.[10] This prohibition is evident in both the positive and negative statements. The positive statement, "Let a woman...receive instruction," is qualified by the manner in which she is to learn: "quietly" and "with entire submissiveness." The woman's learning with full submissiveness must take place under the church's leadership authority, which is the male teacher elders. The negative statement, "But I do not allow a woman to teach or exercise authority over a man," directly forbids women from teaching and leading *men* in the church. Paul is not prohibiting women from teaching absolutely (Titus 2:3; Acts 18:25,26), but specifically from teaching men publicly in the household of God (cf. 1 Cor. 14:34,35). He concludes verse 12 in the same way he began verse 11, insisting on women being silent. "This silence," George Knight insightfully remarks, "is a concrete expression of the principle of submission."[11] Since 1 Timothy 5:17 states that elders lead and teach the church and since women are not to teach or lead *men*, it follows, therefore, that women cannot be elders in the church.

Paul's restriction on women teaching and leading men certainly caused heated criticism, just as it does today. So, as in nearly all other passages on male-female role differences, Paul immediately supports his instruction by reminding his readers of the original creation order. He uses the Old Testament creation account to prove his point: "For it was Adam who was first created, and then Eve. And it was not Adam who was deceived, but the woman being quite deceived, fell into transgression. But women shall be preserved through the bearing of children if they continue in faith and love and sanctity with self-restraint" (1 Tim. 2:13-15).

By stating in verse 13 that Adam was created first, Paul means that in the creation design of male and female Adam, the male, was first among equals. God uniquely designed the man, physically, emotionally, and spiritually, to be head of the relationship and the woman to complement his headship position. It is profoundly significant that God did not create Adam and Eve at the same time. Instead, woman was made after the man, from the man, for the man, brought to the man, and named by the man (Gen. 2:20-23; cf. 1 Cor. 11:8,9).

In verse 14, Paul illustrates from the Fall the necessity of maintaining the creation distinctions between man and woman. He writes, "And it was not Adam who was deceived, but the woman being quite deceived, fell into transgression." Satan shrewdly circumvented Adam—the one God equipped as first among equals to lead in the relationship—and went directly to Eve, whom he rightly perceived to be weaker in resisting his deceptions (2 Cor. 11:3; 1 Peter 3:7; 1 Tim. 4:7; 2 Tim. 3:6). Hence, a major reason that God insists on an all-male eldership is because godly males are more suited by divine design than godly females for leadership, particularly for identifying and fighting off satanic false teaching and subtle, doctrinal deceptions.

Note that immediately following his instruction prohibiting women from teaching and leading men in 1 Timothy 2:11-15, Paul describes the qualifications for those who oversee the local church (1 Tim. 3:1-7). Significantly, the qualifications assume a male subject; thus the overseer is to be "the husband of one wife" and "one who manages his own household well" (1 Tim. 3:2,4). Paul gives no suggestion of women elders in this passage on the qualifications for elders.

First Corinthians 11:2-16

First Corinthians 11:2-16 is a superb example of how Paul supports his instruction of headship and submission with weighty theological and biblical reasons rather than with cultural-social patterns or adaptation to unique circumstances. Paul begins his instruction on male-female role with an explanation of its source: "But I want you to understand that Christ is the head of every man, and the man is the head of a woman, and God is the head of Christ" (1 Cor. 11:3). Woman's submission is part of a series of subordination and headship relationships: God, Christ, man, woman. God is head, Christ is head, and man is head. Only woman is not referred to as head. These relationships have nothing to do with temporal, local circumstances, but follow a divinely constituted hierarchical order.

By stating that "God is the head of Christ," Paul emphasizes the hierarchical relationship that exists in the Godhead. Although equal in substance, Christ obeys and submits Himself to the Father within the relationship of the persons of the Godhead (1 Cor. 15:28). This submission certainly doesn't imply inferiority on the part of the Lord Jesus Christ.

Before the Fall, God created mankind in His own image as male and female, fully equal in terms of personhood. But in terms of relationship among equals, God established a hierarchy of male leadership and female submission. As is the case within the Godhead, the hierarchy of the relationship does not imply inferiority or superiority. The woman is in no way inferior to the man because she subordinates herself to him than Christ is inferior to God the Father because He subordinates Himself to the Father. So the headship-subordination relationship of the man and woman is evidenced in the original creation order and in the greater order, the nature of the Godhead.

With remarkable precision, S. Lewis Johnson, Jr., former professor at Dallas Theological Seminary, summarizes this truth: "The ultimate and telling proof that equality and submission may coexist in glorious harmony is found in the mediatorial mission of the Son of God, 'God from God, Light from Light, true God from true God' (Nicaea), who completed it in the true liberation of submission to His Father (cf. John 8:21-47; 1 Corinthians 15: 24-28; cf. 11:3)."[12]

In verses 7-9, Paul reminds his readers of the original order of creation: "For a man ought not to have his head covered, since he is the image and glory of God; but the woman is the glory of man. For man does not originate from woman, but woman from man; for indeed man was not created for the woman's sake, but woman for the man's sake" (1 Cor. 11:7-9). Paul states that the woman is "the glory of man," which means she was created to directly reflect the man's God-created headship authority by submitting to and supporting his leadership; she is the man's vice-regent. Commenting on these verses and especially the phrase "the woman is the glory of man," David Gooding, former professor of Greek at Queen's University, Belfast, Ireland, best summarizes Paul's thinking in this passage:

> Chapter 1 of that book [Genesis] makes it clear (1:27-28) that as to essential nature and status man and woman were both made equally in the image of God and were intended, both of them, to share dominion over creation. But chapter 2 of Genesis explains (2:18-25) that when it came to their administrative roles there were significant, God-designed, differences between the sexes. The man was made first and had already begun his God-given tasks before the woman was made. He was, moreover, made direct and not out of the woman. As he stood alone, fresh from the hand of God, he was, says the Holy Spirit (1 Cor. 11:7) the image and glory of God, God's viceroy in creation, invested with God's own glory as his official representative. The woman, on the other hand, says the Holy Spirit (11:7-9) is the glory of the man. He is referring to the fact that God made the woman out of the man and designed her role to be that of a partner, help and companion for the man,

> to complement the man in his God-given tasks. The woman, then was the man's glory as the man was God's; and the man felt all that joy and delight in the woman and her role that God felt in the man and his role.
>
> We know all too well how Satan spoiled it and diminished the glories of both their roles. But Christ, the Seed of the Woman, has come to undo the works of the Devil (1 John 3:8). In the church, angels, we are told (Eph. 3:10; 1 Cor. 11:10), are being taught the manifold wisdom of God, as they see man and woman restored to God and to the roles for which the Creator designed them, as they observe men and women out of love for Christ using the symbols which indicate their acceptance of the order which the Redeemer has laid down for them.[13]

An all-male eldership speaks of agreement with and obedience to God's all-important plan for the sexes in which the man uniquely reflects God's image and glory in headship and the woman uniquely reflects the glory of the man by her submission to the man's God-given task of spiritual headship.

First Corinthians 14:33-38

We must mention one final text, 1 Corinthians 14:33-38, which is very similar to 1 Timothy 2 but is directed to a different congregation: "as in all the churches of the saints. Let the women keep silent in the churches; for they are not permitted to speak, but let them subject themselves, just as the Law also says. And if they desire to learn anything, let them ask their own husbands at home; for it is improper for a woman to speak in church...the things which I write to you are the Lord's commandment." Here, as in 1 Timothy 2, Paul prohibits women from taking the lead publicly by speaking in an open, spontaneous church meeting. He again supports his restriction by appealing to the Old Testament Scriptures and a command from the Lord Himself.

Paul's instructions to churches in Ephesus, Corinth, Colossae, and on the island of Crete regarding women's submission remind us that in a sinful world even Christians struggle with the idea of submission.[14] Furthermore, Paul emphasizes male-female roles because it is very common for males to abdicate their spiritual headship responsibility and obligations in the home and church. Male irresponsibility and passivity is an enormous problem that has frustrated and destroyed many wives, families, and churches. Ultimately the abdication of male headship is a refusal to submit to Christ's Word and Lordship. Paul, therefore, had to reaffirm God's original creation order as revealed in the Old Testament Scriptures. Christianity did not abolish God's original design for men and women, rather it brought it into better focus.

EGALITARIAN OPPOSITION TO MALE LEADERSHIP

The rallying cry of all religious feminists, including biblical feminists, is, "There is neither male nor female." They take this cry from their banner text, Galatians 3:28: "There is neither Jew nor Greek, there is neither slave nor free man, there is neither male nor female; for you are all one in Christ Jesus."

Biblical feminists (or Egalitarians) believe that as a result of Christ's redemption, the gospel abolished the old distinctions of male headship and female subordination. They contend that the seven specific passages on women's submission (1 Cor. 11; 14; Eph. 5; Col. 3; 1 Tim. 2; Titus 2; 1 Peter 3) are "problematic," "painfully puzzling," "obscure," "difficult," and "isolated" texts that should be interpreted in light of Galatians 3:28, which they consider to be the clearer, more theologically pertinent text.[15] As a result of their viewpoint, new and creative interpretations have been constructed to explain that the headship-subordination passages do not mean what they appear to say and do not apply to today's churches. Biblical feminists conclude that there are no compelling scriptural reasons for restricting women from serving as elders or as leaders/teachers in any or all church positions.

Flawed methodology

The methods used by biblical feminists to interpret headship-submission passages, however, are seriously flawed. Galatians 3:28, the feminists' principle text, appears in a context that deals with the fundamental issues of salvation, not the concept of headship and submission. The context addresses the purpose of the law, justification by faith, and the lofty position of every Christian in union with Christ. Paul's point is that *all* Christians, no matter what their race, social status, or gender, share equally by faith the glorious, universal privilege of sonship and heirship apart from the works of the Law (Gal. 3:23-29). So, both men and women are one in Christ Jesus based on their faith in Him. All Christians have direct access to God as sons and daughters, are indwelt by Christ through the Holy Spirit, and share equally the eternal promises of God.

As to whether the husband-wife role distinctions or gender-based roles in the larger family of God that are present in the Old Testament still exist under the new covenant, Galatians 3:28 simply doesn't comment. However, the author of Galatians 3:28 comments on this question elsewhere. In his letters to the churches in Ephesus, Colossae, Corinth, and Crete, and to his helpers Timothy and Titus, Paul insists that even among men and women who are now "one in Christ Jesus" as a result of the gospel, there exist functional differences and distinct, gender-based roles in marriage and the local church.

Biblical feminists misuse the Galatians 3:28 passage by pressing the text far beyond its intended meaning and declaring the plain, literal interpretation of the headship-submission passages to be simplistic. Following the same methodology of interpretation as the biblical feminists, so-called Christian homosexuals claim the right to same-sex relationships. Because the Bible says "neither male nor female," they claim that all the specific biblical passages prohibiting homosexuality must be understood culturally and in the light of Galatians 3:28. But does Galatians 3:28 truly abolish all sexual distinctions? Can men now marry men, or women marry women? The conclusions that those who hold an egalitarian viewpoint draw from Galatians 3:28 are plainly at odds with numerous portions of Scripture.

Biblical feminists wrongfully pit one group of verses on women's submission against another group of verses on women's equality. The historic Christian position, however, gives equal weight to both truths. Old Testament scholar Bruce Waltke briefly explains the correct approach to handling both sets of biblical claims: "These truths regarding the equality and inequality of the sexes must be held in dialectical tension, by allowing them the same weight at the same time, and by not allowing one to vitiate the other by subordinating one to the other."[16]

Peter, for example, holds in "dialectical tension" both husband-wife equality and husband-wife role distinctions. The wife, according to Peter, is "a fellow heir of the grace of life" with her husband and is also the "submissive" partner in the husband-wife relationship (1 Peter 3:1-7). Biblical feminists, on the other hand, promote a half truth—emphasizing the equality side of the male-female relationship without recognizing the subordination side. However, we understand the New

Testament correctly only when we allow the Scriptures on male-female equality as well as on male-female role differences to speak with full authority.

The Bible is not ambiguous about this critically important doctrine. In the most straightforward, clear manner, the Bible repeatedly states that male-female role differences exist in relationship to headship and submission. Not only do the apostles Paul and Peter expressly state the headship-submission doctrine, they argue cogently and passionately for it and support the universal application of their teaching from theology and original creation. In the final analysis, Christ's choice of a male apostolate serves as the basis for their teaching.

Chapter 4

Qualified Leadership

"An overseer, then, must be above reproach."

1 Timothy 3:2*a*

In a letter to a young presbyter named Nepotian, dated A.D. 394, Jerome (A.D. 345-419) rebuked the churches of his day for their hypocrisy in showing more concern for the appearance of their church buildings than the careful selection of their church leaders: "Many build churches nowadays; their walls and pillars of glowing marble, their ceilings glittering with gold, their altars studded with jewels. Yet to the choice of Christ's ministers no heed is paid."[1]

A similar error is repeated by multitudes of churches today. Many churches seem oblivious to the biblical requirements for their spiritual leaders as well as to the need for the congregation to properly examine all candidates for leadership in light of biblical standards (1 Tim. 3:10). This failure was dramatically highlighted when a leading evangelical journal in America brought together five divorced pastors and asked them to share their feelings, experiences, and views on divorce and the ministry. The journal's staff published the forum because they believed the growing problem of divorce among ministers needed to be faced openly and honestly. In fact, the article claimed that a recent survey of divorce rates in the United States showed that pastors had the third highest divorce rate—exceeded only by that of medical doctors and policemen![2]

The pastors' thoughts on divorce were presented in the journal through an open forum format. Along with the forum, the journal published the responses of seven well-known evangelical leaders to the divorced pastors' comments. What is astounding about the article is that not one of the seven leaders even mentioned the biblical qualifications for leadership outlined in 1 Timothy or Titus! This article reveals a widespread ignorance within the Christian community concerning Scripture's vigorous insistence on God's qualifications for local church leaders. It also demonstrates that churches and denominations have substituted their own standards for the biblical ones.

THE NEED FOR QUALIFIED SHEPHERD ELDERS

The most common mistake made by churches that are eager to implement eldership is to appoint biblically unqualified men. Because there is always a need for more shepherds, it is tempting to allow unqualified, unprepared men to assume leadership in the church. This is, however, a time-proven formula for failure. A biblical eldership requires biblically qualified elders.

The overriding concern of the New Testament in relation to church leadership is for the right kind of men to serve as elders and deacons. The offices of God's Church are not honorary positions bestowed on individuals who have attended church faithfully or who are senior in years. Nor are they board positions to be filled by good friends, rich donors, or charismatic personalities. Nor are they positions that only graduate seminary students can fill. The church offices, both eldership and deaconship, are open to all who meet the apostolic, biblical requirements. The New Testament is unequivocally emphatic on this point:

- To the troubled church in Ephesus, Paul insists that a properly constituted Christian church (1 Tim. 3:14,15) must have qualified, approved elders:

> It is a trustworthy statement; if any man aspires to the office of overseer, it is a fine work he desires to do. *An overseer, then, must be* above reproach, the husband of one wife, temperate, prudent, respectable, hospitable, able to teach, not addicted to wine or pugnacious, but gentle, uncontentious, free from the love of money. *He must be* one who manages his own household well, keeping his children under control with all dignity (but if

a man does not know how to manage his own household, how will he take care of the church of God?); and not a new convert, lest he become conceited and fall into the condemnation incurred by the devil. And *he must have* a good reputation with those outside the church, so that he may not fall into reproach and the snare of the devil (1 Tim. 3:1-7; italics added).

- Paul also insists that prospective elders and deacons be publicly examined in light of the stated list of qualifications. He writes, "And let these [deacons] also [like the elders] first be tested [examined]; then let them serve as deacons if they are beyond reproach" (1 Tim 3:10; cf. 5:24,25).

- When directing Titus in how to organize churches on the island of Crete, Paul reminds Titus to appoint only morally and spiritually qualified men to be elders. By stating elder qualifications in a letter, Paul establishes a public list to guide the local church in its choice of elders and to empower it to hold its elders accountable:

  For this reason I left you in Crete, that you might set in order what remains, and appoint elders in every city *as I directed you, namely, if any man be* above reproach, the husband of one wife, having children who believe, not accused of dissipation or rebellion. For the *overseer must be* above reproach as God's steward, not self-willed, not quick-tempered, not addicted to wine, not pugnacious, not fond of sordid gain, but hospitable, loving what is good, sensible, just, devout, self-controlled, holding fast the faithful word which is in accordance with the teaching, that he may be able both to exhort in sound doctrine and to refute those who contradict (Titus 1:5-9; italics added).

- When writing to churches scattered throughout northwestern Asia Minor, Peter speaks of the kind of men who should be elders. He exhorts the elders to shepherd the flock "not under compulsion, but voluntarily, according to the will of God; and not for sordid gain, but with eagerness; nor yet as lording it over those allotted to your charge, but proving to be examples to the flock" (1 Peter 5:2,3).

It is highly noteworthy that the New Testament provides more instruction on the qualifications for eldership than on any other aspect of eldership. Such qualifications are not required of all teachers or evangelists. One may be gifted as an evangelist and be used of God in that capacity, yet be unqualified to be an elder. An individual may be an evangelist immediately after conversion, but Scripture says that a new convert cannot be an elder (1 Tim. 3:6). There are three critically important reasons why God demands these qualifications of church elders.

First, the Bible says that an elder must be of irreproachable moral character and capable in the use of Scripture because he is "God's steward," that is, God's household manager (Titus 1:7). An elder is entrusted with God's dearest and most costly possessions, His children. He thus holds a position of solemn authority and trust. He acts on behalf of God's interests. No earthly monarch would dare think of hiring an immoral or incapable person to manage his estate. Nor would parents think of entrusting their children or family finances to an untrustworthy or incompetent person. So, too, the High and Holy One will not have an unfit, unqualified steward caring for His precious children.

As stewards of God's household, elders have access to people's homes and the most intimate details of their lives. They have access to the people who are most vulnerable to deception or abuse. They also have the greatest influence over the doctrinal direction of the church. Therefore, church elders must be men who are well-known by the community, have proven integrity, and are doctrinally sound.

Second, local church elders are to be living examples for the people to follow (1 Peter 5:3). They are to model the character and conduct that God desires for all His children. Since God calls His people to "be blameless and innocent, children of God above reproach in the midst of a crooked and perverse generation" (Phil. 2:15), it is necessary that those who lead His people be morally above reproach and model godly living.

John MacArthur, well-known radio preacher and author, echoes this point when he writes: "Whatever the leaders are, the people become. As Hosea said, 'Like people, like priest' (4:9). Jesus said, 'Everyone, after he has been fully trained, will be like his teacher' (Luke 6:40). Biblical history demonstrates that people will seldom rise above the spiritual level of their leadership."[3] Because people are like sheep, shepherd elders have an extraordinarily powerful impact on the behavior, attitudes, and thinking of the people:

- If the elders have a contentious spirit, the people will inevitably become contentious (1 Tim. 3:3; Titus 1:7).

- If the elders are inhospitable, the people will be unfriendly and cold (1 Tim. 3:2; Titus 1:8).

- If the elders love money, the people will become lovers of money (1 Tim. 3:3).

- If the elders are not sensible, balanced, and self-controlled, their judgment will be characterized by ugly extremes, which will cause the people to be extreme and unbalanced (1 Tim. 3:1,2; Titus 1:8).

- If the elders are not faithful, one-woman husbands, they will subtly encourage others to be unfaithful (1 Tim. 3:2; Titus 1:6).

- If the elders do not faithfully hold to the authority of the Word, the people will not hold to it (Titus 1:9).

Much of the weakness and waywardness of our churches today is due directly to our failure to require that church shepherds meet God's standards for office. If we want our local churches to be spiritually fit, then we must require our shepherds to be spiritually fit.

Third, the biblical qualifications protect the church from incompetent or morally unfit leaders. Some people push themselves into positions of church leadership to satisfy their unholy egos. Others are sadly deceived about their own ability and character. And some are evildoers who are motivated by Satan to infiltrate and ruin churches. The public, objective, God-given qualifications for church leadership protect the congregation from such unfit people.

These observable, objective standards for elders are especially important when churches must deal with dominating, stubborn church leaders who are incapable of truly seeing their sins or heresies and yet must be discharged from office. The elder qualifications empower each congregation and its leaders with the right and the objective means to hold back or remove unfit men from leadership. To refuse to remove a sinful or doctrinally unsound elder, however, is willful disobedience to God's Word that will eventually undermine the moral and spiritual vitality of the whole church as well as the integrity of the leadership council (see chapter 9, page 217). The refusal to remove an erring elder will also damage the church's credibility and gospel witness before an unbelieving community, which is a matter of utmost concern to Paul (1 Tim. 3:7). Thus the God-given standards for elders are essential for protecting the local church's spiritual welfare and evangelistic witness.

Today churches most need men of Christlike character to be in spiritual leadership. The best laws and constitutions are impotent without men who are "just," "devout," "sensible," "self-controlled," "forbearing," "uncontentious," and faithful to sound doctrine. These are precisely the qualities that God requires of those who lead His people. Let us, then, heed the warning of the late author and Christian apologist Francis Schaeffer (1912-1984) who writes, "The church has no right to diminish these standards for the officers of the Church, nor does it have any right to elevate any other as though they are then equal to these which are commanded by God himself. These and only these stand as absolute."[4]

THE QUALIFICATIONS FOR SHEPHERD ELDERS

When we speak of the elders' qualifications, most people think these qualifications are something different from those of the clergy. The New Testament, however, has no separate standards for professional clergy and lay elders. The reason is simple. There aren't three separate offices—pastor, elders, and deacons—in the New Testament local church. There are only two offices—elders and deacons. From the New Testament perspective, any man in the congregation who desires to shepherd the Lord's people and who meets God's requirements for the office can be a pastor elder.

As the three lists below show, God does not require wealth, social status, senior age, advanced academic degrees, or even great spiritual gift of those who desire to shepherd His people. We do the congregation and the work of God a great disservice when we add our arbitrary requirements to God's qualifications. Man-made requirements inevitably exclude needed, qualified men from the pastoral leadership of the church. Roland Allen (1868-1947), well-known Anglican missionary to China and influential missionary author, decried this problem in his day:

> We are so enamored of those qualifications which we have added to the apostolic that we deny the qualifications of anyone who possesses only the apostolic, whilst we think a man fully qualified who possesses only ours. A young student fresh from a theological college lacks many of those qualifications which the apostle deemed necessary for a leader in the house of God, the age, the experience, the established position and reputation, even if he possesses all the others. Him we do not think unqualified. The man who possesses all the apostolic qualifications is said to be unqualified, because he cannot go back to school and pass an examination.[5]

To be faithful to Holy Scripture and God's plan for the local church, we must open the pastoral leadership of the church to all in the church who are called by the Holy Spirit (Acts 20:20) and meet the apostolic qualifications. Although such a plan may be abhorrent to the clerical mind-set, it represents an authentic, apostolic mind-set. According to the New Testament, the elders of the church are all the men of the local church who desire to lead the flock and are scripturally qualified to do so.

The scriptural qualifications can be divided into three broad categories relating to moral and spiritual character, abilities, and Spirit-given motivation. Let us now examine each of these categories.

Comparison of Elder Qualifications

1 Timothy 3:2-7	Titus 1:6-9	1 Peter 5:1-3
1. Above reproach	1. Above reproach	1. Not under compulsion, but voluntary
2. The husband of one wife	2. The husband of one wife	2. Not for sordid gain, but with eagerness
3. Temperate	3. Having children who believe	3. Nor yet as lording it over...but proving to be examples
4. Prudent	4. Not self-willed	
5. Respectable	5. Not quick-tempered	

1 Timothy 3:2-7	Titus 1:6-9	1 Peter 5:1-3
6. Hospitable	6. Not addicted to wine	
7. Able to teach	7. Not pugnacious	
8. Not addicted to wine	8. Not fond of sordid gain	
9. Not pugnacious	9. Hospitable	
10. Gentle	10. Lover of what is good	
11. Uncontentious	11. Sensible	
12. Free from the love of money	12. Just	
13. Manages his household well	13. Devout	
14. Not a new convert	14. Self-controlled	
15. A good reputation with those outside the church	15. Holds fast the faithful Word—both to exhort and to refute	

MORAL AND SPIRITUAL CHARACTER

Most of the biblical qualifications relate to the candidate's moral and spiritual qualities. The first and overarching qualification is that of being "above reproach." What is meant by "above reproach" is defined by the character qualities that follow the term. In both of Paul's lists of elder qualifications, the first specific character virtue itemized is, "the husband of one wife." This means that an elder must be above reproach in his marital and sexual life (see chapter 9, page 192). Pointing out the Bible's emphasis on marital faithfulness and sexual purity, Robertson McQuilkin, author of the excellent book *An Introduction to Biblical Ethics,* writes:

> God's standards on human sexuality are treated in Scripture as the most important of all rules for relations among people. In the Old Testament, teaching against adultery is emphasized second only to teaching against idolatry. In the New Testament, both Christ and the apostles emphasized marital fidelity. Paul includes sexual sins in every one of his many lists of sins, and in most cases they head the list and receive the greatest emphasis.[6]

From the beginning, God sternly warned His people against the corrupt sexual practices of the heathen nations. He commanded His people to be holy and separate from the nations, to be faithful to the marriage covenant, and to be sexually pure. In the eighteenth chapter of Leviticus, Moses details all the sexual sins of the godless nations that would soon surround Israel. God warns His people against the practice of such sins: "Do not defile yourselves by any of these things [depraved sexual practices]; for by all these the nations which I am casting out before you have become defiled....Thus you are to keep My charge, that you do not practice any of the abominable customs which have been practiced before you, so as not to defile yourselves with them; I am the Lord your God" (Lev. 18:24,30). The need for purity was taught in the new covenant community as well. Paul writes, "But do not let immorality or any impurity or greed ev*en be named among you, as is proper among saints"* (Eph. 5:3; italics added).

One of Satan's oldest, most effective strategies for destroying the people of God is to adulterate the marriages of those who lead God's people (Num. 25:1-5; 1 Kings 11:1-13; Ezra 9:1,2). Satan knows that if he can defile the shepherds' marriages, the sheep will follow. The specific marital and family qualifications God requires for elders are meant to protect the whole church. So the church must insist that its leaders meet these qualifications before serving and while serving. If the local church does not insist on these requirements, the people will sink into the toxic wasteland of today's sexual and marital practices.

Tragically, many major Christian denominations have learned nothing from the Old Testament about the certain results of accommodating secular standards of sexual behavior. In nearly every major Christian denomination, God's laws regarding marriage, divorce, sexuality, and gender differences are being discarded and replaced with an acceptance of the most corrupt human practices. Among Christian leaders, adultery and other sexual sins are at epidemic levels.[7] Among the major denominations, clergy divorce and remarriage is hardly an issue. As *Time* magazine aptly describes today's religious landscape, "Denominations that once would not tolerate divorced ministers now find themselves debating whether to accept avowed lesbian ones."[8]

The other character qualities stress the elders' integrity, self-control, and spiritual maturity. Since elders govern the church body, they must be self-controlled in the use of money, alcohol, and in the exercise of their pastoral authority. Since they are to be models of Christian living, they must be spiritually devout, righteous, lovers of good, hospitable, and morally above reproach before the non-Christian community. In pastoral work, relationship skills are preeminent. Thus shepherd elders must be gentle, stable, sound-minded, and uncontentious.

Angry, hot-headed men hurt people. So an elder must not have a dictatorial spirit or be quick-tempered, pugnacious, or self-willed. Finally, an elder must not be a new Christian. He must be a spiritually mature, humble, time-proven disciple of Jesus Christ.

When examining candidates for eldership, most churches address these personal moral qualities only superficially if at all. John H. Armstrong, editor of *Reformation and Revival Journal* and author of *Can Fallen Pastors Be Restored?,* expresses his frustration with the lack of concern churches demonstrate when questioning candidates' personal moral qualities. He writes:

> In all my years of service on councils and committees I have rarely heard a candidate asked: "What about your life morally?" We might discuss a man's marriage, and that often in a rather shallow manner. Almost never did I hear the candidate asked, "Are you sexually pure, at this time, before God?"... We simply do not probe the issue of proven character and personal purity very deeply.
>
> In an age where sexual misconduct is common, both in the culture and in the church at large, I am compelled to ask, "Why do we never ask these kinds of questions before we ordain a man?" We live in a time where the statistics suggest that habits in the church are not that different from those in the general population....
>
> In these professional examination procedures we may ask a dozen doctrinally oriented questions, for every one ethical and moral question. I am not demeaning doctrinal questions, for far too many pastors are fuzzy and unclear in this area as well, but why do we almost totally ignore the areas of sex, money, and power? Is it not in these areas that most of the ethical and moral failures will surface?[9]

Armstrong further comments:

> Some years ago I was asked to chair a committee for my evangelical denomination where the duties included pre-examining men for ordination before the council was convened.... Our job was to test, to question, and then to recommend. We examined a good number of men each year. More than half of

them were unprepared in my own view—doctrinally and/or personally. Several times we recommended that the church not ordain the man.

Often the local church ignored our counsel and proceeded without our approval, finally ordaining the man at a later date. Wh*at was particularly troubling was how infrequently the man or his local church bothered to inquire as to our reasons* (italics added).[10]

ABILITIES

In the catalogs of elder qualifications, three requirements address the elder's abilities to perform the task. He must be able to manage his household well, provide a model of Christian living for others to follow, and be able to teach and defend the faith.

Able to Manage the Family Household Well

An elder must be able to manage his household well. The Scripture states: "He must be one who manages his own household well, keeping his children under control with all dignity (but if a man does not know how to manage his own household, how will he take care of the church of God?)" (1 Tim. 3:4,5). The Puritans referred to the family household as the "little church." This perspective is in keeping with the scriptural reasoning that if a man cannot shepherd his family, he can't shepherd the extended family of the church.

Managing the local church is more like managing a family than managing a business or state. A man may be a successful businessman, a capable public official, a brilliant office manager, or a top military leader but be a terrible church elder or father. Thus a man's ability to oversee his household well is a prerequisite for overseeing God's household.

But what about single men or married men who have no children? Can these men be elders? Most definitely (1 Cor. 7:8-35)! As we will discover in the exposition portion of this book, the qualifications regarding marriage and children should not be construed as commands to marry and have children (see chapter 9, page 190). Rather, because most men are married and have children, the Scripture sets forth God's standard for church leaders who are husbands and fathers. Setting standards for married men who have children is quite a different issue from commanding marriage and fatherhood, which is not always a matter of choice. Single men and childless, married men can certainly be pastor elders. Where they lack experience because of their unmarried or childless status, their fellow elders who are married and have children can fill in the gap. Single and childless men have a unique contribution to make to the flock and the eldership team. Of course the sexual conduct and home management of single and childless men must be above reproach, just as it must be above reproach for married men who have children.

Able to Provide a Model for Others to Follow

An elder must be an example of Christian living that others will want to follow. Peter reminds the Asian elders "to be examples to the flock" (1 Peter 5:3b). If a man is not a godly model for others to follow, he cannot be an elder even if he is a good teacher and manager. Like Peter, Paul also recognized the importance of modeling Christ. He did his utmost to model Christ and expected the people to follow:

- Brethren, join in following my example, and observe those who walk according to the pattern you have in us (Phil. 3:17).

- Be imitators of me, just as I also am of Christ (1 Cor. 11:1).

- For you yourselves know how you ought to follow our example, because we did not act in an undisciplined manner among you...but in order to offer ourselves as a model for you, that you might follow our example (2 Thess. 3:7,9b).

- I exhort you, therefore, be imitators of me (1 Cor. 4:16; cf. Gal. 4:12; 1 Thess. 1:5,6; 1 Tim. 4:12; Titus 2:7).

The greatest way to inspire and influence people for God is through personal example. Character and deeds, not official position or title, is what really influences people for eternity. A quotation by Samuel Brengle concerning the power of personal example, that is quoted by J. Oswald Sanders in his classic work *Spiritual Leadership*, bears repeating: "One of the outstanding ironies of history is the

utter disregard of ranks and titles in the final judgment men pass on each other.... The final estimate of men shows that history cares not an iota for the rank or title a man has borne, or the office he has held, but only the quality of his deeds and the character of his mind and heart."[11] Today men and women crave authentic examples of true Christianity in action. Who can better provide the week-by-week, long-term examples of family life, business life, and church life than local church elders? This is why it is so important that elders, as living imitators of Christ, shepherd God's flock in God's way.

Able to Teach and Defend the Faith

An elder must be able to teach and defend the faith. It doesn't matter how successful a man is in his business, how eloquently he speaks, or how intelligent he is. If he isn't firmly committed to historic, apostolic doctrine and able to instruct people in biblical doctrine, he does not qualify as a biblical elder (Acts 20:28ff; 1 Tim. 3:2; Titus 1:9).

The New Testament requires that a pastor elder "[hold] fast the faithful word which is in accordance with the teaching" (Titus 1:9*a*). This means that an elder must firmly adhere to orthodox, historic, biblical teaching. "Elders must not," as one commentator says, "be chosen from among those who have been toying with new doctrines."[12] Since the local church is "the pillar and support of the truth" (1 Tim. 3: 15*b*), its leaders must be rock-solid pillars of biblical doctrine or the house will crumble. Since the local church is also a small flock traveling over treacherous terrain that is infested with "savage wolves," only those shepherds who know the way and see the wolves can lead the flock to its safe destination. An elder, then, must be characterized by doctrinal integrity.

It is essential for an elder to be firmly committed to apostolic, biblical doctrine so "that he may be able to exhort in sound doctrine and to refute those who contradict" (Titus 1:9*b*). This requires that a prospective elder has applied himself for some years to the reading and study of Scripture, that he can reason intelligently and logically discuss biblical issues, that he has formulated doctrinal beliefs, and that he has the verbal ability and willingness to teach others. There should be no confusion, then, about what a New Testament elder is called to do: he is to teach and exhort the congregation in sound doctrine and to defend the truth from false teachers. This is the big difference between board elders and pastor elders. New Testament elders are both guardians and teachers of sound doctrine.

For this reason, God's book, the Bible, is to be the prospective elder's continual course of study. The Bible is God's complete training manual for all spiritual leaders. Paul reminds Timothy that "from childhood you have known *the sacred writings which are able to give you the wisdom that leads to salvation* through faith in Christ Jesus (2 Tim. 3:15; italics added). Paul further states that "all Scripture is inspired by God [God-breathed], and profitable for teaching, for reproof, correction, for training in righteousness; that *the man of God may be adequate, equipped for every good work* (2 Tim. 3:16, 17; italics added). Thus a man is unequipped for the shepherding task if he has not been schooled in God-breathed Holy Scripture. An elder who doesn't know the Bible is like a shepherd without legs; he can't lead or protect the flock. The probing comment of P. T. Forsyth (1848-1921), an influential British theologian of the early twentieth century, bears repeating: "The real strength of the Church is not the amount of its work but the quality of its faith. One man who truly knows his Bible is worth more to the Church's real strength than a crowd of workers who do not."[13]

How are prospective elders to be educated in God's book? First, if raised in godly, Christian homes, they will have had years of instruction in doctrine and holy living from the most effective teachers in the world, their mothers and fathers (Deut. 6:7; 11:19; Prov. 1:8; 4:1-5; Eph. 6:4; 1 Thess. 2:11; 1 Cor. 14:35; 2 Tim. 1:5; 3:15). John Gresham Machen (1881-1937) was a renowned Presbyterian scholar and educator who brilliantly defended the orthodox doctrine of Christ and the trustworthiness of Scripture during the famous fundamentalist-modernist controversy of the early twentieth century. His books on the virgin birth of Christ and the theological continuity between Paul and Jesus are still classics. On the significance of the Christian home in teaching the Bible, Machen wrote:

> The absence of doctrinal teaching and preaching is certainly one of the causes for the present lamentable ignorance in the church. But a still more influential cause is found in the failure of the most important of all Christian educational institutions. The most important Christian educational institution is not the pulpit or the school, important as these institutions are; but it is

> the Christian family. And that institution has to a very large extent ceased to do its work. Where did those of us who have reached middle life really get our knowledge of the Bible? I suppose my experience is the same as that of a good many of us. I did not get my knowledge of the Bible from Sunday School or from any other school, but I got it on Sunday afternoons with my mother at home. And I will venture to say that although my mental ability was certainly of no extraordinary kind I had a better knowledge of the Bible at fourteen years of age than is possessed by many students in the theological Seminaries of the present day. Theological students come for the most part from Christian homes; indeed in very considerable proportion they are children of the manse. Yet when they have finished college and enter the theological Seminary many of them are quite ignorant of the simple contents of the English Bible.[14]

Second, if the local church fulfills its role as a school for teaching apostolic doctrine, prospective elders will have been taught God's Word by gifted teachers. The Bible says that the local church is "the pillar and support of the truth" and "the household of God" (1 Tim. 3:15). This is why Paul charges Timothy to "give attention to the public reading of Scripture, to exhortation and teaching" (1 Tim. 4:13). Timothy was also to teach "faithful men, who will be able to teach others" (2 Tim. 2:2*b*). When Timothy departed from Ephesus, he expected that "faithful men," like the Ephesian elders, would teach future teachers and pastor elders who in turn would teach others.

Furthermore, the local church is not only a place to learn Scripture, it is the very best place to learn the skills required for shepherding people. It is in the local church that leaders learn to apply God's book to real-life situations. Thus the local church is to be God's school for the spiritual development of His children and the learning of Scripture (Acts 2:42; 11:26).

Third, a prospective elder learns the great truths of God through the consistent reading and study of Scripture and the ministry of the Holy Spirit (1 Cor. 2:12ff; 1 Thess. 4:9; 1 John 2:27). There is no substitute for a disciplined, persistent encounter with God through personal study of and meditation on Holy Scripture. In addition to studying Scripture, a growing Christian should be reading sound doctrinal material written by godly teachers of the Word.

Sadly, however, many churches (and Christian homes) have no vision for serious teaching or training in Scripture and doctrine. Other churches simply do not have the means to train their leaders; they are struggling to survive as a church body. Yet serious-minded believers hunger for in-depth teaching of the Scriptures. That is why Bible schools and seminaries will always be needed. Although there are problems with religious institutions that breed doubt in the authority of Scripture or reinterpret the Bible to agree with the spirit of the age, a good, Bible-believing and teaching school can provide excellent, in-depth training in Scripture.

I must warn, however, against the arbitrary requirement that many denominations impose on their shepherds to earn a master's degree before they are allowed to serve as a church pastor. God does not require advanced academic degrees as a qualification for spiritual leadership. When we set up formal academic standards, we professionalize the government of the church and create, at least in practice, a pastoral office that is separate from the eldership. We do not have God's authorization to establish such standards.

Do not forget that our Lord and Master, Jesus Christ, was not formally trained in a rabbinical school, although such training was available and very much prized in His day. Despite His lack of formal schooling in religion, however, Jesus was eminently educated in Scripture. Indeed, the people were so amazed by Jesus' knowledge and teaching as an untrained layman that they commented: "' How has this man become learned, having never been educated?'" (John 7:15*b*). The same observation was made of Jesus' close disciples: "as they observed the confidence of Peter and John, and understood that they were uneducated and untrained men, they were marveling, and began to recognize them as having been with Jesus" (Acts 4:13).

Unfortunately, many Christian people today are so clergy dependent that they can't imagine how men and women without formal, theological training and the degrees that go with it can know the Bible and teach it effectively. We must remember that degrees are required in the world of business and academia but are not required to minister in the household of God. Some people who are not able to go to school are taught by Christ through the Holy Spirit. They are educated in His Word and thus, according to God's standards, are qualified to lead and teach His people.

SPIRIT-GIVEN MOTIVATION FOR THE TASK

An obvious but not insignificant qualification is the shepherd's personal desire to love and care for God's people. Paul and the first Christians applauded such willingness by creating a popular Christian saying: "If any man aspires to the office of overseer, it is a fine work he desires to do" (1 Tim. 3:1). Peter, too, insisted that an elder shepherd the flock willingly and voluntarily (1 Peter 5:2). He knew from years of personal experience that the shepherding task can't be done by someone who views spiritual care as an unwanted obligation. Elders who serve grudgingly or under constraint are incapable of genuine care for people. They will be unhappy, impatient, guilty, fearful, and ineffective shepherds. Shepherding God's people through this sin-weary world is far too difficult a task—fraught with too many problems, dangers, and demands—to be entrusted to someone who lacks the will and desire to do the work.

A true desire to lead the family of God is always a Spirit-generated desire. Paul reminded the Ephesian elders that it was the Holy Spirit—not the church or the apostles—who placed them as overseers in the church to shepherd the flock of God (Acts 20:28). It was the Spirit who called them to shepherd the church and who moved them to care for the flock. The Spirit planted the pastoral desire in their hearts. He gave the compulsion and strength to do the work and the wisdom and appropriate gifts to care for the flock. The elders were His wise choice for the task. In the church of God, it is not man's will that matters but God's will and arrangement. So the only men who qualify for eldership are those whom the Holy Spirit gives the motivation and gifts for the task.

A biblical eldership, then, is a biblically qualified team of shepherd leaders. A plurality of unqualified elders is of no benefit to the local church. I agree fully with the counsel of Jon Zens, editor of the journal *Searching Together*. He writes, "Better have no elders than the wrong ones."[15] The local church must in all earnestness insist on biblically qualified elders, even if such men take years to develop.

CHAPTER 5

Servant Leadership

"If I then, the Lord and Teacher, washed your feet, you also ought to wash one another's feet. For I gave you an example that you also should do as I did to you."

John 13:14,15

On a Sunday morning after we had publicly commissioned and prayed for a newly installed elder in our church, a brother from another country who had been attending our church during the previous year ran up to me and asked enthusiastically, "How do six such strong, natural leaders work together so harmoniously as you men apparently do?" His question was stirred by the appointment of the new elder because he was a dynamic leader in his own right. The newly appointed elder had planted churches in Spain for twelve years and had previously planted churches in America. So he wasn't, as they say, a "yes man." His strong personality and drive had the potential to create conflict within the eldership team.

I didn't have to think about my reply. "Each of our elders," I explained, "is committed to working together, by the power of the Holy Spirit, in humble, Christlike love." We had thought about and discussed the issue of working together in unity and love for more than twenty years. We didn't think we had an option as to how we were to relate to one another in our work for the Lord. Jesus Christ lived and taught the principles of love, humility, oneness, prayer, trust, forgiveness, and servanthood. After His ascension into heaven, the twelve apostles put these principles into practice by working together humbly and lovingly as a leadership team. Thus they became the first model of collective servant leadership.

Of course we disagree, argue, get angry, and at times think badly of one another. In our own strength we would destroy our eldership team in short order. But Christ's principles of patience, forgiveness, humility, oneness, and love ultimately govern our attitudes and behavior toward one another. When we fail to act toward one another as Christlike disciples (and we do), we repent, confess, and start anew. Eldership will never work if the elders don't understand or fall short of a total commitment to Christ's principles of self-sacrificing love and humble servanthood. To discover how a plurality of elders works together, look and listen to Jesus Christ.

JESUS' TEACHING ON SERVANT LEADERSHIP

Just as Christianity influenced the Roman empire, the Greco-Roman world also affected the course of Christianity. Renowned church historian and professor of Christian missions Kenneth Scott Latourette (1884-1968), when citing pagan influences on early Christianity, states that the Roman concepts of power and rule corrupted the organization and life of the early churches. He observes that "the Church was being interpenetrated by ideals which were quite contrary to the Gospel, especially the conception and use of power which were in stark contrast to the kind exhibited in the life and teaching of Jesus and in the cross and the resurrection."[1] This, Latourette goes on to say, proved to be "the menace which was most nearly disastrous" to Christianity.[2]

I believe it is more accurate to say that the conceptual and structural changes that occurred during the early centuries of Christianity proved disastrous. Christianity, the humblest of all faiths, degenerated into the most power-hungry and hierarchical religion on the face of the earth. After the emperor Constantine elevated Christianity to the status of a state religion in A.D. 312, the once-persecuted faith became a fierce persecutor of all its opposition. An unscriptural clerical and priestly caste that was consumed by the quest for power, position, and authority arose. Even Roman emperors had a guiding hand in the development of Christian churches. The pristine character of the New Testament church community was lost.

When we read the Gospels, however, we see that the principles of brotherly community, love, humility, and servanthood at the very heart of Christ's teaching. Unfortunately, like many of the early Christians, we have been slow to understand these great virtues and especially slow to apply them to church structure and leadership. Because love, humility, and servanthood are pivotal to authentic Christian leadership and the inner life of the Christian community, however, let us briefly survey our Master's teaching on the subject.

MATTHEW 11:29: GENTLE AND HUMBLE. Contrasting Himself with the harsh, self-absorbed religious leaders of His day, Jesus called out to the people, "Take my yoke upon you, and learn from Me, for I am gentle and humble in heart." Through this significant statement, Jesus tells us who He is as a person: He is gentle and humble. Too many religious leaders, however, are not gentle nor are they humble. They are controlling and proud. They use people to satisfy their fat egos. But Jesus is refreshingly different. He truly loves people, selflessly serving and giving His life for them. He expects His followers—especially the elders who lead His people—to be humble and gentle like Himself.

MARK 9:33-35: HUMBLE SERVANTS OF ALL. On the first recorded occasion when the disciples discussed which of them was the greatest, Jesus, the master teacher, answered their age-old question by means of this now-famous paradoxical statement: "If anyone wants to be first, he shall be last of all, and servant of all." Here Jesus begins to transform His disciples' thinking about personal greatness. He declares that true greatness is not achieved by striving for prominence over others or by grasping for power, but by exhibiting a humble, self-effacing attitude of service to *all*—even to the most lowly people.

Charles Colson, who served as Special Counsel to the President of the United States from 1969 to 1973, knows from personal experience the magical enticement of power and high position. He skillfully describes the differences between the worldly view of power and position and the Christian view: "Nothing distinguishes the kingdoms of man from the kingdom of God more than their diametrically opposed views of the exercise of power. One seeks to control people, the other to serve people; one promotes self, the other prostrates self; one seeks prestige and position, the other lifts up the lowly and despised."[3]

Colson's wise warning to Christian leaders bears repeating: "Power is like saltwater; the more you drink the thirstier you get. The lure of power can separate the most resolute of Christians from the true nature of Christian leadership, which is service to others. It's difficult to stand on a pedestal and wash the feet of those below."[4]

MARK 10:35-45: SACRIFICE, SERVICE, AND SUFFERING. In the most blatant display of selfish ambition and total disregard for the good of their ten colleagues, James and John ask Jesus to give them the two most prominent seats in His kingdom: "Grant that we may sit in Your glory, one on Your right, and one on Your left." Their request immediately stirs bad feelings among the other apostles, as selfish ambition always does. Mark records that "the ten began to feel indignant with James and John."

Contrary to the glory James and John were seeking for themselves, Jesus calls the Twelve, in verses 38-45, to "sacrifice, service and suffering."[5] John Stott, author and former rector of All Souls' Church in London, insightfully contrasts the attitudes of James and John with those of Jesus who walked the way of the Cross:

> Yet the world (and even the church) is full of Jameses and Johns, go-getters and status-seekers, hungry for honor and prestige, measuring life by achievement, and everlastingly dreaming of success. They are aggressively ambitious for themselves.
>
> This whole mentality is incompatible with the way of the cross. "The Son of Man did not come to be served, but to serve, and to give...." He renounced the power and glory of heaven and humbled himself to be a slave. He gave himself without reserve and without fear, to the despised and neglected sections of the community. His obsession was the glory of God and the good of human beings who bear his image. To promote these, he was willing to endure even the shame of the cross. Now he calls us to follow him, not to seek great things for ourselves, but rather to seek first God's rule and God's righteousness.[6]

MATTHEW 23:1-12: THE HUMBLE SHALL BE EXALTED. No one understands religious pride like Jesus Christ does. In Matthew 23, Jesus exposes the awful pride, petty selfishness, self-superiority, legalism, and deception of religious hypocrites who love to exalt themselves:

> "And they love the place of honor at banquets, and the chief seats in the synagogues, and respectful greetings in the market places, and being called by men, Rabbi. But do not be called Rabbi; for One is your Teacher, and you are all brothers" (Matt. 23:6-8).
>
> "But the greatest among you shall be your servant. And whoever exalts himself shall be humbled; and whoever humbles himself shall be exalted" (Matt. 23:11,12).

The religious leaders about whom Jesus spoke separated and exalted themselves above the people. They sought for themselves special titles, clothes, and treatment—the chief seats among their fellow men. They loved high-profile, public ministry. They loved the limelight and celebrity status. In marked contrast, Jesus prohibited His disciples from using honorific titles, calling one another Rabbi, exalting themselves in any way that would diminish their brotherly relationship, or usurping the unique place that Christ and the Father have over each believer.[7]

Despite our Lord's repeated teaching on humility, we must concur with Andrew Murray (1828-1917), the beloved devotional writer and missionary statesman from South Africa, that humility is still a neglected virtue among many Christians:

> When I look back on my own religious experience, or on the Church of Christ in the world, I stand amazed at the thought of how little humility is sought after as the distinguishing feature of the discipleship of Jesus. In preaching and living, in the daily activities of the home and social life, in the more special fellowship with Christians, in the direction and performance of work for Christ—how much proof there is that humility is not esteemed the cardinal virtue.[8]

LUKE 22:24-27: ONE WHO SERVES. As unbelievable as it may sound in light of Christ's clear and repeated teaching, the disciples again argued during the Passover meal as to which one of them was regarded as the greatest (Luke 22:24). Again, we witness our Lord patiently teaching them not to think and act like worldly leaders:

> "The kings of the Gentiles lord it over them; and those who

> have authority over them are called 'Benefactors.' But not so with you, but let him who is the greatest among you become as the youngest, and the leader as the servant. For who is greater, the one who reclines at the table, or the one who serves? Is it not the one who reclines at the table? But I am among you as the one who serves" (Luke 22:25-27).

Sadly, the same competitive, self-seeking spirit exhibited by the disciples is alive today. Perhaps its most common form is expressed by the question, "Who has the largest church?" David Prior, in his book *Jesus and Power*, illustrates the carnal striving among churches because of envy and pride over which is bigger and better:

> This rivalry among his disciples was a constant thorn in the side of Jesus. It was endemic in the church at Corinth (cf. 1 Cor. 3:1-15). It is frequently found today among and within large evangelical congregations which strive to be larger, better and more famous than each other. The very size of these congregations often produces an envious attitude among not-so-large churches, an attitude which reveals precisely the same competitive spirit in those churches also. During the last twenty years I have been a member of four congregations with attendances which happen to have been much higher than most in the neighborhood. Being an Anglican, these four have all been Anglican churches. One of the most difficult obstacles to overcome has been the unholy combination of pride-in-numbers in the local church on the one hand, and envy-at-success in the diocese on the other. Competitiveness is a cancer. Jesus recognized it as completely hostile to the reality of power which he was teaching and demonstrating."[9]

JOHN 13:3-17: WASHING ONE ANOTHER'S FEET. That same Passover evening when disciples questioned who among them was the greatest, Jesus illustrated the humble, servant role that is so basic to His ministry and to the ministry of those who follow Him. He demonstrated that role by washing His disciples' feet:

> And so when He had washed their feet, and taken His garments, and reclined at the table again, He said to them, "Do you know

"When we reflect
on the history of the Church,
are we not bound to confess that she
has failed to follow
the example of her Founder?
All too often she has worn
the robes of the ruler,
not the apron of the servant.
Even in our own day it can hardly be said
that the 'brand-image' of the Church
is of a society united in love for Jesus,
and devoted to selfless
service of others."

(Michael Green, *Called to Serve*, 16)

what I have done to you? You call Me teacher and Lord; and you are right, for so I am. If I then, the Lord and the Teacher, washed your feet, you also ought to wash one another's feet" (John 13:12-14).

Here we see that the symbol of our Lord is the servant's towel, not the cleric's robe. If our beloved Teacher and Lord stooped in love to wash His disciples' feet, then we should gladly stoop to minister to the needs and restoration of our fellow brothers and sisters. Only when we learn what it means to wash one another's feet and clothe ourselves in humility will we have any hope of living together in peace and unity.

JOHN 13:34,35: LOVE. The secret to a good eldership team, a healthy church, and all relationships with our brothers and sisters is Christ's new commandment:

> "A new commandment I give to you, that you love one another, even as I have loved you, that you also love one another. By this all men will know that you are My disciples, if you have love for one another" (John 13:34,35).

Thus we are to love one another with the same intensity as Christ loved us.

THREE LESSONS

Our Lord's repeated instruction on love, humility, and servanthood, teaches us three important lessons. First, God hates pride. In the list of seven sins that God especially hates, pride is at the top (Prov. 6:16-19). Proverbs says, "Everyone who is proud in heart is an abomination to the Lord" (Prov. 16:5a). Those are strong words. The Scripture also says, "When pride comes, then comes dishonor, *but with the humble is wisdom*" (Prov. 11:2; italics added). James echoes a similar thought in his writings: "God is opposed to the proud, but gives grace to the humble" (James 4:6). God hates pride so much that He gave Paul a thorn in the flesh to keep him from exalting himself and to force him to be dependent on his Creator (2 Cor. 12:7-10).

One of the awful things about pride is that it deceives us; we may think we are serving God and others, but in reality we are serving ourselves only. John Stott is certainly right when he says, "Pride is without doubt the chief occupational hazard of the preacher."[10] The proud church leader is an offense to the gospel of Jesus Christ, a prime target for the Devil and—no matter how talented and indispensable he may think himself to be—an unfit leader of God's people.

Second, Christ's persistent teaching on love and humble servanthood demonstrates how difficult it is for people to understand and implement this principle. Pride and selfishness continually strive to dominate and deceive the human heart. Tragically, many Christians are more comfortable with Plato's *Republic* and its tough-minded, singular leadership style than with Jesus' style of humble-servant leadership. The past two thousand years of Christian history show that we have advanced little in our understanding of Christ's core teaching. Many of the scandalous divisions, ugly power struggles, wounded feelings, and petty jealousies in our churches and personal relationships exist because pride and selfishness motivate much of our thinking and behavior. The church leader who doesn't understand the Christlike spirit of humility, love, and servanthood is doomed to perpetuate fighting and division.

Third, our Lord's repeated teaching shows that humility, servanthood, and love are essential qualities of the Christian Church. They express the mind and disposition of Christ: "Have this attitude in yourselves which was also in Christ Jesus, who,...taking the form of a bond-servant...humbled Himself" (Phil. 2:5,7,8). Every local church is to be a servant community that is identified by Christ's love. Thus Christian leaders must be servant leaders, not unholy, worldly big shots.

THE PAULINE EXAMPLE OF SERVANT LEADERSHIP

If you can't imagine how a strong, gifted leader can also be a loving, humble servant, consider the life of Paul. The once unyielding, proud Pharisee became the loving, gentle servant of Jesus (2 Cor. 10:1). God had gifted Paul with giant intellectual powers and indomitable zeal. He had also given him extraordinary authority. Yet after his conversion, Paul viewed his giftedness and authority as a means of building up and protecting others, not as a means of controlling and gaining prominence or material advantage for himself (2 Cor. 10:8; 2 Cor. 1:24).

Paul's restraint in his use of authority is a remarkable example of his humble, servant spirit. Paul would rather suffer than risk wounding his children in the faith (2 Cor. 1:23-2:4; 13:7). He would rather appeal than command, choosing to deal with people in love and gentleness rather than "with a rod" (1 Cor. 4:21; 2 Cor. 10:1,2; 13:8-10; Gal. 4:20). Although he used his authority and power when needed to stop false teachers, his patience with erring converts was extraordinary. He so identified with his converts that their discipline, weakness, and humiliation became his (2 Cor. 11:29; 12:21; Gal. 4:12). He would lower and sacrifice himself so that he might raise others in faith and maturity (2 Cor. 11:7,21; 13:9) He sacrificed all personal gain and advantage for others (1 Cor. 10:33). In everything, his converts' spiritual welfare was foremost in his mind.

As a humble servant, Paul avoided self-promotion and self-exaltation. He always promoted Christ, never himself: "For we do not preach ourselves but Christ Jesus as Lord, and ourselves as your bond-servants for Jesus sake" (2 Cor. 4:5). Consider the following example of his humble service. Although he lived in Corinth for a year and a half, he never once mentioned to his new converts his extraordinary experience of being taken up to the third heaven to hear "inexpressible words, which a man is not permitted to speak" (2 Cor. 12:4). He revealed his heavenly experience some four years later only when he was compelled to do so because the proud Corinthians had fallen prey to the boasting of false teachers (2 Cor. 12:1-13). He didn't speak of his heavenly experience prior to that time because he knew the Corinthians would have falsely idolized him. Paul wanted them to exalt Christ, not himself.

The Corinthians' sinful propensity to idolize powerful teachers and form groups around them is addressed in the first four chapters of 1 Corinthians. There Paul says, "So then let no one boast in men" (1 Cor. 3:21*a*; cf. 4:6,7). Paul reminds the Corinthians that he and Apollos are servants, not tin gods: "What then is Apollos? And what is Paul? Servants through whom you believed, even as the Lord gave opportunity to each one. I planted, Apollos watered, but God was causing the growth. So then neither the one who plants nor the one who waters is anything, but God who caused the growth" (1 Cor. 3:6-7).

Paul's servant display of his apostolic authority was, however, misunderstood by many Corinthians, which shows how difficult it is to understand godly humility. Some of them even considered him to be weak and cowardly (1 Cor. 4:18-21; 2 Cor. 10:1-11). But, as the life of Jesus Christ clearly demonstrates, humility is not weakness or cowardliness. Jesus was humble and gentle, yet He taught vast crowds, faced grueling intellectual debate, taught with great authority, and confronted with scorching criticism the hypocritical, religious clerics of His day. In righteous anger, He took a whip and drove the moneychangers out of the temple. Humility is not a symptom of weakness or incompetence, but of true self-understanding, godly wisdom, and self-control.

The humble servant, Paul, was a strong, brave warrior and leader for Christ. He served God and cared for His people with all his might and zeal. During his life he faced many conflicts, debates, and struggles. The man who could say that he "served the Lord with all lowliness of mind" handed over an impenitent believer to Satan for the destruction of his flesh, struck the false teacher Elymus with blindness, rebuked Peter and Barnabas for their hypocrisy, and stood bravely before Roman courts and judges. Despite the many problems he confronted, Paul consistently responded to his brethren in humility and love. He knew that acting in pride would make things worse and divide God's people. That is one reason why Paul's letters, as well as those of Peter, John, and James, are supersaturated with commands concerning love, patience, kindness, prayer, forgiveness, gentleness, and compassion.

ELDERS AS SERVANT LEADERS

Elders are to be servant leaders, not rulers or dictators. God doesn't want His people to be used by petty, self-serving tyrants. Servant elders have chosen a life of service on behalf of others. Like the servant Christ, they sacrifice their time and energy for the good of others. Only elders who are loving, humble servants can genuinely manifest the incomparable life of Jesus Christ to their congregations and a watching world.

A group of elders, however, can become a self-serving, autocratic leadership body. Thus Peter, using the same terminology as Jesus, warns the Asian elders against abusive, lordly leadership: "nor yet as lording it over those allotted to your charge, but proving to be examples to the flock" (1 Peter 5:3). Peter also charges the elders, as well as everyone else in the congregation, to clothe themselves in humility just as Jesus clothed Himself in humility: "all of you, clothe yourselves with humility toward one another, for God is opposed to the proud, but gives grace to the humble" (1 Peter 5:5). With similar concern, Paul reminds the Ephesian elders of his example of humility. In Acts 20:19, he describes his manner of "serving the Lord with all humility" and implies that they, too, must serve the Lord in the same manner. Because of pride's lurking temptation, a new Christian, the Scripture says, should not be an elder: "And not a new convert, lest he become conceited and fall into the condemnation incurred by the devil" (1 Tim. 3:6).

In addition to shepherding others with a servant spirit, the elders must humbly and lovingly relate to one another. They must be able to patiently build consensus, compromise, persuade, listen, handle disagreement, forgive, receive rebuke and correction, confess sin, and appreciate the wisdom and perspective of others—even those with whom they disagree. They must be able to submit to one another, speak kindly and gently to one another, be patient with their fellow colleagues, defer to one another, and speak their minds openly in truth and love. Stronger and more gifted elders must not use their giftedness, as talented people sometimes do, to force their own way by threatening to leave the church and take their followers with them. Such selfishness creates ugly, carnal power struggles that endanger the unity and peace of the entire congregation.

Conflict among elders is a serious, all-too-common problem. It is appalling how little regard some Christians leaders have for the sacredness of the unity of the body of Christ and how quickly they will divide the body in order to gain their own way. In the end they may get their own way, but it is not God's way.

The solution to the problem, however, is not to revert to one-man rule or to leave the church. That is the easy way out. The Christian solution is to humble oneself, love as Christ loved, wash one another's feet, repent, submit, pray, turn from pride, shun impatience, and honor and love one another. I firmly believe that if elders were to spend as much time praying for one another as they do complaining about one another that most of their problems and complaints would disappear. That is the kind of leadership God wants the elders to exemplify for His people.

Elders must understand that the agonizing frustrations, problems, and conflicts of pastoral life are the tools God uses to mold them into the image of the Good Shepherd, the Lord Jesus Christ. If they respond to these difficulties in obedience and faith, they will be molded into Christ's image. And few things in life are more thrilling than to know that one is being transformed into a Christlike pastor.

The humble-servant character of the eldership doesn't imply, however, an absence of authority. The New Testament terms that describe the elders' position and work—"God's stewards," "overseers," "shepherd," "leading"—imply authority as well as responsibility. Peter could not have warned the Asian elders against "lording it over those allotted to your charge" if they had no authority. As shepherds of the church, elders have been given the authority to lead and protect the local church (Acts 20:28-31). The key issue is the attitude in which elders exercise that authority.

Following the Christian model, elders must not wield the authority given to them in a heavy-handed way. They must not use manipulative tactics, play power games, or be arrogant and aloof. They must never think they are unanswerable to their fellow brethren or to God. Elders must not be authoritarian, which is incompatible with humble servanthood. J.I. Packer, noted author and professor of theology at Regent College in Vancouver, Canada, defines authoritarianism and describes its evils:

> Exercise of authority in its various spheres is not necessarily authoritarian. There is a crucial distinction here. Authoritarianism is authority corrupted, gone to seed. Authoritarianism appears when the submission that is demanded cannot be justified in terms of truth or morality....Any form of human authority can degenerate in this way. You have authoritarianism in the state when the regime uses power in an unprincipled way to maintain itself. You have it in churches when leaders claim control of their followers' consciences. You have it in academic work at high school, university or seminary when you are required to agree with your professor rather than follow the evidence of truth for yourself. You have it in the family when parents direct or restrict their children unreasonably. Unhappy experiences of authority are usually experiences of degenerate authority, that is, of authoritarianism. That such experiences leave a bad taste and

> prompt skepticism about authority in all its forms is sad but not surprising.
>
> Authoritarianism is evil, anti-social, anti-human and ultimately anti-God (for self-deifying pride is at its heart), and I have nothing to say in its favor.[11]

When we consider Paul's example and that of our Lord's, we must agree that biblical elders do not dictate, they direct. True elders do not command the consciences of their brethren, but appeal to their brethren to faithfully follow God's Word. Out of love, true elders suffer and bear the brunt of difficult people and problems so that the lambs are not bruised. They bear the misunderstanding and sins of others so that the assembly may live in peace. They lose sleep so that others may rest. They make great personal sacrifices of time and energy for the welfare of others. They see themselves as men under authority. They depend on God for wisdom and help, not on their own power and cleverness. They face the false teachers' fierce attacks. They guard the community's liberty and freedom in Christ so that the saints are encouraged to develop their gifts, to mature, and to serve one another.

In summary, using Paul's great love chapter, we can say that a servant elder "is patient...is kind, and is not jealous...[a servant elder] does not brag...[a servant elder] is not arrogant, does not act unbecomingly...does not seek [his]...own...[a servant elder]is not provoked, does not take into account a wrong suffered, does not rejoice in unrighteousness, but rejoices with the truth; [a servant elder] bears all things, believes all things, hopes all things, endures all things" (1 Cor. 13:4-7).

Part Two

DEFENSE OF BIBLICAL ELDERSHIP

CHAPTER 6

Bible-Based Leadership Structure

"Set in order what remains, and appoint elders in every city as I direct you."

Titus 1:5*b*

For many people, the issue of church government (also referred to as church polity, church structure, church organization, church order, or the ministry) is as irrelevant an issue as the color of the church pews. Indeed, for many people the color of the church pews inspires greater interest! To these people, the organizational structure of the church really doesn't matter. The average church member's disinterest in how the church is governed needs to be challenged, however. Church government is an extremely practical and theologically significant issue. So I ask those of you who have not thought much about this subject, or have assumed that it is unimportant, to consider the following points.

Some of the worst havoc wrought to the Christian faith has been a direct result of unscriptural forms of church structure. Only a few centuries after the apostles' death, for example, Christian churches began to assimilate both Roman and Jewish concepts of status, power, and priesthood. As a result, church government was clericalized and sacralized. Under Christ's name an elaborately structured institution emerged that corrupted the simple, family structure of the apostolic churches, robbed God's people of their lofty position and ministry in Christ, and exchanged Christ's supremacy over His people for the supremacy of the institutional church.

Furthermore, church organizational structure matters because structure determines how people think and act. Ultimately, structure determines how things are done in the local church. I find it ironic that some evangelical leaders in America are more concerned about the structure of the United States government than the structure of the local church. I doubt that many evangelical leaders would say, "It doesn't matter how the U.S. government is structured as long as there is some form of leadership." Yet, that is precisely what I have heard some evangelical leaders say about the local church.

In practical reality, church structure often takes precedence over theology. In his book, *Liberating the Laity,* R. Paul Stevens shares how he tried to equip the people in his church for doing the church's ministry but failed because—as he discovered—the governmental structure of the church required *him* to do "the ministry." He writes, "Structure, I discovered, is important; there is no point in saying that every member is a minister if the structure of the fellowship 'says' the exact opposite—by making it hard for people to discover their gifts or to exercise loving service."[1]

The fact is, no society—religious or secular—can ever afford to be careless about the structure of its government. This is especially true of the Christian community because great and precious principles are at stake. People who are deeply involved in the actual operation of a local church know from personal experience that the government of the church affects every aspect of the inner life of the church and that it is an extremely relevant topic.

There are highly critical doctrinal issues involved in church polity that thinking, concerned Christians cannot avoid without becoming irrelevant Christians. Who would dare call the issue of women's ordination irrelevant? It is without question one of the most dominate issues in church polity today. Interestingly enough, the one stubborn topic that has caused the greatest hindrance to unity for the worldwide ecumenical movement is the issue of church order. The point is, the structure of the church both reflects and determines our theology and beliefs.

Since the structure of the church matters both practically and theologically, we must ask if there is a scriptural base for insisting on one form of church government. I believe there is such a base and that church government by a plurality of elders can be honestly and reasonably demonstrated to be the teaching of the New Testament.

When speaking of the organizational structure of the local church, I have employed, for lack of better terminology, the traditional term *church government*. For many people, the term *government* may communicate bureaucratic and judicial concepts. However, the structure of government the New Testament envisions for the local church is primarily pastoral and familial and involves the spiritual care of all members of the congregation.

The Biblical Base for Government by the Plurality of Elders

Christians who profess the Bible to be God's infallible Word agree that they must establish their church practices and doctrines on the teachings of the Bible. Many contemporary scholars say, however, that the New Testament is ambiguous or silent regarding the topic of church government and conclude that no one can insist upon a biblical model of church government for all churches because the Bible doesn't. George Eldon Ladd (1911-1982), author of *A Theology of the New Testament* and a former professor at Fuller Theological Seminary, expresses this view most concisely: "It appears likely that there was no normative pattern of church government in the apostolic age, and that the organizational structure of the church is no essential element in the theology of the church."[2] Although this is a widely held view among scholars today, it must be challenged because it simply does not fit the biblical evidence.

In its major features, eldership is plainly and amply set forth by the New Testament writers. J. Alec Motyer, former principal of Trinity College in Bristol, England, captures the true spirit of the New Testament when he writes, "it is not as much as hinted in the New Testament that the church would ever need—or indeed should ever want or tolerate—any other local leadership than that of the eldership group."[3]

Not only does the New Testament record the existence of elders in numerous churches, it also gives instruction about elders and to elders. In fact, the New Testament offers more instruction regarding elders than on other important church subjects such as the Lord's Supper, the Lord's Day, baptism, or spiritual gifts. When you consider the New Testament's characteristic avoidance of detailed regulation and church procedures (when compared to the Old Testament), the attention given to elders is amazing. "This is why," writes Jon Zens, "we need to seriously consider the doctrine of eldership; it jumps out at us from the pages of the New Testament, yet it has fallen into disrepute and is not being practiced as a whole in local churches."[4]

A Consistent Pattern of Plural Elders Among the First Churches

To hear some scholars speak, you would think that the Bible doesn't say one word about church elders or church government. But that is not true. The New Testament records evidence of pastoral oversight by a council of elders in nearly all the first churches. These local churches were spread over a wide geographic and culturally diverse area—from Jerusalem to Rome. Consider the consistent pattern of plural leadership by elders that existed among the first Christian churches as it is recorded in the New Testament.

- Elders are found in the churches of Judea and the surrounding area (Acts 11:30; James 5:14,15).

- Elders governed the church in Jerusalem (Acts 15).

- Among the Pauline churches, leadership by the plurality of elders was established in the churches of Derbe, Lystra, Iconium, and Antioch (Acts 14:23); in the church at Ephesus (Acts 20:17; 1 Tim. 3:1-7; 5:17-25); in the church at Philippi (Phil. 1:1); and in the churches on the island of Crete (Titus 1:5).

- According to the well-traveled letter of 1 Peter, elders existed in churches throughout northwestern Asia Minor: Pontus, Galatia, Cappadocia, Asia, and Bithynia (1 Peter 1:1; 5:1).

- There are strong indications that elders existed in churches in Thessalonica (1 Thess. 5:12) and Rome (Heb. 13:17).

Despite this evidence of government by a plurality of elders, it is commonly thought by most Christians that Timothy, Epaphras, and

James are examples of local pastoral leadership by one individual, but such is not the case. Timothy was not a local church pastor in the traditional sense of the term. He was primarily—like Titus, Erastus, and Tychicus—an apostolic delegate. He served as Paul's partner and coworker in spreading the gospel and strengthening the various churches under Paul's care (Acts 19:22). Timothy was an evangelist (1 Thess. 3:2; 2 Tim. 4:5) and did pastoral work in the same sense that Paul did, but he was always under Paul's authority and direction (1 Thess. 3:2; Phil. 2:19,20; 1 Cor. 16:10,11; 1 Tim. 1:3).

Like Timothy, Epaphras was also Paul's apostolic delegate. He ministered on Paul's behalf in the Lycus valley while Paul resided in Ephesus (Col. 1:7). Epaphras was probably the original evangelist of the church in Colossae (Col. 1:7,8; 4:12,13; Philem. 23),[5] but at the time Colossians was written (A.D. 61) he was with Paul in Rome and had no certain plans to return to Colossae (Col. 4:7,8). Although Epaphras did pastoral work among the churches of Colossae, Laodicea, and Hierapolis (Col. 4:13), there is no certain evidence that he was the sole pastor of a church.

James was an apostle who ministered uniquely to the Jews (Gal. 1:19; 2:9). Along with Peter and John, James was considered one of the "pillars" of the church (Gal. 2:9), not "*the* pillar." He was one of the most prominent leaders among the leaders in the church at Jerusalem and among all Jewish Christians (James 1:1; Gal. 2:12). Nevertheless, the New Testament never clearly identifies his official position in the church at Jerusalem. Luke and Paul do not reveal the nature of his formal relationship to the Twelve and the Jerusalem elders. I concur with Bruce Stabbert: "James has been a difficult person to pigeon-hole readily into the categories of ministry in the early church."[6]

In light of John's vision in which he sees seven golden lampstands and seven stars (Rev. 1:12,16,20), some scholars assert that the angels of the seven churches of Revelation were the pastors of the various local churches. The meaning of these symbols, however, is interpreted for us by our Lord Himself: the seven golden lampstands "are the seven churches" and the stars "are the angels of the seven churches" (Rev. 1:20; cf. 1 Cor. 11:10). So "the stars" are "angels" (Job 38:7), not human pastors or messengers.[7] Even if it could be demonstrated that "the stars" represent humans, the reference still doesn't disclose the official position of the human representatives (or messengers) or whether or not the representatives are the sole leaders of their local churches.

Still other scholars draw from the Old Testament and teach that churches should follow what is called the "Moses Model." It is not uncommon to hear them say, "Wasn't Moses the sole leader of Israel and the elders his assistants?" "Isn't the local pastor like Moses, and aren't the elders his assistants?" Yet the pastor of the local church certainly doesn't represent Moses. If anyone today is Moses, it is the Lord Jesus Christ. He leads us in all that we do and is always present with us (Matt. 18:20; 28:20). Christ is our Moses, our great Deliverer!

We must remember that Moses was a unique, one-time deliverer for the nation of Israel. He was not a permanent institution. He is an example to all godly leaders, yet it is hard even to describe his position and role (Deut. 34:10-12; Num. 12:6-8; Ex. 33:11). After the people of Israel settled in their cities, they were no longer to be led by Moses or his successor Joshua. They were to be led primarily by their local elders and the priestly family, with God as their King and Shepherd. Unfortunately, Israel never appreciated this blessed truth (1 Sam. 8).

To argue for pastoral oversight by a plurality of qualified elders is not to deny that God raises up extraordinarily gifted men to teach and lead His people. Certainly there are great evangelists, missionaries, teachers, preachers, and church planters whom God raises up to plant churches, recover truth, write, and correct His people. But this is a different matter from the governmental or organizational structure of the church. The organizational and pastoral oversight of the local church is to be in the hands of a plurality of qualified, pastor elders, not one person. The multi-gifted servants of God described above may or may not be local elders; in many cases they are not. Local elders need to call upon these gifted men for help in evangelism, teaching, and setting the vision for the church.

INSTRUCTION ABOUT ELDERS GIVEN TO THE CHURCHES

Not only does the New Testament provide examples of elder-led churches, it includes explicit instructions to churches about how to care for, protect, discipline, select, restore, obey, and call the elders. The apostles intended these instructions to be obeyed, and they should be regarded as normative teaching for all churches at all times.

- James instructs those who are sick to call for the elders of the church (James 5:14).
- Paul instructs the Ephesian church to financially support elders who labor "at preaching and teaching" (1 Tim. 5:17,18).
- Paul instructs the local church about protecting elders from false accusation, disciplining elders who sin, and restoring fallen elders (1 Tim. 5:19-22).
- Paul instructs the church as to the proper qualifications for eldership (1 Tim. 3:1-7; Titus 1:5-9).
- To the church in Ephesus, Paul states that anyone who desires to be an elder desires a noble work (1 Tim. 3:1).
- Paul instructs the church to examine prospective elders as to their qualifications (1 Tim. 3:10; 5:24,25).
- Peter instructs the young men of the church to submit to the church elders (1 Peter 5:5).
- The writer of Hebrews instructs his readers to obey and submit to the elders (Heb. 13:17).
- Paul teaches that elders are the household stewards, leaders, instructors, and teachers of the local church (Titus 1:7; 1 Thess. 5:12; Titus 1:9).
- Paul instructs the church to acknowledge, love, and live at peace with its elders (1 Thess. 5:12,13).

Instruction and Exhortation Given Directly to Elders

Not only is instruction given to the churches about elders, but Paul, Peter, and James give instructions directly to the elders.

- James tells elders to pray and anoint the sick with oil (James 5:14).

- Peter directly charges elders to pastor and oversee the local congregation (1 Peter 5:1,2).

- Peter warns elders against being too authoritative (1 Peter 5:3).

- Peter promises elders that when the Lord Jesus returns they will receive "the unfading crown of glory" (1 Peter 5:4).

- Peter exhorts elders to be clothed in humility (1 Peter 5:5).

- Paul reminds the Ephesians elders that the Holy Spirit placed them in the church as overseers to pastor the church of God (Acts 20:28).

- Paul exhorts elders to guard the church from false teachers (Acts 20:28) and to be alert to the constant threat of false doctrine (Acts 20:31).

- Paul reminds elders to work hard, help the needy, and be generous like the Lord Jesus Christ (Acts 20:35).

- Paul exhorts elders to live at peace with the congregation (1 Thess. 5:13).

These instructions contradict scholars who try to define the role of the New Testament elder by the Old Testament, Jewish elder.[8] Since, as these scholars see it, Old Testament elders were primarily rulers and judges, they conclude that Christian elders should be church rulers rather than teachers and pastors. Of course there are legitimate and instructive parallels between Old and New Testament elders, but the apostolic elder is not the Old Testament elder in a new age. To try to define the New Testament elder (Pauline elder) by the Old Testament elder or the Jewish synagogue elder (of which we know very little) is to distort the New Testament's teachings on eldership. The work and qualifications of the Christian elder are more clearly defined than those of the Old Testament elder.

New Testament, Christianized elders are not mere representatives of the people; they are, as the passages above show, spiritually qualified shepherds who protect, lead, and teach the people. They provide spiritual care for the entire flock. They are the official shepherds of the church.

Eldership Best Harmonizes with and Promotes the True Nature of the New Testament Church

The local church's structure of government makes a statement about the nature and philosophy of its ministry. The local church is not an undefined mass of people; it is a particular group of people that has a unique mission and purpose. I am convinced that the elder structure of government best harmonizes with and promotes the true nature of the local church as revealed in the New Testament. In Chapter 2, we enumerated three practical reasons for a plurality of elders: (1) balancing people's weaknesses, (2) lightening the work load, and (3) providing accountability. Now we will consider four ways in which the elder structure of government complements the nature of the local church.

The Church Is a Family of Brothers and Sisters

Of the different New Testament terms used to describe the nature of the church—the body, the bride, the temple, the flock—the most frequently used is the family, particularly the fraternal aspect of the family, *brethren.* Robert Banks, a prominent leader in the worldwide, home-church movement, makes this observation in his book, *Paul's Idea of Community*:

> Although in recent years Paul's metaphors for community have been subjected to quite intense study, especially his description of it as a "body," his application to it of "household" or "family" terminology has all too often been overlooked or only mentioned in passing.[9]

Banks further comments on the frequency and significance of these familial expressions:

> So numerous are these, and so frequently do they appear, that the comparison of the Christian community with a "family" must be

> regarded as the most significant metaphorical usage of all....More than any of the other images utilized by Paul, it reveals the essence of his thinking about community.[10]

The reason behind this preference for the familial aspect of the church is that only the most intimate of human relationships could express the love, closeness, privileges, and relationships that exist between God and man, and man and man, as a result of Christ's incarnation and death. The local Christian church, then, is to be a close-knit family of brothers and sisters.

The reality of this strong, familial community supersaturates the New Testament. The New Testament writers most commonly refer to the believers as *brethren.* Peter refers to the worldwide Christian community as "the brotherhood" (1 Peter 2:17; 5:9). The terms *brethren, brother,* or *sister* occur approximately 250 times throughout the New Testament. These terms are particularly abundant in Paul's letters.

The New Testament displays the family character of the Christian brotherhood in many practical ways:

- The early Christians met in homes (Rom. 16:5; 1 Cor. 16:19; Col. 4:15; Philem. 2).

- They shared material possessions (Acts 2:44,45; 4:32; 11:29; Rom. 12:13,20; 15:26; 1 Cor. 16:1; 2 Cor. 8; Gal. 2:10; 6:10; Heb. 13:16; James 2:15,16; 1 John 3:17).

- They ate together (Acts 2:46; 20:11; 1 Cor. 11:20 ff; Jude 12).

- They greeted one another with a holy kiss (Rom. 16:16; 1 Cor. 16:20; 2 Cor. 13:12; 1 Thess. 5:26; 1 Peter 5:14).

- They showed hospitality (Acts 16:15; 21:8,16; Rom. 12:13; 1 Tim. 3:2; 5:10; Heb. 13:2; 1 Peter 4:9; 3 John 5-8).

- They cared for widows (Acts 6:1-6; 9:39; 1 Tim. 5:1-16).

- When appropriate, they disciplined their members (1 Cor. 5-6; 2 Cor. 2:1-11; 2 Thess. 3:6-15; 1 Tim. 5:19,20).

Brotherliness also provided a key guiding principle for the management of relationships between Christians (Rom. 14:15,21; 1 Cor. 6:8; 8:11-13; 2 Thess. 3:14,15; Philem. 16; James 4:11). Jesus insisted that His followers were true brothers and sisters and that none among them should act like the rabbis of His day who elevated themselves above their fellow countrymen:

> But they do all their deeds to be noticed by men; for they broaden their phylacteries, and lengthen the tassels of their garments.
>
> And they love the place of honor at banquets, and the chief seats in the synagogues, and respectful greetings in the market places, and being called by men, Rabbi.
>
> *But do not be called Rabbi*; for One is your Teacher, and *you are all brothers* (Matt. 23:5-8; italics added).

In complete obedience to Christ's teaching on humility and brotherhood, the first Christians and their leaders resisted special titles, sacred clothes, chief seats, and lordly terminology to describe their community leaders. They also chose an appropriate leadership structure for their local congregations—leadership by a council of elders. The first Christians found within their biblical heritage a structure of government that was compatible with their new family and theological beliefs. Israel was a great family, composed of many individual families, and it found leadership by a plurality of elders to be a suitable form of self-government that provided fair representation for its members. The same is true of the local Christian church. The elder structure of government suits an extended family organization like the local church. It allows any brother in the community who desires and qualifies to share fully in the leadership of the community.

The Church Is a Nonclerical Community

Not only is the local church an intimate, loving family of redeemed brothers and sisters, it is a nonclerical family. Unlike Israel, which was divided into sacred priestly members and lay members, the first-century Christian church was a people's movement. The distinguishing mark of Christianity was not found in a clerical hierarchy, but in the fact that God's Spirit came to dwell within ordinary, common people and that through them the Spirit manifested Jesus' life to the believing community and the world.

It is an immensely profound truth that no special priestly or clerical class in distinction from the whole people of God appears in the New Testament. Under the new covenant ratified by the blood of Christ, every member of the Church of Jesus Christ is a holy saint, a royal priest, and Spirit-gifted member of the body of Christ. Paul taught that a wide diversity of gifts and services exists within the body of Christ (1 Cor. 12), but he says absolutely nothing about a mystical gap between sacred clergy and common laity. Surely something as fundamental to the Church as the clergy-laity division should at least be mentioned in the New Testament. The New Testament, however, stresses the oneness of the people of God (Eph. 2:13-19) and the dismantling of the sacred-secular concept that existed between priest and people under the old covenant (1 Peter 2:5-10; Rev. 1:6).

Yet it is deeply ingrained in the minds of many Protestants that only the ordained clergyman is qualified to pastor the church, lead in worship, administer the Lord's Supper, pronounce the blessing, preach, and baptize and that the believing community as a whole is unfit to carry out these functions. Marjorie Warkentin, in an evenhanded and thorough study on the doctrine of ordination, is right when she warns that the practices of many Protestants regarding the ordained clergyman are dangerously close to the sacramental concept of ordination: "The insistence among some that only the ordained may administer baptism and conduct the Lord's Supper demonstrates the persistence of the sacramental view of ordination."[11] Examples of the sacramental clericalism Warkentin describes abound, even among conservative Protestants.

Observe how David and Vera Mace, prominent leaders in the field of marital counseling, refer to the Protestant pastor in their book, *What's Happening to Clergy Marriages?*:

> ...The pastor is not simply a leader, an authority. He also exercises priestly functions that are forbidden to all other members of the church. He administers the sacraments, receiving the power to do so from his ordination. In this capacity he acts directly as the representative of Christ, and this gives him a special aura of holiness.[12]

In an article in the Dallas Theological Seminary journal, *Bibliotheca*

Sacra, John E. Johnson, a Baptist pastor, asserts that the pastor finds his identity and roles in the Old Testament offices of prophet, priest, king, and sage. Regarding the pastor's role as priest, Johnson says, "Like Old Testament priests, pastors are part of a formally designated and consecrated ministry, the nature of which calls for priestly acts at their deepest levels." [13] Without the slightest scriptural support, he further comments:

> Like Old Testament priests, pastors ultimately bear responsibility for the service of worship. While others fulfill certain roles, from arranging flowers to organizing the choir, the pastor carries the responsibility of preserving the dignity of God's house. He is responsible for presiding over worship services, helping others prepare to meet God.[14]

As for the pastor's role as king, Johnson writes, "Part of pastoral identity is wrapped up in climbing the mountain, looking out over the horizon, charting the course, and collecting the people along the way."[15] The Maces' and Johnson's claims for the pastor are unbiblical, wildly exaggerated, and utterly demeaning to the Spirit-indwelt people of God and the work and position of Jesus Christ over His people.

Clericalism does not represent biblical, apostolic Christianity. Indeed, the real error to be contended with is not simply that one man provides leadership for the congregation, but that one person in the holy brotherhood has been sacralized apart from the brotherhood to an unscriptural status. In practice, the ordained clergyman—the minister, the reverend—is *the Protestant priest*.

Biblical eldership cannot exist in an environment of clericalism. Paul's employment of the elder structure of government for the local church is clear, practical evidence against clericalism because the eldership is nonclerical in nature. The elders are always viewed in the Bible as "elders of the people," or "elders of the congregation," never "elders of God." The elders represent the people as leading members from among the people.

When establishing churches, Paul never ordained a priest or cleric to perform the church's ministry. When he established a church, he left behind a council of elders chosen from among the believers to jointly oversee the local community (Acts 14:23; Titus 1:5). Obviously that was all he felt a local church needed. Since the local congregation was composed of saints, priests, and Spirit-empowered servants, and since Christ was present with each congregation in the person of the Holy Spirit, none of the traditional religious trappings such as sacred sites, sacred buildings, or sacred personnel (priests, clerics, or holy men) were needed. Nor could such be tolerated. To meet the need for community leadership and protection, Paul provided the nonclerical, elder structure of government—a form of government that would not demean the Lordship of Christ over His people or the glorious status of a priestly, saintly, body of people in which every member ministered.

The Church Is a Humble-Servant Community

I am convinced that one of the reasons the apostles chose the elder system of government was because it enhanced the loving, humble-servant character of the Christian family. The New Testament provides a consistent example of shared leadership as the ideal structure of leadership in a congregation where love, humility, and servanthood are paramount. When it functions properly, shared leadership requires a greater exercise of humble servanthood than does unitary leadership. In order for an eldership to operate effectively, the elders must show mutual regard for one another, submit themselves one to another, patiently wait upon one another, genuinely consider one another's interests and perspectives, and defer to one another. Eldership, then, enhances brotherly love, humility, mutuality, patience, and loving interdependence—qualities that are to mark the servant church.

Furthermore, shared leadership is often more trying than unitary leadership. It exposes our impatience with one another, our stubborn pride, our bull-headedness, our selfish immaturity, our domineering disposition, our lack of love and understanding of one another, and our prayerlessness. It also shows how underdeveloped and immature we really are in humility, brotherly love, and the true servant spirit. Like the saints at Corinth, we are quick to develop our knowledge and public gifts, but slow to mature in love and humility.

I believe that churches today desperately need a revival of love, humility, and the servant spirit. Such a revival must begin with our leaders, and biblical eldership provides the structure through which leaders learn to work together in mutual love and humility. Since the eldership represents a microcosm of the whole church, it provides a living model of loving relationships and servanthood for the whole body. Thus, leadership by a plurality of elders ideally suits the humble-servant church.

The Church Is Under Christ's Headship

Most important, biblical eldership guards and promotes the preeminence and position of Christ over the local church. Jesus left His disciples with the precious promise that "'where two or three have gathered together in My name, there I am in their midst'" (Matt. 18:20). Because the apostles knew that Jesus Christ, by the Holy Spirit, was uniquely present with them as Ruler, Head, Lord, Pastor, Master, Overseer, High Priest, and King, they chose a form of government that reflected this distinctive, fundamental, Christian truth. This concept was no theoretical idea to the early Christians—it was reality. The first churches were truly Christ-centered, Christ-dependent churches. Christ alone provided all they needed to be in full fellowship with God and one another. Christ's person and work was so infinitely great, final, and complete, that nothing—even in appearance—was to diminish the centrality of His presence among and sufficiency for His people.

So in the first century, no Christian would dare take the position or title of sole ruler, overseer, or pastor of the church. We Christians today, however, are so accustomed to speaking of "the pastor" that we do not stop to realize that the New Testament does not. This fact is profoundly significant, and we must not permit our customary practice to shield our minds from this important truth. There is only one flock and one Pastor (John 10:16), one body and one Head (Col. 1:18), one holy priesthood and one great High Priest (Heb. 4:14ff.), one brotherhood and one Elder Brother (Rom. 8:29), one building and one Cornerstone (1 Peter 2:5ff.), one Mediator, one Lord. Jesus Christ is "Senior Pastor," and all others are His undershepherds (1 Peter 5:4).

To symbolize the reality of Christ's leadership and presence over the local church and its leaders, one church that I know of places an empty chair at the table next to the chairman during all elders' meetings. This is a visual reminder to the elders of Christ's presence and lordship, of their position as His undershepherds, and of their dependence on Him through prayer and the Word.

Conclusion: An Apostolic Directive

Since the elder structure of government was established by Paul among Gentile churches (Acts 14:23) and, most likely, by the Twelve among Jewish churches (Acts 15:6; James 5:14), the New Testament writers assumed eldership to be a fixed, apostolic institution. In Titus 1:5, Paul tells Titus and the churches that a church is not properly ordered until qualified elders (plural) have been appointed. So he orders Titus to install elders: "Appoint elders in every city as I directed you" (Titus 1:5). By doing this, Paul was going against customary cultural practices because in both the Jewish synagogue and in Greco-Roman society one-man oversight was commonly practiced. Thus Paul's choice of the elder structure of government was intentional. He was not simply accommodating himself to current social norms. His instruction to Titus established an apostolic directive that should be followed by Christians today.

Many scholars contend, however, that only the instructions about elders, not the elder structure, are universally binding on churches. They would say that Paul's instructions regarding the qualifications of an elder are binding, but that the structure is not. By making this distinction, they can eliminate the eldership structure from the church and apply the biblical instructions to their self-appointed institutions—the clerical structure or the singular pastorate. But this is an erroneous distinction. How, for example, would a critically important passage like 1 Timothy 5:17,18 apply to the singular pastorate? This instruction makes sense only in the context of a plurality of elders.

I conclude, therefore, that the instructions given to elders and about elders, as well as the eldership structure itself, are to be regarded as apostolic directives (Titus 1:5) that are normative for churches today. Ladd is quite wrong when he claims, "there was no normative pattern of church government in the apostolic age, and that the organizational structure of the church is no essential element in the theology of the church."[16]

We would do well to heed the sober warning against doubting the full sufficiency of Scripture to direct the practices of our churches today that is offered by Alfred Kuen, a Bible teacher at the Emmaus Bible Institute in Switzerland:

> Has not the history of twenty centuries of Christianity proved that the plan of the primitive church is the only one which is suitable for all times and places, is most flexible in its adaptation to the most diverse conditions, is the best able to resist and stand against persecutions, and offers the maximum of possibilities for the full development of the spiritual life?

> Each time that man has believed himself to be more intelligent than God, that he has painstakingly developed a religious system "better adapted to the psychology of man," more conformable to the spirit of our times, instead of simply following the neotestamentary model, his attempt has been short-lived because of failure due to some unforeseen difficulty.
>
> All heresies and deviations in the church spring from the abandonment of the Scripture and of the model for the church which they present.[17]

In short, as Alfred Kuen concludes, "the churches established by the apostles remain the valid models for churches of all times and places."[18]

Part Three

THE EXPOSITION OF SCRIPTURE

CHAPTER 7

The Acts of the Apostles

"Elders for them in every church."

Acts 14:23

The book of Acts, according to New Testament commentator F.F. Bruce (1910-1990), is "the second volume to a *History of Christian Origins*."[1] The Gospel of Luke, of course, is the first volume. Because it records the inspired history of early Christianity and is the only historical backdrop to the epistles, Acts is the logical starting point for the study of Christian elders. The book of Acts provides the foundational material for our study and includes two of the most significant texts on eldership: Acts 14:23 and 20:17-38. Acts also provides helpful examples of the first Christian elders at work and is indispensable to understanding Paul's church planting practices and his distinctive, Christian teaching on eldership.

JEWISH CHRISTIAN ELDERS

At the beginning, the twelve apostles were the official overseers of the Christian community. But at an early, unrecorded date, a body of elders emerged that was fully recognized by the congregation and the apostles as leaders of the community. It is commonly thought that the first Christians borrowed the elder structure of government from the synagogue. Whether or not that is true is difficult to say with certainty, and really is not overly important.[2] No matter how much or how little borrowing occurred, the first Christian congregations clearly weren't reorganized synagogues. For example, the chief, presiding official of the synagogue was called "the ruler of the synagogue" (Luke 8:49; 13:14; Acts 18:8,17), but Christian congregations never adopted this practice. The Christian churches were led by a plurality of elders, not by a chief ruler.

Leadership by a council of men called *elders* predates the synagogue and was very familiar to the Jews and to all readers of the Greek Old Testament. The council of elders was one of Israel's oldest and most fundamental institutions. It was nearly as basic as the family. Israel's elders were the people's official representatives. Hence they are called the "elders of the people" (Ex. 19:7) or the "elders of the congregation" (Judg. 21:16). The elders were the eyes, ears, and voice of the people. To speak to Israel's elders was to speak to the people (Ex. 4:29,31; 12:3,21,27; 19:7,8; Lev. 4:13-15; Deut. 21:3-8; 2 Sam. 5:1,3; 2 Sam. 17:4,14; 1 Chron. 15:25,28).

Israel's elders were not mere figureheads. Although there is no explanation of their origin, appointment, or qualifications, Israel's elders are mentioned approximately one-hundred times in the Old Testament. Their vital leadership role is displayed by their active involvement in every crucial event in Israel's history. From the time they were slaves in Egypt, the elders provided leadership for the people. God acknowledged the elders' leadership role by sending Moses to them first to announce the people's deliverance (Ex. 3:16). Government by elders was particularly well-suited to a patriarchal, family-oriented society such as Israel and continued to exist after Moses and Joshua completed their task of leading the nation into the Promised Land.

When Israel settled in the Land of Promise, each city, each tribe, and the nation as a whole had a council of elders. As community leaders, the elders were to protect the people, exercise discipline, enforce the law of God, and administer justice. According to Mosaic law, as well as by traditional practice, the elders exercised far-reaching authority in civil, domestic, and religious matters. The elders' role as a judicial body is described in the legislative portions of the Old Testament. The book of Deuteronomy especially lays out specific situations that required the elders' judgment and counsel—from hearing murder cases to judging the most intimate family matters (Deut. 19:11,12; 21:1-8, 18-20; 22:16-19; 25:7-9; Josh. 20:2-4). The elders were to know the law, to bear (along with the priests) responsibility of communicating the law to the people regularly and publicly, and to ensure that the law was obeyed (Deut. 27:1-8; 31:9-11).

The Old Testament elders were preeminently men of counsel and wisdom. The concept of wisdom and discernment is implied in the word, *elder,* itself: "Wisdom is with aged men, with long life is understanding" (Job 12:12, also 1 Kings 12:8,13). To be an elder is to be a wise man and counselor. The prophet Ezekiel wrote that visions belong to the prophet, law to the priest, and counsel to the elders: "Disaster will come upon disaster, and rumor will be added to rumor; then they will seek a vision from a prophet, but the law will be lost from the priest and counsel from the elders" (Ezek. 7:26). Job refers to the sovereign God who takes away the discernment of the elders (Job 12:20; cf. Pss. 105:22; 119:100; Lam. 2:10; 5:14).

At the time of Christ, there were local and national Jewish elders. Luke mentions local Jewish elders only once: "And a certain centurion's slave, who was highly regarded by him, was sick and about to die. And when he heard about Jesus, *he sent some Jewish elders* asking Him to come and save the life of his slave. And when they had come to Jesus, they earnestly entreated Him, saying, 'He is worthy for You to grant this to him; for he loves our nation, and it was *he who built us our synagogue.*'" (Luke 7:2-5; italics added). Exactly who these local elders were and what their relationship to the synagogue was, however, we don't know.

All other references to nonChristian, Jewish elders that occur in the Gospels and Acts are associated with the Sanhedrin of Jerusalem. The Sanhedrin was the supreme court of the Jewish people, and the New Testament indicates a threefold classification of its members: high priests, scribes, and elders. Their frequent appearance is due to their leading role in the rejection and death of Christ: "And He began to teach them that the Son of Man must suffer many things and be rejected by the elders and the chief priests and the scribes" (Mark 8:31). Judging from the meager historical information available, it appears that these elders were part of the nonpriestly nobility, heads of important, wealthy Judean families. Joseph of Arimathea, whom Matthew identifies as a rich man of Arimathea was one such elder (Matt. 27:57). In addition, the entire Sanhedrin is referred to three times in the New Testament as the council of elders (*presbyterion*, Luke 22:66; Acts 22:5; *gerousia,* Acts 5:21). The eldership structure of government, therefore, was very familiar to the Jewish Christians.

In adopting this familiar form of government, we can be certain that the apostles' choice was no arbitrary decision. Prayer and the Spirit's leading guided the twelve apostles and the first Jewish Christian community to establish leadership by a council of elders. As the church's official community leaders, the elders received money for the poor and were responsible for its proper administration. They judged doctrinal issues, provided counsel, and spoke for the congregation.

Luke mentions these Jewish Christian elders three times in his history of beginning Christianity. Let us now examine what Luke reveals about the elders' role through these historic events.

THEY RECEIVE AND ADMINISTER MONEY

Luke mentions Christian church elders for the first time in Acts 11:30:

> Now at this time some prophets came down from Jerusalem to Antioch. And one of them named Agabus stood up and began to indicate by the Spirit that there would certainly be a great famine all over the world. And this took place in the reign of Claudius. And in the proportion that any of the disciples [in Antioch] had means, each of them determined to send a contribution for the relief of the brethren living in Judea. And this they did, sending it in charge of Barnabas and Saul to the elders [*presbyterous*] (Acts 11:29,30).

It was to the Jewish Christian elders that the Christians in Antioch sent their contribution for the poor (A.D. 47). The elders' actual role in the distribution of the funds is not explained by Luke, but the fact that money was placed into their care reveals that they were the church's official representatives. As such, they received the offering on behalf of the church and were responsible for its proper administration.

Word Study on Presbyteros

The Greek word for "elder" is *presbyteros*, which is derived from the adjective *presbys,* which means "old." *Presbyteros* is the comparative form, meaning "older" (Luke 15:25). However, in many cases the comparative force disappears and *presbyteros* simply means "old" or "old man." The term *presbyteros* also carries a twofold sense as a designation for age and a title for office. In a few contexts it is hard to know which of these designations is intended, but in most cases the intended meaning is clear. Depending on the context, then, *presbyteros* can mean:

(1) "older man" or "old man," as in 1 Timothy 5:1: "Do not sharply rebuke an older man [*presbyteros*]."

(2) a title for a community official, an "elder," as in 1 Timothy 5:17: "Let the elders [*presbyteroi*] who rule well be considered worthy of double honor."

Although the strict sense of advanced age is eliminated from the meaning of elder when referring to a community leader, certain connotations such as maturity, experience, dignity, authority, and honor are retained. Thus the term *elder* conveys positive concepts of maturity, respect, and wisdom. When *presbyteros* is used of a community leader, it is most commonly used in the plural form, *presbyteroi*. This is because the elder structure of leadership is leadership by a council of elders.

THEY JUDGE DOCTRINAL ISSUES

Jerusalem was the first center and hub of Christianity. It was also home base for the twelve apostles. But by A.D. 41, the gospel message had expanded to the great city of Antioch in Syria, the third largest city of the Roman empire (Acts 11:19-22). Antioch lay 310 miles north of Jerusalem. Unlike the church in Jerusalem, the church in Antioch comprised both Jews and a large population of Gentiles. It was, as F.F. Bruce says, "the citadel of Gentile Christianity."[3] Two of its leading teachers were Paul and Barnabas, the preeminent pioneers of the Gentile gospel mission (Acts 13:1-14:27; Gal. 2:7-10).

Trouble brewed between these two great centers of early Christianity. In Jerusalem and Judea, legalistic, zealous Jews worried about Gentile salvation apart from the law and circumcision (Acts 15:5; 21:20-26; Gal. 2:1-12). Eventually some of these agitators made their way to Antioch. Their appearance prompted Luke's second mention of the Jewish Christian elders:

> And some men came down from Judea and began teaching the brethren, "Unless you are circumcised according to the custom of Moses, you cannot be saved." And when Paul and Barnabas had great dissension and debate with them, the brethren determined that Paul and Barnabas and certain others of them should go up to Jerusalem to the apostles and elders concerning this issue (Acts 15:1,2).

Alarmed by this teaching on Antiochene soil, Paul and Barnabas strenuously debated these Judaizing teachers. But because these Jewish teachers were from Judea and claimed the church of Jerusalem as their home, and possibly as their authority (Acts 15:24), the church in Antioch decided to press the debate back to its home ground—Jerusalem.

> And when they arrived at Jerusalem, they were received by the church and the apostles and the elders, and they reported all that God had done with them (Acts 15:4).

> And the apostles and the elders came together to look into this matter (Acts 15:6).

"It was true wisdom, therefore," states biblical commentator William Kelly (1821-1906), "to transfer the further discussion of the question to the source from which the mischief had come."[4]

It is essential to note that the decision to go to Jerusalem was a voluntary decision on the part of the church in Antioch. There is no biblical evidence to suggest that there was an established, supreme court in Jerusalem to which all Christian churches were answerable. Rather, the leaders of the church in Jerusalem needed to publicly clarify their position and policies regarding Gentile evangelization and fellowship. So for the sake of unity among the churches, respect for Jerusalem and the apostles, the future Gentile mission, and the defeat of the false gospel, the church in Antioch sent its key leaders to Jerusalem to further debate the issue (Acts 15:2). Antioch, not Jerusalem, initiated the conference.

This momentous meeting in Jerusalem in A.D. 49 is sometimes called "the Apostolic Council." This terminology might imply to some readers that only the apostles deliberated together. This, however, was not the case. Luke writes that "the apostles and the elders came together to look into this matter" (Acts 15:6). Plainly "the apostles and the elders," as the church's official leaders, jointly shared in these deliberations.

The elders' close association with the apostles demonstrates their significant position and role in the church at Jerusalem. Even though the elders could not claim the same distinction as the apostles, they represented at that time the leadership of the church in Jerusalem. The apostles' unique, universal commission required them to travel. So as the apostles gradually left Jerusalem, the daily supervision of the church became the elders' responsibility. The elders' role, therefore, was absolutely essential in combating any legalistic error that might emanate from Jerusalem (Acts 15:5).

Because of the Jerusalem elders' close association with the twelve apostles, their leadership of the first Christian church, and their conservative Jewish character, they possessed a unique status and influence among the churches. The disavowal of the Judaizers' legalistic gospel by the apostles and the Jerusalem elders was of utmost importance to Gentile Christians. Yet there is no clear evidence from the New Testament that the Jerusalem elders had formal jurisdiction over Gentile churches.

Furthermore, the decision reached at this conference was the decision of the apostles, elders, and church in Jerusalem.[5] It was not a joint decision by all the churches of Judea, Syria, or Cilicia. The "church" mentioned in verses 4 and 22 is the church in Jerusalem, not Antioch. The resulting letter makes this clear:

> Then it seemed good to the apostles and the elders [of Jerusalem], with the whole church [in Jerusalem, vv. 4, 12], to choose men from among them [Jerusalem] to send to Antioch with Paul and Barnabas...and they sent this letter by them, "The apostles and the brethren who are elders, to the brethren in Antioch and Syria and Cilicia who are from the Gentiles, greetings. Since we have heard that some of our number to whom we gave no instruction have disturbed you with their words, unsettling your souls, it seemed good to us, having become of one mind, to select men to send to you with our beloved Barnabas and Paul...For it seemed good to the Holy Spirit and to us to lay upon you no greater burden than these essentials" (Acts 15:22-25,28).

I emphasize these historical facts because Acts 15 is often misused to justify the authority of church councils and permanent church courts above the local church. For example, Presbyterian scholar James Bannerman (1807-1868) wrote, "Now, in this narrative [Acts 15] we have all the elements necessary to make up the idea of a supreme ecclesiastical court, with authority over not only the members and office-bearers within the local bounds of the congregations represented, but also the Presbyteries or inferior Church courts included in the same limits."[6]

Bannerman's conclusions, however, represent ecclesiastical dogma rather than historical, biblical fact. His conclusions certainly have no support in the teachings of the epistles. First Timothy is the primary New Testament epistle on church order. Yet it says nothing about an organizational structure or court that has authority over a local congregation. When one considers the serious doctrinal disruptions in the church at Ephesus, the absence of any mention of church courts above the local church (if such existed) is unthinkable.

It is historical fact that no formal interchurch federation, denominational union, or fixed organizational framework linked churches together for the first two hundred years of the Christian era. In his classic work, *The Organization of the Early Christian Churches*, renowned church historian and classical scholar Edwin Hatch (1835-1889) demonstrates that no superior individual or organizational body ruled over local Christian congregations. Each congregation was self-governing and independent, with the jurisdiction of its elders restricted to the local congregation:

> In the course of the second century the custom of meeting in representative assemblies began to prevail among the Christian communities....
>
> At first these assemblies were more or less informal. Some prominent and influential bishop invited a few neighbouring communities to confer with his own: the result of the deliberations of such a conference was expressed sometimes in a resolution, sometimes in a letter addressed to other Churches. It was the rule for such letters to be received with respect: for the sense of brotherhood was strong, and the causes of alienation were few. But so far from such letters having any binding force on other Churches, not even the resolutions of the conference were binding

> on a dissentient minority of its members. Cyprian [died A.D. 258], in whose days these conferences first became important, and who was at the same time the most vigorous of early preachers of catholic unity—both of which circumstances would have made him a supporter of their authoritative character if such authoritative character had existed—claims in emphatic and explicit terms an absolute independence for each community. Within the limits of his own community a bishop has no superior but God.
>
> But no sooner had Christianity been recognized by the State than such conferences tended to multiply, to become not occasional but ordinary, and to pass resolutions which were regarded as binding upon the Churches within the district from which representatives had come, and the acceptance of which was regarded as a condition of other provinces....
>
> It was by these gradual steps that the Christian Churches moved from their original state of independence into a great confederation.[7]

In the face of overwhelming historical evidence for the "original completeness and autonomy"[8] of each local church, Acts 15 cannot be made to justify interchurch organizations or courts with authority over the local church. Although each local church originally was a separate and complete entity that was dependent on no higher court or person, there were varied and important links between the first Christian churches. Churches were to seek to conform to universal church practices as taught by the apostles (1 Cor. 7:17; 4:17; 14:33,36). Churches sacrificially shared their finances with poorer churches. Churches sent greetings and letters to one another. Teachers traveled freely among the congregations, and all believers had the responsibility to offer hospitality to traveling Christians and preachers. Believers from all churches were to pray for one another and love one another; they were to view themselves as a worldwide brotherhood that transcended all cultural and racial boundaries.

We can learn from Acts 15 important information about the elders' responsibilities and position, however. Church elders hear and judge doctrinal issues. They help resolve conflict. They protect the church from false teachers. They bear responsibility for the doctrines taught by the members of their flock. Elders, therefore, must be men who know God's Word. In a hostile world filled with satanic lies and false teachings, churches desperately need shepherd elders who are sound in judgment and possess the knowledge of the truth.

THEY PROVIDE COUNSEL AND RESOLVE CONFLICT

Paul's appearance in Jerusalem in A.D. 57 to deliver the Gentiles' offering for the poor furnishes the background for Acts' third mention of the Jewish Christian elders:

> And now the following day Paul went in with us to James, and all the elders were present. And after he had greeted them, he began to relate one by one the things which God had done among the Gentiles through his ministry. And when they heard it they began glorifying God; and they said to him, "You see, brother, how many thousands there are among the Jews of those who have believed, and they are all zealous for the Law; and they have been told about you, that you are teaching all the Jews who are among the Gentiles to forsake Moses, telling them not to circumcise their children nor to walk according to the customs.
>
> What, then, is to be done? They will certainly hear that you have come.
>
> Therefore do this that we tell you. We have four men who are under a vow; take them and purify yourself along with them, and pay their expenses in order that they may shave their heads; and all will know that there is nothing to the things which they have been told about you, but that you yourself also walk orderly, keeping the Law.
>
> But concerning the Gentiles who have believed, we wrote, having decided that they should abstain from meat sacrificed to idols and from blood and from what is strangled and from fornication" (Acts 21:18-25).

The reference to James at the beginning of this passage naturally prompts several questions: "Who was James?" "What was his position in the church?" and "What was the official relationship between James and the elders?" The answers to these questions give insight into the nature of the church and Christian leadership.

The James referred to here is "James, the Lord's brother," as Paul calls him (Gal. 1:19; 2:9,12; 1 Cor. 15:7). Although we may be inclined to wonder what position James held in the church, Luke seems to have little interest in James' title or official position. A major reason for this disinterest is found in the revolutionary teachings of Jesus concerning brotherhood in the community of the risen Christ. Jesus sternly warned His disciples against the prideful obsession with titles and positions that characterized the typical religious leaders of His day. He forbade them from taking honorific titles in the fraternal community: "But do not be called Rabbi; for One is your Teacher, and *you are all brothers*" (Matt. 23:6-12; italics added).

The practical implementation of Jesus' teaching is found throughout the New Testament, and this passage is a good example of the biblical writers' basic disinterest with formal titles and rank. Although Luke mentions James four times in the book of Acts, he does not once identify his position in the church (Acts 1:14; 12:17; 15:13-21; 21:18). Galatians 1:19 seems to classify James as an apostle, yet there is some uncertainty about the statement concerning James' apostleship that appears in that passage. Many in Jerusalem considered James to be of equal status with Peter and John as one of the "pillars" of the church (Gal. 2:9). At the Jerusalem council, James spoke as one of the chief spokesmen of the council and church (Acts 15:13-21). James' letter "to the twelve tribes who are dispersed abroad" (James. 1:1) reveals his widespread influence and great stature among Jewish Christians. It also exhibits his outstanding personal character and remarkable prophet-like teaching. James was so highly esteemed by the believers that Jude could identify himself simply as the "brother of James" (Jude 1). The first Christians had high esteem for the brothers of Jesus (1 Cor. 9:5). Peter's command to notify James of his deliverance from prison (Acts 12:17), James' leading role at the Jerusalem council, and Paul's encounters with him all reveal James' unquestionable leadership position and prominence among his Jewish Christian brethren, yet his exact title and position remains unspecified.

The question regarding the official relationship between James and the elders has long been debated. In the early centuries of Christianity, it was commonly thought that James was the bishop of Jerusalem and the elders were his clergy. Others claimed that James was the twelfth apostle. These ideas have no basis in Scripture, however.

Scripture reveals (in Acts 15) that "the apostles and elders" met together as a council and it identifies James as one of the principle speakers. Unfortunately, Acts 15 doesn't identify the group to which James belonged. There is a slight indication, however, that he was counted among the elders because Luke most frequently uses the term "apostles" to refer to the Twelve. This would be especially true in Acts 15, but for a possible exception to this see Acts 14:4,14. It is possible, then, that James was both an apostle (Gal. 1:19) and an elder (Acts 15). If that is true, then he was *primus inter pares* ("first among equals") among the elders.

Although the account begins with James as the central person, the dialogue is clearly between Paul and the assembly of brothers (Acts 21:18-25). Note that Luke uses the plural form throughout this passage: "And after he had greeted *them...a*nd when *they* heard it *they* began glorifying God...and *they* said unto him...therefore do this that *we* tell you...*we* have...*we* wrote."

The meeting between Paul and James and the Jerusalem elders was a critical one. Luke recalls that all the elders were present, although he doesn't give a specific number. This statement demonstrates clearly that a distinct, recognizable body of elders existed. At the meeting, the bond of Christian fellowship between Paul, James, and the elders was renewed. It had been five years since Paul was last in Jerusalem (A.D. 52). They rejoiced at Paul's report of what God was doing among the Gentiles, but their own pressing problems—created by their zealous fellow Jews—quickly dominated the meeting. The elders explain the situation they faced:

> You see, brother, how many thousands there are among the Jews of those who have believed, and they are all zealous for the Law; and they have been told about you, that you are teaching all the Jews who are among the Gentiles to forsake Moses, telling them not to circumcise their children nor to walk according to the customs (Acts 21:20,21).

This was a critical problem that James and the elders had to resolve. The elders were under titanic pressure from both believing and nonbelieving Jews concerning Gentile fraternization and threats to the Law of Moses. Rumors spread by anti-Pauline teachers had poisoned even the Jewish believers' attitude toward Paul. It was said that Paul was teaching Jewish Christians not to circumcise their children and to forsake Moses. Such rumors, of course, were distortions of Paul's teachings. The elders were clearly caught in the middle—a place elders frequently find themselves. Nevertheless, as the church's leaders, they had to face the problems and provide answers to sensitive, theological questions. They walked a fine line trying to protect Paul, the Gentile mission, and the church in Jerusalem. So they had to be wise counselors, judges, peacemakers, and arbitrators.

To help calm an explosive situation, James and the elders devised a plan, recorded in verses 23-25, whereby Paul could publicly disavow false criticism before his Jewish brethren, and the elders could maintain their previous counsel regarding Gentile salvation and peaceful, Jew-Gentile coexistence (Acts 15:11,19,28,29).[9] Paul judged the elders' counsel to be a wise plan for shedding false rumors and establishing peace, and acted upon it.

ELDERS OF THE GENTILE CHURCHES

Acts chapters 13 and 14 record the first missionary journey of Paul and Barnabas (A.D. 48-49), a momentous turning point in the history of Christianity. In a bold, new way, their gospel mission opened "the door of faith to the Gentiles" (Acts 13:46,48; 14:27). After preaching the gospel and planting churches in the cities of Pisidian Antioch, Iconium, Lystra, and Derbe, Paul and Barnabas, before returning to Antioch in Syria, visited their newly founded churches. What is profoundly significant to our study is that upon their visit, they appointed elders in every church. Luke records:

> And when they had appointed elders for them in every church, having prayed with fasting, they commended them to the Lord in whom they had believed (Acts 14:23).

This text records the first appearance of Christian elders among Gentile churches. It reveals who decided on the eldership structure of government for the churches and who appointed the elders. No information like this exists concerning the origin of elders in either the Old Testament or among the Jewish Christian churches. Most important, the passage provides indispensable historical information on Paul's method of organizing churches. Although this is the only time Luke records that Paul appointed elders, the account is most likely intended to be a summary statement on Paul's customary method of organizing his churches.

Scholars have long recognized the significance of this passage. Sir William Ramsay (1851-1939), the pioneer New Testament archaeologist and expert on Luke's historical research, states:

> It is clear, therefore, that Paul everywhere instituted elders in his new churches; and on our hypothesis as to the accurate and methodical expression of the historian [Luke], we are bound to infer that this first case is intended to be typical of the way of appointment followed in all later cases. When Paul directed Titus (1:5) to appoint Elders in each Cretan city, he was doubtless thinking of the same method which he followed here.[10]

J.B. Lightfoot (1828-1889), Anglican bishop and one of the most learned New Testament and patristic scholars of his time, also noted:

> On their very first missionary journey the Apostles Paul and Barnabas are described as appointing presbyters in every church. The same rule was doubtless carried out in all the brotherhoods founded later; but it is mentioned here and here only, because the mode of procedure on this occasion would suffice as a type of the apostles' dealings elsewhere under similar circumstances.[11]

Because Paul was Christ's special apostle and teacher of the Gentiles (1 Tim. 2:7), what he did in these newly planted churches should be of paramount importance to us. In the sovereign will and gifting of God, Paul was a "wise master builder" (1 Cor. 3:10) who successfully laid the foundation of these first Gentile churches. Roland Allen reminds us that "in little more than ten years St. Paul established the Church in four provinces of the Empire, Galatia, Macedonia, Achaia and Asia. Before A.D. 47 there were no Churches in these provinces; in A.D. 57 St. Paul could speak as if his work there was done."[12] The fact that Paul saw the establishment of elders as strategically important is therefore of great significance.

The historical information provided by Acts 14:23 is also vital because in his letters to the churches, Paul does not use the term *elder* or indicate that he appointed elders. For example, in writing to the Galatians in A.D. 49 (that is, to the churches of Pisidian Antioch, Iconium,

Lystra, and Derbe) for the purpose of correcting serious doctrinal error, Paul never once mentions elders or any other leaders. He writes directly to the members of the congregations. We know only from Acts 14:23 that there were officially appointed elders in these churches, so the text provides invaluable historical data for both the study of eldership and the Pauline letters.

Appointing Elders for the Churches of Galatia

Paul and Barnabas knew that each local church needed some structure for governing itself in their absence. Although the churches existed for a short time without elders, they still were recognized as churches (Acts 14:23). Thus, the ministry of elders is not essential to the existence of a local church; the Holy Spirit's presence is the only essential element. But God doesn't neglect the basic human need for leadership. No society can operate without leadership and structure, and the local Christian church is no exception. Even in heaven, around the throne of God, twenty-four elders sit on thrones (Rev. 4:4). So as Spirit-led, wise church planters, Paul and Barnabas chose the elder system of government and appointed a body of elders for each church.

Luke writes, "And when they had appointed elders [plural] for them in every church [singular]." The phrase "in every" represents the Greek preposition *kata*. Here it is used in the distributive sense, meaning "in each individual church."[13] Literally the passage reads: "having appointed for them *church by church*, elders." Thus each local church had apostolically appointed elders.

By establishing elders for each church, Paul followed the practice of the church in Jerusalem and other Jewish congregations (James 5:14). We can be sure that Paul's choice of eldership was a Spirit-led, carefully calculated decision. He could easily have appointed one person as "chief ruler" of the local church, as was the case in all the Jewish synagogues, but he didn't. Instead, he chose eldership because it best suited the nature of the local Christian church (see chapter 6).

Paul chose elders from among the members of each new church. The reason Paul could appoint elders so soon after their conversion was that these men were already schooled in the Old Testament Scriptures and the life of the synagogue. These God-fearing Gentiles and

Jewish converts already knew God and the Scriptures, which is not true of all newly planted churches.

The word "appointed" is from the Greek verb *cheirotoneō*. Here the verb means "appoint," "designate," or "choose." Unfortunately this word has often been misinterpreted, causing much confusion and debate. Early churchmen, like the famous Greek orator and commentator John Chrysostom (A.D. ca. 344-407), used the word to mean ordination by laying on of hands.[14] In Luke's day, however, the word had nothing to do with ordination or the laying on of hands. In fact, Luke elsewhere employs a distinct Greek verb (*epitithēmi*) to designate the laying on of hands, which he doesn't use here (Acts 6:6; 8:17,19; 9:12,17; 13:3; 19:6; 28:8). Nothing stated or implied in this passage (Acts 14:23) suggests the laying on of hands or a special rite of ordination.

Other commentators have insisted that the word's root meaning indicates election by popular vote (*cheirotoneō* is composed of the two words, "hand" (*cheir*) and "to stretch" (*teinō*), thus "to extend the hand").[15] They claim that the founders merely presided over the churches' election of elders. This claim, however, is contrary to the plain language of the text. *Cheirotoneō* can mean to vote, but it also means to appoint or choose without reference to voting. Context and usage, not etymology, determine the word's meaning, and in this case the context is conclusive that "appoint" is the only possible meaning.

In contrast to these interpretations, all Greek lexicons and dictionaries, as well as all modern English Bible translations, agree on the meaning of *cheirotoneō* as "appoint."[16] Thus there should be no debate over the meaning of this term in the Acts 14:23 context. Ordination, laying on of hands, or election of elders by the congregation cannot be proven from this term or passage. Luke used a perfectly good Greek word to state that Paul and Barnabas appointed elders for the churches. The problem in interpretation is not with Luke's choice of words, but with biblical interpreters who erroneously trifle with etymology.

"The verb itself," as F. F. Bruce accurately states, "tells us nothing about the method of appointment."[17] Luke simply does not reveal what part the congregation played in the process of appointing these new elders. It is possible that Luke expected his readers to understand that the appointing of the Seven in Acts 6:1-6 established the pattern followed by all later appointments to church offices. Thus the verb "appointed" summarizes the whole process of selecting, examining, and installing into office.

If this assumption is true, then Paul and Barnabas, acting as the only official leaders of the churches, would have guided the whole process of elder appointment, just as the apostles did in Acts 6. Paul and Barnabas would have formally placed the first elders into office, but the congregation would have examined and selected qualified candidates (see chapter 14, page 282).

Word Study on Cheirotoneō

The word *cheirotoneō* is made up of two words, "hand" (*cheir*), and "to stretch" (*teinō*), thus "to stretch out the hand," and that for the purpose of voting. The word could then mean to elect or vote, as in the two examples below:

Isocrates, at the end of *Areopagiticus* (ca. 355 B.C.) says, "but it is for you to weigh all that I have said and cast your votes according to your judgment of what is best for Athens."

Plutarch (A.D. 45-120), in his *Life of Phocion*, writes, "But Hagnonides read aloud an edict which he had prepared, in accordance with which the people were to vote by show of hands whether they thought the men to be guilty, and the men, if the show of hands was against them, were to be put to death" (34,34).

But *cheirotoneō* was also used more generally to mean "appoint" or "designate" without reference to the manner of choosing. In Luke's day, Philo, the Jewish philosopher (ca. 20 B.C.-A.D. 50), uses the word without reference to voting:

- "Nor yet, when he [Joseph] was appointed to be the king's viceroy" (*On Joseph* 248).
- "A king appointed not by men but by nature" (*On Dreams* 2, 243).
- "His wish to honor the ruler whom He [God] had appointed" (*Moses* 1, 198).

The first-century Jewish historian Josephus uses the word in the same way:

- "Samuel said to Saul, 'know that thou art king, elected [appointed] of God to combat the Philistines'" (*Antiquities* 6, 54).
- "Ask Claudius Caesar to give him [Herod] authority over

the temple and the holy vessels and the selection of the high priests" (*Antiquities* 20, 14).

In the New Testament, the verb is used in a compound form to convey the meaning "chosen beforehand by God:" "God raised Him up on the third day, and granted that He should become visible, not to all the people, but to witnesses who were chosen beforehand [*procheirotoneō*] of God, that is, to us" (Acts 10:40,41). In 2 Corinthians 8:19, the only other place in which the verb is used, the churches chose a well-known brother to travel with Paul: "and not only this, but he has also been appointed by the churches to travel with us." Although the procedure for choosing was undoubtedly different from that of Acts 14:23, the word itself does not indicate a difference. The point is, *cheirotoneō* means to choose or to appoint, with or without reference to a show of hands. The context is perfectly clear that *appoint* is the only possible meaning in Acts 14:23. Consider the following two points:

(1) The first contextual indicator that *appoint* is the intended meaning of the verb is its subject, "they." Certainly, the word *they* refers to Paul and Barnabas, not to the churches. If interpreters insist on the root meaning of the verb (they had stretched forth the hands), then the subject must be the voter, because the subject can never preside over the votes of others. The action is always predicated of the verb's subject (*cheirotoneō* is here in the active voice, not the middle). Therefore, only Paul and Barnabas raised their hands in voting, not the church. But such an interpretation doesn't make sense. Henry Craik (1805-1866), an able student of the Hebrew and Greek languages and co-pastor with George Müller, remarks:

> The verb *cheirotoneō* so far as I am aware, is nowhere else employed in the sense of electing or appointing by the votes of others. Had the historian told us that the members of the Christian communities chose their elders by vote, we should have necessarily understood him to mean that they themselves voted for his appointment. No such statement is made in the passage under review. I cannot, therefore, rest upon the passage as evidence for popular election (*New Testament Church Order*, [Bristol: W. Mack, 1863], p. 51).

(2) The pronoun *them* (*autois*), following the verb "appointed," also confirms this conclusion. Paul and Barnabas appointed elders *for* them (that is, the disciples), not *by* them.

Although we have concentrated our study on the first half of Acts 14:23, we ought not to overlook the second half of the verse. It records a solemn farewell meeting in which "having prayed with fasting, they commended them to the Lord in whom they had believed." Some commentators think that Paul and Barnabas commended only the elders to the Lord, thus "them" refers to the newly appointed elders. However, it seems best to interpret "them" as a reference to the disciples in general, including the elders, because this interpretation fits best with the flow of thought (beginning in verse 22) concerning the new disciples.

Paul and Barnabas knew that false teachers, persecution, and internal conflict would confront these new disciples. So in verse 22 they warned their new brothers and sisters that "through many tribulations we must enter the kingdom of God." Before departing, they earnestly prayed and fasted, thereby commending their new converts to the Lord's safekeeping. (The clause, "having prayed with fasting," relates to the verb "commended," not to the verb "appointed.") The verb "commended" (*paratithēmi*) implies entrusting something valuable to the care of another, and nothing was more valuable to the apostles than their new converts. The apostles knew that the Lord Jesus Christ, "in whom they [the disciples] had believed," was the only sure protection in the apostles' absence. And prayer was the means whereby the apostles entrusted the disciples to the risen Lord's protection, guidance, and care.

It is important to note that Paul and Barnabas did not leave the new congregations in the care of apostles, priests, clerics, or even the newly appointed elders. They placed the new congregations in the care of Christ. The new believers had entered the life of faith, the life of prayer, and the life of obedience to and dependence on the Lord Jesus Christ. They would grow only as they depended on Him for everything. Like Abraham, and all the other great men and women of God before them, they had to learn to live by faith.

The prayers of Paul and Barnabas were accompanied by "fasting," which adds intensity and urgency to prayer (Ezra 8:21-23; Acts 13:1-3). "Fasting is one of those things," writes William Kelly, "in which the body shows its sympathy with what the spirit is passing through; it is a means of expressing our desire to be low before God, and in the attitude of humiliation."[18] The apostles put aside their natural needs, giving themselves completely to the occasion in order to concentrate on God. Their fasting demonstrated their earnestness and dependence on God.

Paul's Farewell to the Ephesian Elders

As Paul concluded his third missionary journey and headed toward Jerusalem to arrive for the feast of Pentecost (May, A.D. 57), his ship docked for several days in the harbor of Miletus to unload and load its cargo. Since Miletus is but forty miles south of the city of Ephesus, Paul seized the opportunity to summon the Ephesian elders to meet him in Miletus for a final farewell. His speech to the Ephesian elders is a virtual manual for pastor elders. It is the only record of Paul speaking directly to elders. It records his final words of exhortation and warning to the church elders, providing a dramatic description of who they are and what they are called by God to do. In short, this sermon provides us with an excellent synopsis of the uniquely Pauline, Christianized teaching on church elders.

Every elder, then, should master thoroughly the content of Paul's apostolic message to the Ephesian elders. History amply demonstrates that the truth of Paul's message cannot be overstated or repeated too often. The appalling, centuries-long failure to stop false teachers from invading churches can be traced directly to disobedience to or ignorance of Paul's warning to the Ephesian elders. Every new generation of elders must grasp afresh the prophetic message to the Ephesian elders: Guard the church—wolves are coming!

The Church and the Elders

In Paul's day, a council of elders pastored the Ephesian church. This is clear from the way in which Luke records Paul's summon to the elders:

> And from Miletus he [Paul] sent to Ephesus and called to him the elders [plural] of the church [singular] (Acts 20:17).

"He shared all possible truth
with all possible people
in all possible ways.
He taught the whole gospel
to the whole city
with his whole strength.
His pastoral example must have been
an unfailing inspiration
to the Ephesian pastors."

(John Stott, *The Spirit, the Church, and the World: The Message of Acts*, 328)

Nearly sixty years after Paul's meeting with the Ephesian elders, Ignatius, overseer of the church in Antioch of Syria, wrote to "the church which is in Ephesus," calling special attention to the preeminence of the overseer (*episkopos*) of Ephesus whose name was Onesimus (ca. A.D. 115).[19] At the time of Paul's farewell address, however, there was no single overseer to call upon. There was only a body of elders. Like the churches of Galatia (Acts 14:23), the church in Ephesus was at that time led by a council of elders, not a council of elders and an overseer.

Some scholars reject the concept of multiple elders within a single congregation. They try to explain the plurality of elders by saying that there were various house churches that made up the citywide church in Ephesus, that each house church had one presiding overseer, and that these house-church overseers (sometimes collectively called elders) presided over the citywide church. Lea and Griffin maintain this view. In their writing on the Pastoral Epistles in the *The New American Commentary* series, they state: "Probably the overseer served over a single house-church with the group of overseers from within a city constituting 'the overseers [elders]'" (brackets mine)[20] In a similar vein, R. Alastair Campbell, an instructor at Spurgeon's College in London, writes:

> We may then envisage the situation as follows. The church at Ephesus has grown to the point where it has a number of *episkopoi* [overseers], each, we may suppose, the head of his own house-church. Together they are the elders of the church, and it is [as] such that Paul summons them and reminds them of their responsibilities. They are the elders of the church because they are the overseers of the household congregations of which it is comprised.[21]

Such claims are pure guesswork, however. The fact is, there is absolutely no biblical evidence that a single overseer presided over an individual house church. There is, indeed, evidence to the contrary. A number of prominent commentators believe that the Epistle to the Hebrews was written to a house church in Rome.[22] If they are correct, the house church is exhorted to obey and submit to a plurality of leaders, not to a single overseer: "Obey your leaders and submit to them; for they keep watch over your souls (Heb. 13:17; cf. 1 Thess. 5:12). There is certainly no reason why a house church could not have two or three elders.

Furthermore, Luke doesn't refer to the "churches of Ephesus," he refers to the "church" (Acts 20:17). Later he refers to the "flock," not "flocks," over which the Holy Spirit placed the elders (Acts 20:28). The natural reading of the passage, then, indicates that there is one church in Ephesus and one body of elders to oversee it. The same is true nearly forty years later when John addresses "the church in Ephesus," not the churches (Rev. 2:1). And nearly twenty years after John's letters, Ignatius also writes to "the church which is in Ephesus."[23] This is not to deny that there were house churches in Ephesus, because there were (1 Cor. 16:19). But the biblical information on the interrelationship of the house churches is very sparse, so we are unable to recreate a detailed working model. What we do know from Acts 20 is that a council of elders was responsible for the pastoral oversight of the church (singular) in Ephesus. How that eldership organized itself among the various house churches, however, we simply do not know.[24]

The same single-church concept describes the church in Jerusalem. Although there were thousands of believers in Jerusalem (Acts 4:4; 5:14; 6:1,7; 21:20), the inspired historian speaks only of the *church* in Jerusalem, not *churches* (Acts 5:11; 8:1,3; 11:22; 12:1,5; 15:4,22; 18:22). Luke portrays the believers in Jerusalem as viewing themselves as one united congregation (Acts 2:44,46; 5:12; 6:2) under the leadership of twelve apostles and later the elders and James (Acts 2:42; 4:35,37; 5:2 ff; 6:2-4,6; 8:14-17; 9:27; 15:4 ff.). Until times of severe persecution, the first Christians in Jerusalem met regularly on the east side of the outer court of Herod's Temple, in a place referred to as Solomon's colonnade:

- And all those who had believed were together, and had all things in common.... And day by day continuing with one mind in the temple. (Acts 2:44,46*a*).

- And at the hands of the apostles many signs and wonders were taking place among the people; and *they were all with one accord in Solomon's portico* (Acts 5:12; cf. 3:11; italics added).

- And every day in the temple and from house to house, they kept right on teaching and preaching Jesus as the Christ (Acts 5:42).

What was more natural for God's family than for all those in geographic proximity (the city boundary being the most natural) to assemble themselves together in unity under one body of leaders? At the same time, small groups of Christians in Jerusalem also gathered in private homes (Acts 2:46; 5:42; 12:12):

- And when they had entered, they went up to the upper room, where they were staying...(a gathering of about one hundred and twenty persons was there together)...(Acts 1:13*a*,15*b*).

- And day by day continuing with one mind in the temple, and breaking bread from house to house, they were taking their meals together with gladness and sincerity of heart (Acts 2:46).

- And every day in the temple and from house to house, they kept right on teaching and preaching Jesus as the Christ (Acts 5:42).

- And when he [Peter] realized this, he went to the house of Mary, the mother of John who was also called Mark, where many were gathered together and were praying (Acts 12:12).

So according to Acts, Jerusalem had one citywide church, many house churches, and one body of leaders. This also appears to be the case in Antioch (Acts 11:26; 13:1; 14:27; 15:3,30) as well as in Ephesus.

The Elders' Duty: Protect the Church

As he bid them farewell, Paul reminded the Ephesian elders that he had taught them the complete counsel of God. He held back nothing that he had received by revelation from God: "For I did not shrink from declaring to you the whole purpose of God" (Acts 20:27). Paul repeats this theme in verses 20 and 27 to emphasize that he had thoroughly executed his duty as Christ's apostle. The responsibility for the defense of the gospel and the welfare of the church now belonged to the elders, so Paul was free to press on to new lands.

> I did not shrink from declaring to you anything that was profitable, and teaching you publicly and from house to house....Therefore I testify to you this day, that I am innocent of the blood of all men. For I did not shrink from declaring to you the whole purpose of God. Be on guard for yourselves and for all

> the flock, among which the Holy Spirit has made you overseers, to shepherd the church of God which He purchased with His own blood (Acts 20:20,26-28).

Paul begins his exhortation to the Ephesian elders with the warning "be on guard for yourselves and for all the flock." The verb rendered "be on guard" (*prosechō*) means "to keep watch" or "pay strict attention." This verb is often used in the context of false teaching (Deut. 12:30; Matt. 7:15; 16:6,12; Luke 20:46). It is an imperative verb, and the tense used here indicates continuous action. So Paul is saying, "keep a constant watch over yourselves and all the flock." The opposite would be to neglect the flock, to be inattentive, or to be preoccupied with other matters so as to be unaware of the problems and dangers confronting the flock. In contrast, "Unceasing vigilance is the essential requirement in shepherds."[25]

In order to fulfill their task, the elders must first vigilantly protect their own spiritual condition. An elder cannot guard the spiritual lives of others if he cannot guard his own soul. Matthew Henry (1662-1714), one of the most frequently read commentators during the past two hundred years, states: "Those are not likely to be skillful or faithful keepers of the vineyards of others who do not keep their own."[26] So Paul wisely charges the elders to first keep watch over their own spiritual lives. The well-known Puritan writer Richard Baxter (1615-1691), in his classic work *The Reformed Pastor,* sounds the alarm that Satan "has a special eye" for the guardians of the flock. Satan knows that if he can destroy the shepherds, he can swiftly invade and devour the flock:

> Take heed to yourselves because the tempter will make his first and sharpest attack on you.... He knows what devastation he is likely to make among the rest if he can make the leaders fall before their eyes. He has long practiced fighting, neither against great nor small, comparatively, but against the shepherds—that he might scatter the flock.... Take heed, then, for the enemy has a special eye on you. You are sure to have his most subtle insinuations, incessant solicitations and violent assaults. Take heed to yourselves, lest he outwit you. The devil is a greater scholar than you are, and a more nimble disputant.... And whenever he prevails against you, he will make you the instrument of your own ruin.... Do not allow him to use you as the Philistines used

> Samson—first to deprive you of your strength, then put out your eyes, and finally to make you the subject of his triumph and derision.[27]

Elders, therefore, must take whatever action is necessary to guard their daily walk with God. They must faithfully engage in daily prayer and Scripture reading. They must guard against any hint of indifference to divine truth. Peter warns, "be on your guard lest, being carried away by the error of unprincipled men, you fall from your own steadfastness" (2 Peter 3:17). In the same vein, former Regent College professor Michael Green reminds us that "error has many attractive faces by which even the most experienced may be beguiled."[28] Elders must also guard themselves against being ensnared by the pleasures and cares of this world. They must guard against bitterness of heart, discouragement, spiritual laziness, and unbelief. They must keep their minds and hearts fixed firmly on Jesus Christ (Heb. 12:1-3).

In addition to guarding themselves, elders must guard "all the flock," that is, the local Christian congregation. To effectively communicate his exhortation, Paul employs the familiar, Old Testament imagery of the flock-shepherd relationship. He describes the local church as a flock of sheep that the elders are to shepherd and, especially, to protect from wolves. The sheep-shepherd image beautifully illustrates the church's need for leadership and protection. An essential part of this metaphor is the inseparable relationship between the sheep and the shepherd. Because sheep are defenseless, an unguarded flock is in danger. So there must always be shepherds to keep watch over the flock. Throughout Scripture, a shepherdless flock is deplored and lamented (Num. 27:17; 1 Kings 22:17; Zech. 10:2; Matt. 9:36).

The command to guard the flock means that the elders must keep their minds on the church. They must be watchful and observant. They must be attentive at all times to the spiritual well-being of the people. They must watch for people who have wandered off from the flock or for new believers who are struggling to survive. They must constantly be alert to dangers both from outside the flock and from within it. They must know about new trends and doctrines that will influence the people. Great King Solomon gives the same counsel when he writes, "Know well the condition of your flock, And pay attention to your herds" (Prov. 27:23).

Finally, we must not overlook Paul's use of the significant, little word "all." The elders are responsible to protect *all* the sheep—the whole flock, not just their favorite portion of the flock. None must be neglected, for all are precious. The word *all* points out the difference between the elder's role and the role of others who also faithfully minister in the local flock: the elder's role entails the overall management of the entire flock, not just a part of it.

Like every other member of the congregation, an elder will have personal interest in and involvement with a specific ministry such as a small group Bible study, music, youth, Sunday School, counseling, missions, or evangelistic outreach. These ministries have a limited number of people and responsibilities to attend to, and one does not need to be an elder to do them. But the role of the church elder involves the individual and corporate responsibility to care for the whole flock with all its people, programs, and problems. So most elders carry a number of specific responsibilities, as well as the responsibility of the body of elders to assume the overall management of the entire flock. Not everyone qualifies for this responsibility (1 Tim. 3:1-13). It is a heavy load that few men care to accept.

The Elders' Divine Commission

Having stated his main charge to "guard the flock," Paul goes on to reinforce it in the rest of verse 28 and verses 29-31. In typical Pauline fashion, he explains the underlying doctrinal bases for his command to guard the flock: the Spirit's sovereign will, the immense value of the Church, the Cross of Jesus Christ, and the inevitable onslaught of false teachers.

Paul reminds the elders that it was God, the Holy Spirit, who made them overseers for the express purpose of pastoring the flock. The verb "made" comes from the Greek word *tithēmi*, which generally means "put" or "placed." In this case the translation "placed" or "set" seems to fit the context best: the local flock they are to guard is the very one the Holy Spirit placed them in as overseers. The verb's middle voice expresses the wonderful truth that the Holy Spirit did this for His own wise purposes.[29] Moreover, the verb is used in the New Testament to indicate a special theological sense of divine appointment or placement (Acts 13:47; 1 Tim. 1:12; 2 Tim. 1:7,11). This is clearly the intent in 1 Corinthians 12 where Paul writes, "But now God has placed the members, each one of them, in the body, just as He desired" (12:18;

cf. 12:28). Thus these men are overseers by divine placement, initiative, and design.

Paul stresses the personality and will of God the Holy Spirit in determining who oversees the church of God. It was not the church nor the apostles that placed these men as overseers. Although human means were not excluded from the process, the placement was ultimately made by a divine person, God the Holy Spirit. So as God's overseers, the elders must guard the church with their lives. To do anything less would be to disobey the One who ultimately appointed them.

Following the reference to "elders" in verse 17, we might expect to read that the Holy Spirit set these men as "elders" to shepherd the church of God (verse 28). Instead, verse 28 refers to the elders as "overseers." Paul has just exhorted the elders to keep watch over the flock, so it is appropriate for him to call them "overseers." As the word indicates, overseers are responsible for the overall supervision, protection, management, and care of the flock of God. The *New American Standard Bible* accurately translates the Greek word *episkopoi* as "overseers," which is an exact translation. Although some English Bibles translate *episkopoi* as "bishops," this rendering conveys concepts that are not present in Paul's thought and creates misunderstanding for modern readers.

Word Study on Overseer

The Greek word *overseer* (*episkopos*) is a general term like our English words supervisor, manager, or guardian. In ancient Greek society, the word was a well-known designation of office. It was broadly used to describe any official who acted as a superintendent, manager, guardian, controller, inspector, or ruler. "More commonly," states Hermann W. Beyer, "the *episkopoi* are local officials or the officers of societies."[30]

The Greek Old Testament (the *Septuagint*) used *overseer* in much the same way to refer to various officials. Beyer says, "There is no closely defined office bearing the title *episkopos* in the LXX. But the term 'overseer' is freely used in many different ways."[31] A few examples of Old Testament overseers include the following: superintendents responsible for temple repair (2 Chron. 24:12,17), army officers (Num. 31:14), temple guardians (2 Kings 11:18), leaders supervising the people (Neh. 11:9), and tabernacle overseers (Num. 4:16).

The purpose for which the Holy Spirit placed the elders in the flock as overseers was "to shepherd the church of God." The verb "shepherd" (*poimainō*) means "to tend as a shepherd," which encompasses the complete shepherding task of leading, folding, feeding, and guarding the sheep. This image of shepherding perfectly fits the Holy Spirit's purpose for the elders.

The shepherd imagery blends the ideas of authority and leadership with self-sacrifice, tenderness, wisdom, hard work, loving care, and constant watchfulness. Shepherding requires long hours of work and complete attention—the shepherd must always be with the sheep. It demands knowledge of the sheep, good management skills, and courage in the face of danger. Most important, it demands love for the sheep. Thus, "to shepherd" means to govern the church of God, to provide leadership and guidance for the church, to teach and correct from God's Word, and to provide protection from all dangers that threaten the life of the church.

We should note that in the New Testament the verb *shepherd* is used three times in the context of Christian leaders: (1) Jesus charged Peter to shepherd His sheep (John 21:16); (2) Peter charged the Asian elders to shepherd the flock of God (1 Peter 5:1*a*,2*a*); and (3) Paul reminded the Ephesian elders that the Holy Spirit placed them as overseers to shepherd the church (Acts 20:28). Twice, then, elders are given the mandate to shepherd, that is, to pastor, the local church.

The noun *shepherd*, however, is used only once to describe Christian leaders. In Ephesians 4:11 Paul lists five spiritual gifts, and one is the gift of shepherding: "And He gave some as apostles, and some as prophets, and some as evangelists, and some as pastors [shepherds] and teachers." So just as there are gifted evangelists and teachers, there are gifted shepherds. It is also noteworthy that in the New Testament, the term *shepherd* (pastor) is never used as a title for a church leader. Christ alone is given the title of shepherd.

The flock the elders pastor is a flock of unspeakable worth. It is special because it is "the church of God." It is God's congregation of people. It does not belong to the elders, the apostles, or any man. God called His flock into being and He is the One who cares for it, sustains it, and provides for it. Paul further expresses the magnitude of the worth of "the church of God" by the clause, "which He hath purchased with His own blood." Bible translators disagree over both the correct Greek text and the proper translation of this clause,[32] but we must not permit these technical problems to detract from the statement's intent and impact. Whatever the correct rendering may be, the point regarding the immeasurable worth of God's church is still made. "With this," says Gooding, "we touch the mainspring of all true defence and shepherding of the church: the cost at which God bought it."[33]

The price one is willing to pay for an object demonstrates its value. For the Church, God gave His only Son as a sin-bearing sacrifice. The Son bled and died for the Church. How could God have paid more for His Church? He has paid an incalculable price. How God must love the Church! How much it must mean to Him when His chosen elders earnestly care for His blood-bought children. Richard Baxter dramatically captures the passion of Paul's persuasive reasoning when he states,

> Can you not hear [Christ] saying, "Did I die for these people, and will you then refuse to look after them? Were they worth My blood, and are they not worth your labor? Did I come down from Heaven to seek and to save that which was lost, and will you refuse to go next door, or to the next street or village to seek them? How small is your labor or condescension compared to Mine! I debased Myself to do this, but it is your honor to be so employed. Have I done and suffered so much for their salvation, and will you refuse that little that lies upon your hands?"
>
> Everytime we look out upon our congregations, let us believingly remember that they are purchased by Christ's blood, and that therefore they should be highly regarded by us.[34]

What an immense honor it is to shepherd the church of God! It is a most serious matter when a pastor elder is inattentive to the needs of the church of God, yet this remains a common, worldwide problem. I am convinced that one of the key reasons elders neglect the congregation and many men lack the desire to be elders is that they fail to comprehend the inestimable value of the church of God and fail to appreciate the Cross of our Lord Jesus Christ (2 Cor. 5:14,15). When men grasp the eternal value of God's flock and the nearly unimaginable price paid for our salvation, they should be inspired to commit their lives wholeheartedly to caring for the church of God. As the great hymn writer Isaac Watts wrote: "Love so amazing, so divine, demands my soul, my life, my all."

The Elders' Archenemy: False Teachers

Following his plea for the elders to keep a vigilant watch over God's blood-bought flock, Paul fuels the fire of his exhortation. He explains the chief fear that motivates his concerns:

> I know that after my departure savage wolves will come in among you, not sparing the flock; and from among your own selves men will arise, speaking perverse things, to draw away the disciples after them. Therefore be on the alert, remembering that night and day for a period of three years I did not cease to admonish each one with tears (Acts 20:29-31).

Paul knew the enemy so well that he could say, "I know…savage wolves will come." There was no question about it. It was going to happen. Since the local church is figuratively called a flock, it follows that its enemies are "wolves," the proverbial predators of sheep. The wolves Paul speaks about are false teachers who stalk the flock. They are called "savage wolves," a pack of large, fierce wolves who will not spare the flock from destruction. They are strong and cunning. They are persistent, and they come from every side. They are insatiable and merciless in their appetite for devouring Christians. Their presence can only bring death, confusion, and destruction.

Paul's presence was a powerful force against the "savage wolves" of false doctrine (Acts 15:1). He fought tirelessly against the infiltration of false teachers. His whole life was spent in defense of the gospel (Phil. 1:7). When it came to the truth of the gospel, Paul would not budge for anyone (Gal. 2:5). His most scathing anathema fell on those who attempted to add to Christ's gospel (Gal. 1:7-9). For three years, Paul had thoroughly proclaimed and defended the gospel in Ephesus, and his departure marked a crucial moment for the church in Ephesus. Now that he was gone, it was the Ephesian elders' duty to protect the flock of God.

Paul goes on to predict something even more subtle and frightening than wolves; he warns that false teachers will arise from within the congregation! Not only will wolves come in to destroy the flock, men from within God's flock—professing Christians—will emerge as false teachers. Such men expose themselves by teaching "perverse things." Paul means that they will teach perversions of God's holy truth—twisted, distorted, heretical doctrine. They will not out-and-out deny the truth of God's Word, for that would be too obvious and ineffective for Satan's purposes. Instead, they will pervert truth. As masters of subtlety and novelty, they will mix truth with error, reinterpret the truth, and change the meaning of words to give the illusion of truth.

Such false teachers want followers, so they seek "to draw away the disciples after them." They try to tear Christians away from the flock and its Spirit-placed overseers (Gal. 4:17). They care nothing for the church's unity or safety. They care only for themselves. How different they are from Christ's true servants who "preach...Christ Jesus as Lord" and consider themselves as the "bond-servants" of His people (2 Cor. 4:5).

Paul's solution to the ominous threat of false teachers is: "Therefore be on the alert." The word "alert" is from the Greek word *grēgoreō,* which literally means "keep awake" or "not sleep" (Matt. 26:38; Luke 12:37). It is most often used figuratively in the New Testament to mean "be watchful," "be vigilant," "stay awake and ready for action." In this instance it is a present tense, imperative verb of command that means, "keep on being alert and ready for action." It implies a conscientious effort, a mental and spiritual attitude of alertness.

The verb "alert" fits well the pastoral imagery of Paul's exhortation. A good shepherd is always alert to danger. He is not caught unaware. He is vigilant and ready to act in order to protect the sheep.

To strengthen and clarify his exhortation to be alert, Paul calls upon the elders to remember his example: "remembering that night and day for a period of three years I did not cease to admonish each one with tears." He is saying that his own life is a study of pastoral vigilance in action. In fact, the greater portion of Paul's speech to the elders is a rehearsal and defense of his personal example while in Ephesus. David Gooding comments: "Paul's address to the Ephesian elders is remarkable for this, that his exhortation to defend the church of God occupies scarcely more than four verses; but the model he offers of how the defence should be conducted occupies at least thirteen. The model he offers is of course himself and his behaviour towards the church during the years he was with them."[35]

Paul's vigilant protection of the flock entailed a ministry of admonition (*noutheteō*), which means "to warn," "advise," or "counsel." To admonish is to exert a corrective influence in a positive, caring way. According to Kittel's dictionary, "The basic idea is that of the well-meaning earnestness with which one seeks to influence the mind and disposition by appropriate instruction, exhortation, warning and correction."[36] In the present context, admonishing involves instructing believers about the persistent, dangerous attacks of false teachers and the human tendency to become inattentive to this danger.

Paul's admonitions started when he first arrived in Ephesus. He didn't wait until his departure to warn about the sure dangers of false teachers. He admonished them "night and day" for a period of three years. Paul used every contact with them—not just official occasions—for admonition. Furthermore, "tears" filled Paul's admonitions because the damage done by false teachers caused him much heartache: "For many walk, of whom I often told you, and now tell you even weeping, that they are enemies of the cross of Christ" (Phil. 3:18). Finally, Paul's admonition was inclusive. He never ceased "to admonish each one." His eye was on every single sheep. Oh, that elders today might warn and equip each saint with such thoroughness and devotion!

The reason for being alert is not just to be informed, but to act. Both imperative commands, "be on guard" (v. 28) and "be on the alert" (v. 32), imply action. A good shepherd is never passive. He knows the necessity for acting quickly and decisively in the face of danger. He knows when he must fight and when he must stand his ground. To be aware of danger and not to act is to be a lazy, cowardly shepherd who betrays the flock.

Elders must act because God has given them the authority to lead and protect the flock. They do not do this work on their own authority. Since the Holy Spirit placed the elders as overseers in the flock for the purpose of shepherding the church, they have the authority to act as shepherds and overseers. They are God's undershepherds who act in accordance with their God-given shepherding authority to protect the flock and to stop false teachers.

The Elders' Double Resource

Paul knew that the Ephesian elders would face many trials and fierce battles, so he concludes his message by entrusting them not to any earthly authority or human organization but to God and His life-sustaining Word:

> And now I commend you to God and to the word of His grace, which is able to build you up and to give you the inheritance among all those who are sanctified (Acts 20:32).

David Gooding aptly calls this a "double resource."[37] Referring to this double resource, namely God and His Word, William Kelly states: "It is not commendation to one only, but to both. Without God before the heart the word becomes dry and sapless, and we grow discouraged and impatient; without the word to direct the life, we are in danger from the will and the wisdom, or from the folly of man."[38]

Paul had complete confidence in God and the Word to keep his beloved co-laborers safe. He knew that the same God who had sustained two million Israelites for forty years in the barren wilderness of Sinai could sustain these elders in their shepherding ministry. The Old Testament Scriptures, which they all knew, were a powerful witness to the power of God to care for His people in the worst possible circumstances:

> He led you through the great and terrible wilderness, with its fiery serpents and scorpions and thirsty ground where there was no water; He brought water for you out of the rock of flint. In the wilderness He fed you manna which your fathers did not know, that He might humble you and that He might test you, to do good for you in the end (Deut. 8:15,16).

> For the Lord your God has blessed you...He has known your wanderings through this great wilderness. These years the Lord your God has been with you; you have not lacked a thing (Deut. 2:7).

The fundamental principle that every child of God must learn and relearn many times throughout life is to depend on the God who is absolutely trustworthy. The Christian life is the life of faith—faith in an all-powerful and all-loving God who is the source of all life and grace. Yet, like Israel, there is nothing with which we struggle more than with self-sufficiency and unbelief (Ps. 78:17-22).

The troubles, failures, and problems that were to come were intended to drive these elders to greater trust in God, to a deeper and more intimate relationship with the living God. Paul had experienced this trust in Ephesus: "indeed, we had the sentence of death within ourselves in order that we should not trust in ourselves, but in God who raises the dead" (2 Cor. 1:9). The elders would have to learn, as Paul did, "that we are [not] adequate in ourselves to consider anything as coming from ourselves, but our adequacy is from God" (2 Cor. 3:5).

Paul entrusted the elders not only to God, but to "the word of His grace." With Paul's frightening predictions of wolves, false teachings, and divisions, the elders desperately needed "the word of His grace," which is the full gospel story (Acts 13:43;14:3; 20:24). The gospel is the story of the wonderful Lord Jesus Christ, His person and His work; it is the story of God's love and grace to undeserving sinners; it is the message of forgiveness, the promise of the Holy Spirit, and eternal life. The elders must rest in this living, supernatural message and continue to learn of its infinite riches and depths.

The elders heard "the word of His grace" through Paul's preaching. Elders today can read the same message as it is recorded in the New Testament. Paul was confident that God's Word was perfectly sufficient to provide guidance, comfort, and strength for these hard-working shepherds. He knew, as Moses declared long ago to Israel, "that man does not live by bread alone, but man lives by everything that proceeds out of the mouth of the Lord" (Deut. 8:3*b*). The absolute sufficiency of God's precious Word to sustain His children through all the struggles of life is splendidly expressed by C. H. Mackintosh (1820-1896) in his classic devotional exposition on the Pentateuch:

> Here [Deut. 8] we have the only true, the only safe, the only happy attitude for man, namely, hanging in earnest dependence upon "every word that proceedeth out of the mouth of the Lord...." We may well say there is nothing like it in all this world. It brings the soul into direct, living, personal contact with the Lord Himself.... It makes the Word so absolutely essential to us, in every thing; we cannot do without it.
>
> There is not a single crisis occurring in the entire history of the Church of God, not a single difficulty in the entire path of any individual believer, from beginning to end, which has not been perfectly provided for in the Bible. We have all we want in that blessed volume, and hence we should be ever seeking to make ourselves more and more acquainted with what that volume contains, so as to be "thoroughly furnished" for whatever may arise, whether it be temptation of the devil, an allurement of the world, or a lust of the flesh; or, on the other hand, for equipment

> for that path of good works which God has afore prepared that we should walk in it.
>
> And it never fails those who simply cleave to it and confide in it. We may trust Scripture without a single shade of misgiving. Go to it when we will, we shall always find what we want....A few sentences of holy Scripture will pour in a flood of divine light upon the heart and conscience, and set us at perfect rest, answering every question, solving every difficulty, removing every doubt, chasing away every cloud, giving us to know the mind of God, putting an end to conflicting opinions by the one divinely competent authority.
>
> What a boon, therefore, is holy Scripture! What a precious treasure we possess in the Word of God! How we should bless His holy name for having given it to us! Yes? And bless Him, too, for everything that tends to make us more fully acquainted with the depth, fullness, and power of those words of our chapter, "Man shall not live by bread only, but by every word that proceedeth out of the mouth of the Lord doth man live."[39]

In order to effectively guard the flock from wolves, elders need to be strong and well skilled in the things of God. Paul promises that the Word would build them up and make them strong. As a source of divine power, the Word is "profitable for teaching, for reproof, for correction, for training in righteousness; that the man of God may be adequate, equipped for every good work" (1 Tim. 3:16,17). If elders, then, neglect to read, study, meditate on, and obey the Word, they will become weak and the flock will be in danger. Only strong overseers can withstand the pressure. Only the living power of the Word can give elders the strength needed to protect the flock from false teachers. What a marvelous blessing it is to have elders who are spiritually alert, strong in the Word, and rest fully upon God for all their decisions and activities.

The Elders' Duty: To Work Hard and Help the Needy

Nothing is more apt to bring sinister charges against the Lord's servants than money, so Paul's farewell includes a disavowal of all greedy motives:

> I have coveted no one's silver or gold or clothes. You

> yourselves know that these hands ministered to my own needs and to the men who were with me. In everything I showed you that by working hard in this manner you must help the weak and remember the words of the Lord Jesus, that He Himself said, "It is more blessed to give than to receive" (Acts 20:33-35).

Few people can honestly make such a confident, open-hearted confession. Note that Paul did not say he took no one's gold, because he did accept money from the saints. (The church in Philippi was especially faithful in sharing financially with Paul, as recorded in Phil. 1:5; 4:15,16; 2 Cor. 11:8,19.) Paul's claim is even more profound. He is saying that greed has no control over him and that he has no inner, secret desire for material profit from his converts.

Anyone, even the greedy, can say, "I have coveted no one's silver." Greedy people can be self-deceived. But Paul appeals to an unusual aspect of his work in verse 34: "You yourselves know that these hands ministered to my own needs and to the men who were with me." By this reminder, Paul reveals that his normal practice was to provide his own lodging, food, and necessities through his own manual labor (1 Cor. 9:4-6; 2 Cor. 11:7; 1 Thess. 2:9; 2 Thess. 3:8-10). Even more amazing, Paul also supported his co-workers in the gospel by working as a tentmaker (Acts 18:3). Thus, working with his "hands" was no token gesture on Paul's part. He labored both night and day (1 Thess. 2:9; 2 Thess. 3:8).

Like the life of his Lord (Mark 3:20,21), Paul's life was characterized by arduous, ceaseless labor. Paul labored at his trade and his preaching. The phenomenal results of his service in the gospel were the Spirit's doing, not the result of self-serving desires (1 Cor. 3:5-9; 2 Cor. 4:7). His life was proof enough that he had no desire for the wealth of others.

Christians, especially Christian leaders, must display Christ's love by sharing their resources with the poor and needy. Paul presents to the elders his own selfless example of hard work, self-support, and sharing his resources: "In everything I showed you that by working hard in this manner you must help the weak." He mentions the same idea of working in order to help the poor in Ephesians 4:28: "Let him who steals steal no longer; but rather let him labor, performing with his own hands what is good, in order that he may have something to share with him who has need." So Paul implores the elders to have a similar concern for the weak in body and in material necessity, always remembering "the words of the Lord Jesus, that He Himself said, 'It is more blessed to give than to receive.'"

The elders, then, like Paul, are to be characterized by hard work. They are to be employed in order to support financially their families and help the needy. They are to give considerable time to shepherding God's church. By doing these things, they will be examples to the congregation of the type of life God intends for all His people.

At the conclusion of Paul's fervent exhortation, Luke records a touching farewell scene:

> And when he had said these things, he knelt down and prayed with them all. And they began to weep aloud and embraced Paul, and repeatedly kissed him, grieving especially over the word which he had spoken, that they should see his face no more. And they were accompanying him to the ship (Acts 20:36-38).

Paul was not a church hireling; he was a true spiritual shepherd. These elders had worked intimately with Paul and been inspired by his amazing, single-minded devotion to Jesus Christ. Prayer, then, was the only fitting conclusion to their gathering.

As they "knelt down and prayed," the elders looked to God alone for strength and guidance for the future. We can imagine that as a mighty man of prayer, Paul prayed for the spread of the gospel in Asia, for protection from false teachers, for the growth of the church, and for the Ephesian elders' labors and trials. Although Paul didn't command the Ephesian elders to pray, he could not have set a clearer example for them. It is God's intention that those who guard His flock utilize, as Paul did, persistent prayer—the greatest means of spiritual protection (Acts 6:4).

Summary of the Elders' Work

The work of the Christian elders that Paul describes is "to shepherd the church of God." These elders are not board elders; they are shepherd elders. As shepherd elders, they are called to guard the flock from its archpredator—the false teacher. Moreover, shepherd elders are called to be spiritually alert and to constantly admonish the congregation about the subtle dangers of false teachers and their divisive, false doctrines. Like Paul, Christian elders are to guard the gospel and teach the whole counsel of God. Thus elders must be doctrinally sound leaders who are able to defend and teach the Word.

Elders are also obligated to guard "all the flock," that is, every single member. Hence Christian elders are required to know and be involved in the personal lives of the people they shepherd. Furthermore, they are to sacrificially care for needy, suffering members of the flock. Like the life of Paul, the life of an elder must be marked by hard work, generosity, and a life of service on behalf of others.

Finally, shepherd elders must take their duty seriously because the Holy Spirit Himself has sovereignly placed them in the flock as overseers for the purpose of shepherding God's precious, blood-bought people. Elders, then, are Spirit-placed overseers. The kind of oversight Paul has in mind is shepherding: guarding, feeding, leading, and caring for God's flock. In short, Pauline, Christian elders are responsible for the pastoral oversight of the local church.

CHAPTER 8

Paul's Letters to the Churches

"Live in peace with one another"

1 Thessalonians 5:13b

Before examining the letters of 1 Thessalonians and Philippians, we must address an issue that troubles many biblical scholars. The problem is that the book of Acts and the letters of 1 Timothy and Titus say that Paul appointed elders and include detailed instructions about elders, yet in none of Paul's nine letters to the churches does he mention specifically the term *elder* (Romans, 1 and 2 Corinthians, Galatians, Ephesians, Philippians, Colossians, and 1 and 2 Thessalonians). As a result of this omission, most liberal scholars conclude that during Paul's lifetime there were no officially designated elders in any of the churches he founded. They maintain that Luke's claims about elders in the Pauline churches is unhistorical and that the letters to Timothy and Titus were written by someone other than Paul.

Clearly articulating this view, Ernst Käsemann, a German theologian and commentator, writes, "For we may assert without hesitation that the Pauline community had no presbytery during the Apostle's lifetime. Otherwise the silence on the subject in every Pauline epistle is quite incomprehensible."[1] Hans Küng, a Roman Catholic theologian and author, also asserts, "At all events Luke is making an unhistorical addition—either theologically conditioned, or based on a tradition which had developed in the meantime—when he maintains that Paul and Barnabas 'appointed elders…in every church' (Acts 14:23; cf. especially 20:17-35), for this is not borne out by the letters of Paul himself."[2]

Despite what these scholars have said about the absence of any mention of elders in Paul's letters to the churches, elders are addressed in the opening of Paul's letter to the Philippians, where he uses the alternative title, *overseer*. Paul writes: "Paul and Timothy, bond-servants of Christ Jesus, to all the saints in Christ Jesus who are in Philippi, including the overseers [elders] and deacons" (Phil. 1:1). So it is not accurate to say that Paul never addresses elders in his letters to the churches.

To claim that Acts, even in part, is historically unreliable and that 1 Timothy and Titus are fictitious Pauline letters is to deny the doctrine of divine inspiration, which in short states, "All Scripture is God-breathed and is useful for teaching…so that the man of God may be thoroughly equipped for every good work" (2 Tim. 3:16*a*,17; NIV). If Luke records that Paul appointed elders and spoke to the elders (an event to which Luke was an eyewitness), when in truth he didn't, then Luke's history is detrimental to the truth and misleading to the people of God. How could the first Christians have confidence in Luke's historical record, which claims to have "investigated everything carefully" (Luke 1:3), if it states that Paul appointed elders when in fact he did not?

Moreover, those who deny the authenticity of 1 Timothy and Titus and the historical reliability of Acts have an incomplete, skewed picture of Paul and his churches. If we are to accurately understand Paul and his church practices, we must trust the complete historical record as delivered by the Holy Spirit of God. This record includes Paul's nine letters to the churches, his inspired letters to Timothy, Titus, and Philemon, as well as Luke's inspired historical accounts.

Paul's so-called failure to specifically address the elders in his letters to the churches can be explained by his profound understanding of the new covenant people of God. Because all members of the local congregation are saints, priests, and Spirit-empowered ministers, all are responsible for life in the community. Therefore, Paul's customary practice was to address the whole community of saints when he wrote letters to local congregations. The New Testament offers multiple examples of this Christ-centered ecclesiology in practice:

- On the first missionary journey, Paul and Barnabas appointed a body of elders in all the churches of Pisidian Antioch, Iconium, Lystra, and Derbe. Yet in his letter to these churches, Paul doesn't once address the elders (assuming that the churches of Acts 13:14-14:21 are the same as those of Gal. 1:2). Instead, Paul writes: "Brethren [brothers and sisters] even if a man [or woman] is caught in any trespass, *you who are spiritual* [not just elders], restore such a one in a spirit of gentleness; each one looking to yourself, lest you too be tempted. Bear one another's burdens, and thus fulfill the law of Christ" (Gal. 6:1,2; italics added).

- Disorder and sin in the church at Corinth had to be dealt with, yet in Paul's letter to the church, he calls upon no one person or group to resolve the problems. Does this mean there was no one to call upon? Not at all! Paul could have called upon the dedicated Stephanas (1 Cor. 16:15-18); Gaius, in whose home the church met (Rom. 16:23); Erastus, the city treasurer (Rom. 16:23); Crispus, a converted chief ruler of the synagogue (Acts 18:8); or a number of other gifted men and prophets (1 Cor. 1:5,7). He could easily have asked one of these men to help the congregation resolve its problems, but, as always, he addresses the entire gathering of holy saints (1 Cor. 1:2).

- In 1 Thessalonians 5:12,13, Paul calls upon the congregation to highly esteem and love those who take the lead and give instruction. Hence we know that some form of leadership was in place in the church. But in his two letters to the Thessalonians, Paul never calls upon these leading men to correct problems within the church. Instead, he says, "Therefore encourage one another, and build up one another, just as you also are doing" (1 Thess. 5:11).

- The letter to the Philippians best illustrates Paul's practice of addressing the entire congregation. Despite his brief greeting to the overseers and deacons (Phil. 1:1), Paul addresses the rest of the letter (except for 4:2,3) "to all the saints."

- Peter and James also address the churches in the same manner. Each one writes to congregations in which the presence of elders

> is well documented, but they always address the entire congregation, not just the officials (James 5:14; 1 Peter 1:1; 5:1).

There are, therefore, no contradictions between Acts, 1 Timothy, Titus, and Paul's letters to the churches. The differences noted in these accounts reflect three different recipients and approaches, all of which are essential to understanding Paul's practices. Acts presents historical facts (what Paul did). First Timothy and Titus address Paul's personal assistants (church leaders, colleagues) who must act on his behalf to deal with various groups within the church and to order the life of the church. The letters to the churches teach and exhort the entire gathering of God's congregation. It is to two of these letters that we now turn to study the doctrine of eldership.

PAUL'S FIRST LETTER TO THE THESSALONIANS (5:12,13)

Because elders aren't mentioned by name in this passage, it is often overlooked in the study of eldership. Yet this passage is highly relevant to the subject of biblical eldership. The exhortations contained in 1 Thessalonians 5:12,13 most certainly apply to elders, or in the case of a new church, to potential elders.

The arrival of Paul and his missionary colleagues in Thessalonica is recorded in Acts 17:1-9. Because of fierce hostility to the gospel, however, Paul and his co-workers were able to stay in Thessalonica only a short period of time—one to three months. Several months after their hasty departure from Thessalonica, they wrote the letter of 1 Thessalonians from Corinth. The letter begins, "Paul and Silvanus and Timothy to the church of the Thessalonians in God the Father and the Lord Jesus Christ: Grace to you and peace" (1 Thess. 1:1).

Although the church in Thessalonica was but a few months old and lacked its founding fathers—Paul, Silas (probably an apostle, 1 Thess. 2:6), and Timothy (Paul's personal assistant and special emissary)—a group of men from within the congregation was providing leadership. Paul exhorts the infant congregation to recognize and love these leaders:

> But we request of you, brethren, that you appreciate those who

> diligently labor among you, and have charge over you in the Lord and give you instruction, and that you esteem them very highly in love because of their work. Live in peace with one another (1 Thess. 5:12,13).

Exactly who these laboring brethren were, the text does not reveal. It is possible that these laboring brethren were elders appointed by Paul and his fellow workers before they fled the city. It seems more likely, however, that they were Spirit-empowered volunteers who were able and willing to care for the church in the missionaries' absence. What is obvious is that some form of church leadership was in place. One didn't need apostolic appointment to love and sacrificially serve God's people. In accordance with Paul's practice (Acts 14:23), he, or one of his representatives, would return to Thessalonica to appoint from among such proven leaders official elders for the church.

GIVE PROPER RECOGNITION TO YOUR LEADERS

In verse 12, the missionaries appeal to their new brothers and sisters in Christ to give proper recognition to those who lead and instruct the congregation: "But we request of you, brethren, that you appreciate those who diligently labor among you, and have charge over you in the Lord and give you instruction." There is disagreement over the translation of the Greek verb *eidenai,* which usually means "to know" but in this case is rendered "appreciate" by the *New American Standard Bible.* "To know" is certainly a possible rendering for *eidenai* and is the choice of the *Authorized* (*King James*) *Version.* However, this meaning seems inadequate in the context. The people would surely know those who lead and instruct them, so the context demands a different verbal sense. Although it is difficult to be certain of the original intent, the renderings "to acknowledge" or "to give proper recognition" fit the context well.

In a similar context (1 Cor. 16:15-18), Paul uses another Greek verb for "know" (*epiginoskō*) that conveys the sense of "recognize" or "acknowledge." He writes, "And I rejoice over the coming of Stephanas and Fortunatus and Achaicus.... For they have refreshed my spirit and yours. Therefore acknowledge [*epiginōskete*] such men" (1 Cor.

16:17,18). Immediately preceding this instruction, Paul urges the congregation to submit to all those who devote themselves to caring for the church:

> Now I urge you, brethren (you know the household of Stephanas, that they were the first fruits of Achaia, and that they have devoted themselves for ministry to the saints), that you also *be in subjection to such men* and to everyone who helps in the work and labors (1 Cor. 16:15,16; italics added).

The exhortation in 1 Corinthians 16:16*a*, "be in subjection to such men," appears to be a parallel statement to "acknowledge such men" in verse 18*b*.[3] So although 1 Thessalonians 5:12 doesn't explicitly exhort believers to submit to those who labor among them, the exhortation to acknowledge certain people as leaders certainly implies, as in 1 Corinthians 16:16,18, a submission to their leadership and instruction. In other words, the people are to respond appropriately to their leadership and position.

To better appreciate Paul's exhortation to the Thessalonians to acknowledge these church leaders, we must remember that there were at that time no distinctions between clergy and laity, there was no officialism, and there were no priestly garments to distinguish certain members. Furthermore, we should not assume that anyone from within the congregation was at this time financially supported full time in the service of the congregation. Therefore, these humble, servant brethren (or at least some of them) could easily be overlooked and their service underestimated. Furthermore, as the plural verbs indicate, a number of brothers provided leadership for the church. So the missionaries' request is that all those who labor, not just one prominent person, be acknowledged.

Those who deserve recognition are first described as "those who diligently labor among you." The word "labor" (*kopiaō*) is a term used to describe manual labor (Luke 5:5; 1 Cor. 4:12; Eph. 4:28). It is a strong word denoting toil and strenuous work that results in weariness and fatigue. It is a favorite Pauline word. The phrase "diligently labor" then, reveals a vitally important aspect of eldership: hard work. In assessing this phrase, John Calvin adds the pungent comment, "It follows from this that all idle bellies are excluded from the number of pastors."[4] Caring for people's spiritual welfare is stressful work. It is

emotionally draining, time-consuming, and often monotonous and discouraging. It requires a great deal of personal dedication and sacrifice.

The prepositional phrase "among you" shows that the labor is on behalf of the local congregation, not labor for personal employment. These brethren were working hard in the church. So a biblical eldership is not a church board that conducts business for two or three hours a month—it is a hard-working, pastoral body.

It might appear to some readers that Paul refers to three separate groups of individuals in verse 12: those who labor diligently, those who direct the congregation, and those who give instruction. However, the structure of the Greek clause makes it clear that one group of individuals who discharges three functions is the intended meaning.[5] Furthermore, the second and third terms—leading and instructing—most likely explain the first term, "diligently labor." These brethren, then, labor at leading and instructing.

The plural forms of these three present participles should not be overlooked. A *team* of men labors at leading and instructing the congregation. Highlighting this point, Scottish theologian and biblical commentator James Denney (1856-1917) writes: "At Thessalonica there was not a single president, a minister in our sense, possessing to a certain extent an exclusive responsibility; the presidency was in the hands of a plurality of men."[6]

These brethren worked hard to provide leadership for the congregation. The clause "have charge over" translates the Greek word *prohistēmi*, which can range in meaning from "lead," "preside," "govern," and "manage" to "support" and "care for," or can combine the ideas of caring for and leading.[7] Paul uses this term in other places to describe a father's management of the home, a spiritual gift, and the work of the elders:

- He uses *prohistēmi* to describe a father's management of his family, particularly the proper control of his children: "He [the elder] must be one who manages [*prohistēmi*] his own household well keeping his children under control with all dignity (but if a man does not know how to manage [*prohistēmi*] his own household, how will he take care of the church of God?" (1 Tim. 3:4,5). In this usage, *prohistēmi* combines both the ideas of ruling and providing care.

- Paul also speaks of the spiritual gift of leading: "And since we have gifts that differ according to the grace given to us, let each exercise them accordingly...he who teaches, in his teaching; or he who exhorts, in his exhortation; he who gives, with liberality; he who leads [*prohistēmi*], with diligence; he who shows mercy, with cheerfulness" (Rom. 12:6*a*,7*b*,8). Undoubtedly, some of the Thessalonians had the gift of leadership and were using it for the edification of the church.

- Of special interest is the fact that Paul uses the same term to describe the elders' work in 1 Timothy 5:17: "Let the elders who rule well [*prohistēmi*] be considered worthy of double honor."

In the context of 1 Thessalonians 5:12,13, which addresses the congregation's proper response to those who diligently labor at providing leadership, care, and instruction, *prohistēmi* is best translated as: "those who take the lead among you in the Lord." In its verbal form, *lead* describes what these brothers do; it is not used as a title. E.K. Simpson, a biblical commentator and specialist in Hellenistic Greek literature, refers to this term as being "expressive of superintendence."[8] Expositors who dispute Paul's appointment of elders normally render this verb as "care for" or "aid" in order to avoid any notion of a formal leadership role. Those who affirm that Paul appointed elders and was concerned about the appointment of elders, however, render this term as "take the lead" or "lead and care for."

The phrase, "in the Lord," defines the elders' unique sphere of leadership—not in civil government, but in matters that pertain to the Lord and His people who are in spiritual union with Him and with one another. The fact that the phrase "in the Lord" is added only to the term "have charge over" further suggests that leading is the sense in which Paul is using the term. These new believers must remember that some of their fellow members have authority over them in spiritual matters. Thus these leaders should be recognized and loved for their important work. And those who lead must not forget that their authority is "in the Lord." Everything they do must be done in accordance with the Lord's authority and in the Lord's ways. The church is not their kingdom, and they are not lords over the people.

In addition to leading the congregation, these brethren also work hard at instructing the church. "Instruction" translates the Greek word *noutheteō*, which would be better rendered "admonish." To instruct in the sense of "admonish" means to warn or correct improper behavior or attitudes through sound teaching. John R.W. Stott illuminates the meaning of this word when he writes that it "is almost invariably used in an ethical context. It means to warn against bad behavior and its consequences, and to reprove, even discipline, those who have done wrong. Being a negative word, it is often coupled with 'teaching'...Moreover *noutheteō* does not denote a harsh ministry. As Leon Morris has put it, 'while its tone is brotherly, it is big-brotherly.'"[9] Christian admonition, then, is not angry scolding. It is loving correction and warning based on God's Word for the purpose of protecting and building up a brother or sister (1 Cor. 4:14).

Serious shepherd elders spend considerable time dealing with people's sins, failures, and offenses. It is not a part of the shepherding task that men naturally like, but it is an indispensable element of true spiritual care. James Denney emphatically underscores the need for the ministry of admonition and the people's proper response to those who must admonish:

> We are certain to bring a good deal of the world into the Church without knowing it; we are certain to have instincts, habits, dispositions, associates perhaps, and likings, which are hostile to the Christian type of character; and it is this which makes admonition indispensable.... But we should remember that, as Christians, we are pledged to a course of life which is not in all ways natural; to a spirit and conduct which are incompatible with pride; to a seriousness of purpose, to a loftiness and purity of aim, which may all be lost through willfulness; and we should love and honour those who put their experience at our service, and warn us when, in lightness of heart, we are on the way to make shipwreck of our life. They do not admonish us because they like it, but because they love us and would save us from harm; and love is the only recompense for such a service.[10]

Church leaders who fail to admonish God's people because they are afraid that people will leave the church or stop giving financially dishonor God, disobey His Word, and fail miserably at spiritual care.

ESTEEM AND LOVE YOUR LEADERS

In verse 12, Paul appeals to the congregation to acknowledge all those who lead and admonish the body, and in verse 13 he appeals to the congregation to "esteem them very highly in love." The magnitude to which the church is to esteem its leaders is expressed by the intensive adverb "very highly," which means "superabundantly" or "most exceedingly." Biblical commentator George G. Findlay (1849-1919) speaks of this exuberant word as "the strongest intensive possible to the language. So deep and warm should be the affection uniting pastors and their flocks."[11] William Hendriksen, founder and leading author of the *New Testament Commentary* series, adds this masterful comment: "Note the piling up of prefixes in this word: the ocean of esteem having reached its outermost perimeter, reaches even higher and begins to flow outward, overflowing its banks."[12] The church, then, has a divine obligation to highly esteem its spiritual leaders.

God cares about how people treat those who are in authority. The Bible exhorts us not only to obey, but to honor our rulers (Rom. 13:7; 1 Peter 2:17). When Paul, for example, realized he had spoken rudely to the high priest, Ananias, he apologized by saying, "I was not aware, brethren, that he was high priest; for it is written, 'You shall not speak evil of a ruler of your people'" (Acts 23:5). If the disobedience and ingratitude of people toward their civil leaders concerns God deeply, imagine how much greater is His concern that His people properly honor their spiritual leaders!

Our natural tendency is to take our leaders for granted, forget what they have done for us, complain rather than be thankful, accentuate the bad, and disregard the good. For example, God gave Israel some of the greatest leaders in human history—men like Moses and David. Yet during difficult times, the people were ready in a moment to stone both Moses and David. Due to our basic ingratitude and complaining spirit, the Scripture exhorts us to highly honor our spiritual leaders.

To the injunction to "esteem them very highly," Paul adds the beautiful and comprehensive phrase, "in love." We usually emphasize the importance of church shepherds loving the people, and that is necessary, but here Paul turns the tables and charges the people to love their shepherds. To Paul, love is the divine glue that holds the leaders and congregation together through all the disagreements and hurts of congregational life.

No group of elders is perfect. All elders have weaknesses, and each believer has a unique perspective on how elders should operate. As a result, there is always some degree of tension between leaders and followers. Even the best elders are inevitably accused of pride, wrong judgment, doing too much or too little, moving too slowly or too quickly, changing too much or not enough, and being too harsh or too passive. As commentator E.J. Bricknell observes, "The exercise of authority is always apt to provoke resentment."[13]

Difficult situations arise in which leaders cannot avoid angering some part of the congregation. Conflict between leaders and the led can at times become severe. Ultimately, however, God uses these conflicting situations to show us our pride, selfishness, and lovelessness. Paul E. Billheimer, well-known radio Bible teacher and author, is right in noting that the local church—with all its problems, stresses, and conflicts—is actually a testing ground for our growth in love and preparation for future ruling with the Lord:

> The local church, therefore, may be viewed as a spiritual workshop for the development of *agape* love. Thus the stresses and strains of a spiritual fellowship offer the ideal situation for the testing and maturing of the all-important qualification for sovereignty.
>
> Most controversies in local congregations are produced, not primarily by differences over essentials, but by unsanctified human ambitions, jealousy, and personality clashes. The real root of many such situations is spiritual dearth in individual believers, revealing lamentable immaturity in love. Therefore the local congregation is one of the very best laboratories in which individual believers may discover their real spiritual emptiness and begin to grow in *agape* love. This is done by true repentance, humbly confessing the sins of jealousy, envy, resentment, etc., and begging forgiveness from one another. This approach will result in real growth in the love that covers.[14]

Believers who love their shepherds will have greater understanding and tolerance for their shepherds' mistakes. In love, believers will view difficult situations in the best possible light. In love, believers will be less critical and more responsive to the elders' instruction and admonition. It cannot be emphasized enough that the best thing a congregation can do for its leaders is to love them. Love (and only love) suffers long (1 Cor. 13:4,6). Love covers a multitude of sins (1 Peter 4:8).

In his remarkably penetrating booklet, *The Mark of the Christian*, Francis Schaeffer reminds us that the real issue to be dealt with in most of our conflicts is not the issue at hand but our lack of Christlike love toward our fellow Christians:

> I have observed one thing *among true Christians* in their differences in many countries: What divides and severs true Christian groups and Christians—what leaves a bitterness that can last for 20, 30, 40 years (or for 50 or 60 years in a son's or daughter's memory)—is not the issue of doctrine or belief that caused the differences in the first place. Invariably, it is a lack of love—and the bitter things that are said by true Christians in the midst of differences.[15]

Love and esteem are due leaders "because of their work." Leaders are not to be loved and esteemed because they are older men, hold special religious titles, have received an apostolic appointment, or have winning personalities. Rather, they are to be loved "because of their work." This point is all too easily overlooked. Leon Morris, one of the most prolific biblical commentators of this century, ably captures the idea when he states: "A special kind of love within the brotherhood is love for the leaders; they are to be loved because of their work, not necessarily because of their personal qualities."[16]

Caring for people's problems, handling their seemingly endless complaints, refereeing interpersonal conflicts, confronting sins, and encouraging people toward maturity in Christ is work indeed. It nearly buried Moses, a man of enormous strength and ability. So people need to understand that leading a church is tough work. Only a few people are able or even care to bear this weighty responsibility. Those who do it certainly deserve to be loved and, as Leon Morris wisely points out, followers have significant responsibilities in the leader-follower relationship:

> It is a matter of fact that we are often slow to realize to this day that effective leadership in the church of Christ demands effective following. If we are continually critical of them that

are set over us, small wonder if they are unable to perform the miracles that we demand of them. If we bear in mind "the work's sake" we may be more inclined to esteem them very highly in love.[17]

LIVE IN PEACE

It is not easy to live in peace, even with fellow Christians. Satan does all he can to create warfare and division among God's people, and Christians often help him by acting in pride and selfishness rather than in humility and love. In fact, so many churches are marked by fighting and quarreling that a church at peace seems like an oasis in the desert. Yet the testimony and spiritual growth of a church is intricately tied to the measure of peace it enjoys. So Paul appropriately concludes his exhortation with a command directed to both the leaders and congregation: "Live in peace with one another."

The relationship between a congregation and its leaders always involves a delicate tension that can easily erupt into misunderstanding, ill feeling, or even division, such as occurred many times between Moses and the people of Israel. Both the leaders and the led must be fully aware of potential conflicts and their solemn duty to conscientiously work for peace. Thus the New Testament repeatedly exhorts and teaches Christians about the importance of peacemaking:

- Blessed are the peacemakers (Matt. 5:9).
- Be at peace with one another (Mark 9:50).
- So then let us pursue the things which make for peace (Rom. 14:19).
- Live in peace (2 Cor. 13:11).
- Being diligent to preserve the unity of the Spirit in the bond of peace (Eph. 4:3).
- And let the peace of Christ rule in your hearts (Col. 3:15).
- Now may the Lord of peace Himself continually grant you peace in every circumstance (2 Thess. 3:16).
- And the seed whose fruit is righteousness is sown in peace by those who make peace (James 3:18).
- Let him seek peace and pursue it (1 Peter 3:11).

Concerning the New Testament's emphasis on peace, biblical scholar F.J.A. Hort (1828-1892) writes that Paul "is giving instruction on the very essence of membership when in each of the nine Epistles addressed to Ecclesiae [churches] he makes the peace of God to be the supreme standard for them to aim at, and the perpetual self-surrender of love the comprehensive means of attaining it."[18]

Despite certain debatable details, the main points of Paul's exhortations to the church at Thessalonica are perfectly clear: to acknowledge and esteem in love those who work hard at leading and admonishing the church. Furthermore, his plea goes out to all members of the church—leaders and congregation alike—to work for peace. This divine instruction is all too easily forgotten when we face the pressures, hurts, and conflicts of life. Referring to the need to obey this inspired exhortation, Scottish commentator John Eadie (1810-1876) writes, "On obedience to it depended, in no small measure, the peace and the spiritual prosperity of the church."[19]

PAUL'S LETTER TO THE PHILIPPIANS (1:1)

Unlike 1 Thessalonians, which was written to an infant church, Philippians was written to a church that was more than ten years old. It was a model of spiritual maturity and faithfulness. At the time he wrote Philippians, Paul was under house arrest in Rome (A.D. 60-62). The Philippians dearly loved Paul, and while he was in custody they sent a generous loving offering and their personal envoy, Epaphroditus, to communicate their love to him. Paul responded by writing the letter of Philippians.

Among Paul's letters to the churches, Philippians is unique in that Paul greets both "the overseers and deacons" in his salutation:

> Paul and Timothy, bond-servants of Christ Jesus, to all the saints in Christ Jesus who are in Philippi, including the overseers and deacons (Phil. 1:1).

Paul's brief mention of overseers and deacons provides a wealth of valuable information for our study on eldership. It confirms, as Luke states, that elders were established in the Pauline churches. It also confirms that there were elders in the churches of Macedonia (Europe), not just in Asia Minor and Palestine as Acts records.

The most likely reason Paul mentions the overseers and deacons in his opening salutation is that they had a special part in initiating and organizing the church's financial contribution to him. Perhaps a letter, signed "the overseers and deacons," accompanied the offering. For example, in the letter to the churches of the Gentiles from Jerusalem, the apostles and elders (representing the whole church in Jerusalem) wrote: "The apostles and the brethren who are elders, to the brethren in Antioch and Syria and Cilicia who are from the Gentiles, greetings" (Acts 15:23). If the Philippian overseers and deacons followed the same practice, then Paul acknowledges their special part. Of course, there may have been other reasons for greeting the church officials in this manner, but this seems to be the most obvious.

Paul's usage of the terms *overseers* and *deacons* indicates a generally accepted recognition of official designations for church leadership positions (offices). Some commentators, however (usually those who reject Luke's record of Paul's appointment of elders), claim that the terms *overseers* and *deacons* are used functionally to designate all the people who supervise and serve the local church. They deny that Paul is referring to specific church offices. They support this view by the absence of the definite article before the terms *overseers* and *deacons*. But the absence of the definite article in Greek is insufficient reason to assign a purely functional sense to these terms. The context itself makes the terms definite. If Paul wanted to speak generally, he would not have used the noun forms as he did. He would most likely have used the participial forms, *overseeing* and *serving*.

The nouns *episkopos* and, to a lesser extent, *diakonos* were recognized, official designations in Greek society. Ernest Best, former professor of biblical criticism at the University of Glasgow, makes this point emphatically clear:

> I say "officials" because *episkopos* at any rate could not have been used in any other way than as a designation of an office.... A first century Greek could not have used it in a purely functional sense without suggesting that the person who exercised oversight held "official" status. There is also some, though less, evidence that *diakonos* was used in the same way. The fact that one was

> certainly used in the sense of a group of officials implies that the other was also.[20]

Finally, there is obvious similarity between the joint use of the words *overseers* and *deacons* in this passage and those found in 1 Timothy 3:1-13. Both letters were written in the early to mid sixties (A.D. 62-66). We know there were overseers and deacons at Ephesus during this time (1 Tim. 3:1-13), so it is likely that there were officially recognized overseers and deacons at Philippi as well. The interpretation, then, that assigns merely a functional sense to Paul's usage of *overseers* and *deacons* in this instance is confusing and nearly meaningless.

It is also significant that only two separate groups of officeholders, "overseers and deacons," appear in Paul's salutation to the Philippians. Some fifty years after Paul's letter to the Philippians, Polycarp wrote a letter to the church at Philippi in which he gave instructions concerning the leaders of the church. Polycarp, who was born around A.D. 70 and died A.D. 156, was the overseer of the church in Smyrna in Asia Minor. He was a disciple of John the apostle and a distinguished martyr for Christ. It is immensely relevant to us that in his letter to "the Church of God which sojourneth at Philippi" (ca., A.D. 115), Polycarp refers to only two groups of officials: elders and deacons. He comments considerably on elders, even mentioning one elder (Valens, who had fallen into sin because of greed) by name:

> Wherefore it is right to abstain from all these things, submitting yourselves to the presbyters [elders] and deacons as to God and Christ....
>
> And the presbyters also must be compassionate, merciful towards all men, *turning back the sheep that are gone astray*, visiting all the infirm, not neglecting a widow or an orphan or a poor man: but *providing always for that which is honorable in the sight of God and of men,* abstaining from all anger, respect of persons, unrighteous judgment, being far from all love of money, not quick to believe anything against any man, not hasty in judgment, knowing that we are all debtors of sin.[21]

Polycarp makes no mention of a chief overseer (bishop) in his letter, demonstrating that there was no such individual at Philippi. In fact, although Polycarp was called "the overseer of Smyrna" by his friend Ignatius,[22] he refers to himself simply as Polycarp in his own letter to the Philippians. He clearly places himself with the elders: "Polycarp and the presbyters that are with him."[23] From these two letters, we can conclude that in Paul's day and for the next fifty years there were only two recognized groups of officials at Philippi: overseers (who are elders) and deacons. There is no evidence of the three office bearers that are found in the second century (overseer, elders, and deacons).[24]

Paul's usage of the plural nouns indicates that Philippi had a plurality of overseers and deacons. The use of "overseers" (plural) has profound implications. In one stroke, the plural form utterly confounds later theories of church government. However, in their efforts to explain away the plurality of overseers in the church at Philippi, some scholars claim that there were several congregations in Philippi, each of which had a single overseer. But this view has no basis in the text or in the historical record, as we have already shown (see chapter 7, page 142). Fifty years after its founding, Polycarp writes to the church (not churches) at Philippi and counsels it to submit to its deacons and elders.

Although Paul singles out overseers and deacons for special mention in his greeting, he speaks to the whole community throughout the body of the letter. Without this brief, introductory reference, there would be no way to know, either from the rest of the letter or from Acts, that the Philippian church had overseers and deacons. It is clear that the overseers and deacons are accorded no elevated status above the congregation. The letter is written "to all the saints…in Philippi," and the terms "overseers and deacons" are subjoined to this phrase. The shepherds can be mentioned after the sheep because they are also part of the sheep. They are first among equals, not clerics over lay people.

Contrasting the obvious organizational changes that took place in the second century with Philippians 1:1, John Eadie succinctly concludes: "The mention of *episkopoi* in the plural, and the naming of both classes of office-bearers after the general body of members, indicate a state of things which did not exist in the second century."[25]

IDENTIFYING THE OVERSEERS

The first Gentile Christians and their leaders utilized the common Greek title, *overseer* (*episkopos*), to describe their community leaders. The term was a well-known designation of office equivalent to our word *superintendent*. In the Greek New Testament, *episkopos* appears four times to describe local church officials:

- And from Miletus he sent to Ephesus and called to him the elders of the church.... "Be on guard for yourselves and for all the flock, among which the Holy Spirit has made you overseers [*episkopoi*], to shepherd [pastor] the church of God" (Acts 20:17,28*a*).

- Paul and Timothy, bond-servants of Christ Jesus, to all the saints in Christ Jesus who are in Philippi, including the overseers [*episkopoi*] and deacons (Phil. 1:1).

- An overseer [*episkopos*], then, must be above reproach (1 Tim. 3:2*a*).

- For the overseer [*episkopos*] must be above reproach as God's steward (Titus 1:7*a*).

So who are the church overseers? It is evident from the rest of the New Testament that the individuals referred to as *overseers* are the same as those called *elders*. Although both terms apply to the same body of men, *elder* reflects the Jewish heritage that stresses dignity, maturity, honor, and wisdom, while *overseer* reflects a Greek-speaking origin that stresses the work of oversight. The following Scriptures confirm that the terms *overseer* and *elder* were used interchangeably in New Testament times:

- *Acts 20:17,28.* Luke writes that Paul sent for the elders of the church at Ephesus. But in the sermon to the same elders, Paul says that the Holy Spirit made them—the elders—"overseers." This plainly indicates that elders and overseers represent the same group of leaders.

- *Titus 1:5-7.* In verse 5, Paul mentions his previous directive that Titus appoint elders in every city. In verse 6, Paul begins to list the elders' qualifications and interjects the word "overseer" in verse 7. Since there is no clear indication that Paul has changed subjects, "overseer" must be another term for elder.

- *1 Peter 5:1,2.* Peter exhorts elders to oversee the church. Since elders oversee the local church, they are also overseers.

- *1 Timothy 3:1-13; 5:17-25.* In 1 Timothy 5:17, Paul speaks of the leading role and great value of "elders who rule well...especially those who work hard at preaching and teaching." But in 1 Timothy 3:1-13, he lists the qualifications of overseers and deacons, making no mention of elders. All the questions are resolved when we understand that the word "overseer" in 3:1 is a generic, singular form for overseers, and that "overseers" is used interchangeably for elders. Thus, 1 Timothy 3 and 5 refer to only two groups of men—elders and deacons.

Unfortunately, the terms *elders* and *overseers,* which occur interchangeably in the New Testament, later came to refer to two completely separate officials: the overseer and the council of elders.[26] Jerome, one of the greatest students of the original biblical languages (Greek and Hebrew) in the early centuries of Christianity, boldly asserted against all the traditions of his day that bishops and elders originally were the same:

> A presbyter and a bishop are the same...the churches were governed by a joint council of the presbyters.... If it be supposed that it is merely our opinion and without scriptural support that bishop and presbyter are one...examine again the words the apostles addressed to the Philippians.... Now Philippi is but one city in Macedonia, and certainly in one city there could not have been numerous bishops. It is simply that at that time the same persons were called either bishops or presbyters.[27]

Jerome was not the only early biblical commentator to affirm that elders and bishops were originally the same. J.B. Lightfoot writes:

> But, though more full than other writers, [Jerome] is hardly more explicit. Of his predecessors the Ambrosian Hilary had discerned the same truth. Of his contemporaries and successors, Chrysostom, Pelagius, Theodore of Mopsuestia, Theodoret, all

> acknowledge it. Thus in every one of the extant commentaries on the epistles containing the crucial passages, whether Greek or Latin, before the close of the fifth century, this identity is affirmed. In the succeeding ages bishops and popes accept the verdict of St. Jerome without question. Even late in the medieval period, and at the era of the reformation, the justice of his criticism or the sanction of his name carries the general suffrages of theologians.[28]

I conclude with Lightfoot's classic evaluation: "It is a fact now generally recognized by theologians of all shades of opinion, that in the language of the New Testament the same officer in the Church is called indifferently 'bishop' (*episkopos)* and 'elder' or 'presbyter' (*presbyteros).*"[29]

CHAPTER 9

Paul's Instruction to Timothy

"What I say is true: Anyone wanting to become an elder desires a good work"

1 Timothy 3:1 (*New Century Version*)

First Timothy is one of the most relevant New Testament letters for understanding the mission, organization, and life of the local church. It demands reform, correction, and discipline for many of the problems that trouble churches today. This Spirit-inspired, New Testament letter confronts such highly contemporary issues as:

- Disciplining church leaders (5:19-25)
- Qualifications for church leaders (3:1-13)
- Women in leadership (2:9-15)
- The spiritual disciplines of a church leader (1:18,19; 4:6-16)
- The teaching ministry of the church (4:14; 5:17,18)
- Care for the poor and the senior members of the congregation (5:1-6:2; 6:18,19)
- Confronting false teachers and cults (1:3-11,18-20; 4:1-5; 6:3-6)
- The prayer ministry of the church (2:1-8)
- The issues of wealth and materialism (6:5-19)
- The proclamation and protection of the gospel message (3:7,15,16)

Furthermore, 1 Timothy is the most important letter of the New Testament for the study of biblical eldership. It contains more direct, detailed, systematic teaching on eldership than any other New Testament letter. It also addresses two topics that are closely intertwined with the study of elders—deacons (3:8-13) and women (2:9-15). For these reasons, the largest portion of this book's expositional material centers around 1 Timothy. If we are to fully comprehend the teachings of this letter, however, we must first understand the disruptive situation in the church at Ephesus that prompted its writings.

THE HISTORICAL SETTING

For three years, Paul labored in the city of Ephesus and established a sound church (A.D. 53-56). When he was about to leave Asia Minor, Paul summoned the Ephesian elders for a final farewell meeting (A.D. 57). Gathered with the elders on the shore of Miletus, Paul solemnly warned the elders to be on guard because savage wolves would soon come. Acts 20 records this apostolic sermon:

> For I did not shrink from declaring to you the whole purpose of God. Be on guard for yourselves and for all the flock, among which the Holy Spirit has made you overseers, to shepherd the church of God which He purchased with His own blood. I know that after my departure savage wolves will come in among you, not sparing the flock; and from among your own selves men will arise, speaking perverse things, to draw away the disciples after them. Therefore be on the alert, remembering that night and day for a period of three years I did not cease to admonish each one with tears (Acts 20:27-31).

Five or six years after this prophetic warning to the Ephesian elders, the church in Ephesus was caught in the deathly grip of false teachers. The letter of 1 Timothy seems to indicate that the heresy had erupted from within the church. Paul's ominous words had come true: "and from among your own selves men will arise, speaking perverse things" (Acts 20:30).

We cannot be positive about Paul's exact movements following his release from Roman imprisonment (A.D. 62; Acts 28), but we do know that he and Timothy visited Ephesus. Their visit was not pleasant. False teachers were poisoning the church with deadly doctrines. In order to stop these teachers, Paul took radical action. He excommunicated the two leading perpetrators, Hymenaeus and Alexander (1 Tim. 1:19,20). Paul then moved on to Macedonia, leaving Timothy in Ephesus to help the embattled church and particularly to stop the advancement of false teachings: "As I urged you upon my departure for Macedonia, remain on at Ephesus, in order that you may instruct certain men not to teach strange doctrines" (1 Tim. 1:3).

Paul knew that Timothy faced a difficult assignment. He was keenly aware of the tough problems Timothy would encounter. Like tough, deeply rooted weeds, false teaching is hard to pull out once it has taken root. The opposition at Ephesus was fiercely argumentative (1 Tim. 6:3-5,20), so Paul wrote the letter of 1 Timothy to formally reinforce his verbal instructions to Timothy and to the church.

Given this background, it is easy to understand why a strong sense of urgency permeates the entire letter. "The church that Paul addresses," writes commentator Philip Towner, "had been torn apart by the false teachers, and much of this letter is aimed at putting the pieces back together."[1] The letter is all business. Biblical commentator and former principal of St. Edmund Hall, Oxford, J.N.D. Kelly writes, "Throughout [1 Timothy] we get the impression of acute dissatisfaction with conditions in the Ephesian church."[2] Paul even omits his usual thanksgiving that is found at the beginning of most of his letters and does not conclude the letter with his customary greetings from other saints. First Timothy lacks the intensely personal elements found in 2 Timothy. Whatever personal elements exist relate to Timothy's duties in Ephesus.

Although Timothy was Paul's intimate friend and personal assistant, this letter is written in a formal, official, and authoritative manner. The opening words illustrate this point and set the tone for the rest of the letter: "Paul, an apostle of Christ Jesus according to the commandment of God our Savior...." This is the only salutation in which Paul states that he is an apostle "according to the commandment of God." Paul's use of a formal salutation in a letter to a beloved friend prompts Patrick Fairbairn (1805-1874), a Scottish theologian and commentator, to write: "It was right, therefore, he [Timothy] should feel that necessity was laid upon him; that the voice which speaks to him is that not merely of a revered instructor or a spiritual father, but of a Heaven-commissioned ambassador, who has a right to declare the divine will and rule with authority in the Christian church."[3] As Christ's ambassador, Paul was under divine orders. So, too, Timothy was under orders from God and Christ's apostle to perform his duty faithfully in a time of crisis. The letter was meant, then, to authorize Timothy to act as Paul's representative in Ephesus.

The church in Ephesus urgently needed corrective discipline. Senseless, destructive doctrines were being taught that disrupted the entire inner life of the church. Christians were acting unlovingly toward one another. Quite likely, unqualified men had become elders and fallen into sin. Some women were crudely flaunting their wealth and newfound knowledge. Exclusive ideas and fighting among men had adversely affected the church's prayers. Needy widows were forsaken by their selfish families and forced to rely on the church for support. Sin was ignored. But worst of all, the gospel message and its reputation in the unbelieving community was seriously threatened. As a result of these problems, Paul spells out in the letter of 1 Timothy (1) how Timothy should faithfully execute his duties, (2) how he should handle the false teachers, and (3) how the local church should conduct itself as God's household and the pillar and foundation of the truth.

This last point is of direct interest to our study. In 1 Timothy 3:14,15, Paul states:

> I am writing these things to you [Timothy], hoping to come to you before long; but in case I am delayed, I write so that you may know *how one ought to conduct himself* in the household of God, which is the church of the living God, the pillar and support of the truth (italics added).

The "these things" mentioned in verse 14 are the instructions Paul writes to Timothy and the church, which begin in chapter two (1 Tim. 2:1-3:13). They are the God-given principles for ordering the life of the church. The word "conduct" (*anastrephō*) in verse 15 means "behavior," "one's manner of life and character," or, as one Greek lexicon puts it: [to] "*live* in the sense of the practice of certain principles."[4] The conduct, then, of every single member of the church family must conform to these apostolic principles.

The reason for insisting upon proper conduct and order is that the local church is "the household of God," "the church of the living God," and "the pillar and support of the truth." "The gist of Paul's message," writes J.N.D. Kelly, "is that order, in the widest sense of the term, is necessary in the Christian congregation precisely because it is God's household, his chosen instrument for proclaiming to men the saving truth of the revelation of the God-man, Jesus Christ."[5]

As in any successful household, but especially God's, proper structure, responsible behavior, discipline, and love are required. An unruly, dysfunctional household ruins the lives of its members and is an offense to the community. God's household should enrich and protect its members and be an inviting testimony of the gospel's truth to the unbelieving world. High on Paul's list for the proper governing of God's household are qualified, godly elders (1 Tim. 3:1-7,10; 5:17-25). If the elders of God's household deviate from sound doctrine or are of reproachable character, the entire household will suffer.

Not only is the local church God's household, it is "the pillar and support [foundation] of the truth." The truth that the church holds up before the world and supports is the gospel message of Christ:

> And by common confession great is the mystery of godliness:
> He [Christ] who was revealed in the flesh,
> Was vindicated in the Spirit,
> Beheld by angels,
> Proclaimed among the nations,
> Believed on in the world,
> Taken up in glory (1 Tim. 3:16)

The description of the local church as the pillar and foundation of the truth reveals the church's mission: to safeguard and proclaim the gospel of Christ. Every local church is to be a gospel lighthouse, missionary agency, and gospel school. Hence, for the local church to be ridden with heresy and false teachers is unspeakable. Such a church delivers a bankrupted testimony to a world that needs the truth of Christ.

The conduct of the believing community, therefore, must speak well of the gospel and of Jesus Christ. Of paramount importance, its spiritual leaders must be men of irreproachable character (1 Tim. 3:2) and "have a good reputation with those outside the church" (1 Tim. 3:7). Elders cannot teach and defend the gospel if their lives discredit the gospel. So of utmost concern in the governing of the household of God, the pillar and foundation of the truth, is that its spiritual leaders are credible witnesses to the truth of the gospel.

Although the church in Ephesus had been governed by elders for more than five years, problems existed within the eldership. Quite possibly unfit men had become elders since Paul had left the church, and some of the elders may have become false teachers. It is obvious that the elders weren't able to stop the false teachers, which is why Timothy had to remain in Ephesus. Even for Timothy, stopping these strong-minded men and women was difficult. Therefore, Paul felt the church needed fresh instruction on eldership, particularly on the character and discipline of elders.

The fact that the elders at Ephesus had failed should not surprise us, however. It is not easy to stop determined and energetic false teachers. The elders of the churches of Galatia were also unable to stop the invasion of false teachers. The tragic history of Christianity demonstrates the inability of many Christian leaders to keep churches pure from doctrinal error. The desperate need for sound teaching leads Paul to address one of the most important issues of the local church—the moral and spiritual qualifications of its elders.

The Qualifications for an Overseer

Paul sets the stage for his catalog of elder requirements with what he calls a "trustworthy statement." This is one of five trustworthy sayings in Paul's letters to Timothy and Titus (1 Tim. 1:15; 3:1; 4:9; 2 Tim. 2:11; Titus 3:8). Each saying is given special attention by the formula, "a trustworthy statement" (or "faithful is the saying"). This quotation formula both emphasizes and makes a positive commendation about the saying with which it is associated. In effect, it says that what is stated is indeed true and deserves constant repeating among the Lord's people: "It is a trustworthy statement; if any man aspires to the office of overseer, it is a fine work he desires to do" (1 Tim. 3:1). Although we don't know whether this saying originated with Paul or within the collective body of early Christians, the "trustworthy statement" indicates a widely accepted view that the work of the office of overseer is a fine work.

The phrase, "the office of overseer," represents one word in Greek, *episkopē*, which can be literally rendered "overseership." It represents the position and function of the church official called the overseer (*episkopos*) who is mentioned in verse 2. The overseer of verse 2 is not someone different from the elders of 1 Timothy 5:17-25 who lead and teach the church. Paul plainly demonstrates that *overseer* is used interchangeably for *elder* when he switches from the term "elders" to the term "overseer" within the Titus list of elder qualifications (Titus 1:5,7).

The singular form of the word "overseer" does not imply that there was only one overseer in the church at Ephesus. We know that in Paul's previous speech to the Ephesian elders (the same church leaders mentioned in 1 Timothy), he addresses a plurality of overseers (Acts 20:17,28); to the church in Philippi, Paul greets a plurality of "overseers." The reason that the term "overseer" in 1 Timothy 3:2 and Titus 1:7 is singular is because Paul uses a generic singular, that is, the singular name representing an entire class or type when speaking about the overseers. Thus, the singular "overseer" stands for *all* overseers—*all* elders.

This use of the generic singular is not an unusual way for Paul to express himself. Paul freely uses the generic singular—"woman," "widow," "elder," and "the Lord's servant"—when referring to special classes of people (1 Tim. 2:11-14; 5:5,19, and 2 Tim. 2:24). The only occasions that Paul uses "overseer" in the singular are in his lists of qualifications for the office (1 Tim. 3:2; Titus 1:7). In both cases, *overseer* is preceded by the singular construction "if any man" (1 Tim. 3:1; Titus 1:6). When he addresses the overseers directly, however, he uses the plural form because he is addressing a council of overseers, not a single overseer (Phil. 1:1; Acts 20:28). From Paul's use of singular and plural constructions, we can conclude that the church structure of 1 Timothy is pre-Ignatian and still follows the simple, brotherly, elder system of oversight that is recorded in Acts.

Paul goes on to say that overseership is "a fine work." "Fine" renders the Greek word *kalos*, which here conveys the idea of "excellent," "good," "worthwhile," or "noble." "Work" is used in the sense of a specific "task" or "job." Acts 20:28 explains why overseership is an excellent work: overseers shepherd God's Church that He purchased with His own blood. To God, the Church is the most precious thing on earth. In the face of many problems and labors, the greatest encouragement and incentive an elder can have is to know that he performs an exceedingly excellent work—one that is worthy of the sacrifice of one's life.

In brief, this early Christian saying declares the great value of the work of the office of overseer (eldership) while also encouraging those who desire this work. It is equally important that congregations today realize the worthwhile character of the elders' task. They need to realize its significance so they will support and encourage the elders in their work on behalf of the church.

Since God declares the office of overseer to be an excellent work, it follows that an overseer must be a man of excellent Christian character. A noble task naturally demands a noble person. To assure that only men of good character assume the role of overseer, Paul provides the local church with public, observable qualifications to protect both the office and the church:

> An overseer, then, must be above reproach, the husband of one wife, temperate, prudent, respectable, hospitable, able to teach, not addicted to wine or pugnacious, but gentle, uncontentious, free from the love of money. He must be one who manages his own household well, keeping his children under control with all dignity (but if a man does not know how to manage his own household, how will he take care of the church of God?); and not a new convert, lest he become conceited and fall into the condemnation incurred by the devil. And he must have a good reputation with those outside the church, so that he may not fall into reproach and the snare of the devil (1 Tim. 3:2-7).

The verb "must be" is an imperative. So the overseer "must be" of a certain moral and spiritual character or he doesn't qualify to be an overseer. Paul skillfully emphasizes this point because this is probably where the church tragically failed, as many churches do today. God wants us to know that a properly qualified elder is a nonnegotiable requirement for the government of God's household.

God provides objective, observable qualifications to test the subjective desire of all who seek the office of overseer. Desire alone is not enough; it must be matched by good character and spiritual capability. In his summary of Paul's fourteen specific qualifications, George Knight writes: "The items focus on two areas: (1) personal self-discipline and maturity, and (2) ability to relate well to others and to teach and care for them. These two are intertwined, although there seems to be a tendency to move from the personal to the interpersonal."[6]

ABOVE REPROACH: Heading the list of qualifications stands the general, overarching, "all-embracing"[7] qualification: "above reproach" (*anepilēmptos*). To be above reproach means to be free from any offensive or disgraceful blight of character or conduct, particularly as described in verses 2-7. When an elder is irreproachable, critics cannot discredit his Christian profession of faith or prove him unfit to lead others (Neh. 6:13). He has a clean moral and spiritual reputation. Since all God's people are called to live holy and blameless lives (Phil. 2:15; 1 Thess. 5:23), since the world casts a critical eye at the Christian community (1 Peter 3:15,16), and since Christian leaders lead primarily by their example (1 Peter 5:3), an irreproachable life is indispensable to the Christian leader. Job, for example, was an elder among his people (Job 29:7,21,25; 31:21), and he, the Scripture says, was morally above reproach: "There was a man in the land of Uz, whose name was Job, and that man was blameless, upright, fearing God, and turning away from evil" (Job 1:1).

Paul now begins to delineate concrete, observable qualities that define what it means to be irreproachable.

THE HUSBAND OF ONE WIFE: In both of Paul's qualification lists, he places the qualification "the husband of one wife" immediately after "above reproach." So the first and foremost area in which an elder must be above reproach is in his marital and sexual life.

The phrase, "the husband of one wife," and its related phrase, "the wife of one man," occur four times in the New Testament. Each occurrence is in the context of qualifications for overseers, deacons, or widows:

- An overseer, then, must be above reproach, the husband of one wife, temperate, prudent, respectable, hospitable, able to teach (1 Tim. 3:2).

- Let deacons be husbands of only one wife, and good managers of their children and their own households (1 Tim. 3:12).

- Let a widow be put on the list only if she is not less than sixty years old, having been the wife of one man (1 Tim. 5:9).

- If any man be above reproach, the husband of one wife, having children who believe, not accused of dissipation or rebellion (Titus 1:6).

The phrase "husband of one wife" is made up of three words in Greek: *mias gynaikos andra*. The words literally mean:

- *mias,* one
- *gynaikos,* wife or woman
- *andra,* husband or man

The phrase "of one wife" is placed first in an emphatic position to stress the idea of "one wife." It modifies the noun "husband." Thus we can translate the phrase in the following ways: "one-wife husband," "one-woman man," or "husband of one wife." There is broad disagreement, however, on the proper interpretation of this little phrase. We will consider four possibilities:

- elders must be married
- elders must not be polygamists
- elders may marry only once
- elders must be maritally and sexually above reproach

It's not uncommon to hear people say that an elder must be married because Scripture says he must be "the husband of one wife." This, however, is not an accurate interpretation. If Paul requires elders to be married, he flatly contradicts what he teaches in 1 Corinthians 7 where he outlines the distinct advantages of singleness in serving the Lord and even encourages singleness for the purpose of more effective, undivided service (1 Cor. 7:32-35; cf. Matt. 19:12). If an elder is required to be married, Paul should have qualified his statements about the advantage of singleness because singleness would disqualify an aspiring elder or deacon. However, Paul didn't write, "an elder must be a man who has a wife." Rather, he says that an elder must be a *one-wife man,* which is quite a different point.

Using similar logic, some people also conclude that an elder must have children because of the qualification that an elder manage "his own household well, keeping his children under control" (1 Tim. 3:4). I've talked with some men, for example, who don't believe they can serve as elders or deacons because they have only one child. They say that Paul's qualification requires "children." Paul, however, is not requiring an elder to father two or more children. We must realize the limitations of Paul's language. He wouldn't use "child" because people would then think that an elder could have only one child. He is simply saying that an elder who has offspring must manage his home well.

The fact is, most men are married and have children. Scripture requires that these men have their homes in order and that their marital relationships exemplify what Christian marriage should be. These qualifications obviously don't apply to elders who are single or childless.

A number of biblical commentators believe that the phrase, "the husband of one wife," means "married to one wife." They say that Paul's intent was to prohibit polygamy—having two or more wives at the same time—and conclude that elders must not be polygamists.

This seems like a good interpretation on the surface, but the related phrase, "the wife of one man" (1 Tim. 5:9), makes this interpretation nearly impossible. First Timothy 5:9 lists the qualifications for widows who receive living assistance from the church, and specifies that a woman must have been "the wife of one man." Certainly Paul wasn't referring to women who had two or more husbands at one time, which is called polyandry. Polyandry was abhorrent to Jews as well as to Romans and definitely was not a problem in the church. So it is unlikely that the phrase, "the husband of one wife," is intended primarily to address polygamy.

Some prominent biblical commentators believe that this phrase means "married only once in a lifetime." Paul, they say, prohibits remarriage for any reason, even remarriage following the death of a spouse. Thus a man who was divorced and remarried or a widower who had remarried wouldn't qualify to be an elder or deacon. This interpretation, however, is plainly at odds with the rest of the Bible's teaching on the sanctity of marriage.[8] "Nowhere else in the N.T.," writes biblical expositor J.E. Huther, "is there the slightest trace of any ordinance against second marriages."[9]

By itself, the phrase "the husband of one wife" doesn't indicate whether Paul means one wife in an entire lifetime or one wife at a time. This phrase must be interpreted within the larger context of Paul's overall teaching on marriage. It must never be allowed to contradict God's clear, general teaching on marriage. Therefore, from a New Testament perspective it is unthinkable that this phrase is meant to disqualify remarried widowers. A remarried widower could still be called "the husband of one wife."

Other commentators interpret this phrase to mean that men who have remarried following a divorce cannot be elders. Among Jews,

Romans, and Greeks, it was easy to divorce and remarry. In the case of remarriage following a divorce, two or three living women could have been married to the same man. Some have termed this *successive polygamy.* They believe Paul prohibits a remarried, divorced man from office because of the potentially embarrassing situations his ex-wife (or ex-wives) creates for the elder and the congregation.

The correctness of this interpretation seems impossible to prove one way or the other. In fact, the problem with this interpretation as well as the previous ones is that they create more problems than they solve. The interpretation, married only once in a lifetime, particularly raises a hornet's nest of mind-puzzling theological and marital questions. Regarding the issue of whether or not a divorced or divorced and remarried man (whether the divorce took place before or after his conversion) can become an elder, the New Testament doesn't directly comment. Commentator Philip H. Towner is on target when he writes, "the point is not how often one can be married, nor precisely what constitutes a legitimate marriage (that the marriage of the candidate is legitimate is assumed), but rather how one conducts himself in his marriage."[10]

A final interpretation, and the one favored here, is the simplest and least problem creating. It contends that the phrase "the husband of one wife" is meant to be a positive statement that expresses faithful, monogamous marriage. In English we would say, "faithful and true to one woman" or "a one-woman man." This latter phrasing closely follows the Greek wording.

Negatively, the phrase prohibits all deviation from faithful, monogamous marriage. Thus it would prohibit an elder from polygamy, concubinage, homosexuality, and/or any questionable sexual relationship. Positively, Scripture says the candidate for eldership should be a "one-woman man," meaning he has an exclusive relationship with one woman. Such a man is above reproach in his sexual and marital life.

What does 1 Timothy say about sexual and marital sins committed before a person's conversion to Christ? What about people who have legally divorced and remarried (assuming the local church allows for such)? What about the forgiveness and restoration of a fallen spiritual leader? These and many other painful and controversial questions are not answered directly here. They must be answered from the whole of Scripture's teaching on divorce and remarriage, forgiveness, grace, and restoration, as well as its teaching on leadership example and the full spectrum of elder qualifications.

All deviations from God's standard of marital behavior confuse and perplex us. Sin always confuses, distorts, and divides, so there will always be diverse opinions on questions such as these. This in no way, however, diminishes the local church's obligation to face these issues and make wise, scripturally sound decisions. In all these heartbreaking situations, the honor of Jesus' name, faithfulness to His Word, and prayer are the supreme guides.

TEMPERATE: In Greek, the word "temperate" (*nēphalios*) can mean sobriety in the use of wine. Here, however, it is used to mean mental sobriety.[11] "Temperate" denotes self-control, balanced judgment, and freedom from debilitating excesses or rash behavior. Negatively, it indicates the absence of any personal disorder that would distort a person's judgment or conduct. Positively, it describes a person who is stable, circumspect, self-restrained, and clear-headed.

It is necessary that elders, who face many serious problems, pressures, and decisions, be mentally and emotionally stable. Elders who lack a balanced mental and emotional perspective can easily be snared by the devil or false teachers.

PRUDENT: Similar to the word "temperate," "prudent" (*sōphrōn*) also stresses self-control, particularly as it relates to exercising good judgment, discretion, and common sense. To be prudent is to be sound-minded, discreet, and sensible, able to keep an objective perspective in the face of problems and disagreements. Prudence is an essential quality of mind for a person who must exercise a great deal of practical discretion in handling people and their problems. Prudence tempers pride, authoritarianism, and self-justification.

RESPECTABLE: "Respectable" (*kosmios*) is associated with the word "prudent" (1 Tim. 2:9). A sensible-minded person will also be a well-behaved person. *Kosmios* conveys the ideas of self-control, proper behavior, and orderliness. Although the word is used to describe properness in outward demeanor and dress in 1 Timothy 2:9, its usage here conveys the more general meaning of "'orderly'…'well-behaved,' or 'virtuous'…that which causes a person to be regarded as 'respectable' by others."[12] An elder cannot expect people to follow him if he is not respectable.

HOSPITABLE: It is also necessary for an elder to be hospitable. Hospitality is a concrete expression of Christian love and family life. It is an important biblical virtue:

- Job, the exemplary Old Testament elder, was a model of hospitality: "The alien has not lodged outside, For I have opened my doors to the traveler" (Job 31:32).

- Paul exhorts the Christians at Rome to pursue hospitality (Rom. 12:13).

- Peter writes, "Be hospitable to one another without complaint" (1 Peter 4:9).

- The author of Hebrews bids his readers: "Do not neglect to show hospitality to strangers, for by this some have entertained angels without knowing it" (Heb. 13:2).

These New Testament commands to practice hospitality are all found within the larger context of Christian love. Unfortunately, most Christians, and even some Christian leaders, are unaware that hospitality is a biblical requirement for pastoral leadership in the church. Some may even argue against such a seemingly insignificant point being a requirement for church shepherds.

Such thinking, however, shows an inadequate understanding of authentic Christian community, agape love, and the elder's work. For an elder to be inhospitable is a poor example of Christian love and care for others. The shepherd elder is to give himself lovingly and sacrificially for the care of the flock. This cannot be done from a distance—with a smile and a handshake on Sunday morning or through a superficial visit. Giving oneself to the care of God's people means sharing one's life and home with others. An open home is a sign of an open heart and a loving, sacrificial, serving spirit. A lack of hospitality is a sure sign of selfish, lifeless, loveless Christianity.

In my work as a pastor elder, I have found my home to be one of the most important tools I possess for reaching out to and caring for people. Although the shepherd's ministry of hospitality may seem like a small thing, it has an enormous, lasting impact on people. If you doubt this, ask those to whom a shepherd has shown hospitality. Invariably they will say that it is one of the most important, pleasant, and memorable aspects of the shepherd's ministry.

In His mysterious ways, God works through the guest-host relationship to encourage and instruct His people. So we must never underestimate the power of hospitality in ministering to people's needs. Those who love hospitality love people and are concerned about them. If the local church's elders are inhospitable, the local church will also be inhospitable and indifferent toward the needs of others.

ABLE TO TEACH: Like Israel, the Christian community is built on Holy Scripture. So those who oversee the community must be able to guide and protect it by instruction from Scripture. According to Acts 20, the elders must shepherd the flock of God. A major part of shepherding the flock involves feeding it the Word of God. Therefore, elders must be "able to teach" in order to do their job.

The ability to teach entails three basic elements: a knowledge of Scripture, the readiness to teach, and the ability to communicate. This doesn't mean that an elder must be an eloquent orator, a dynamic lecturer, or a highly gifted teacher (of which there are very few). But an elder must know the Bible and be able to instruct others from it.

In his parallel list of elder qualifications in Titus, Paul expands on the meaning of "able to teach." He writes, "holding fast the faithful word which is in accordance with the teaching, that he [the elder] may be able both to exhort in sound doctrine and to refute those who contradict" (Titus 1:9). An elder, then, must be able to open his Bible and exhort and encourage others from it. He must also be able to discern false doctrine and refute it with Scripture. God's Word brings growth to the church and protects it from falsehood. Therefore, shepherd elders must be able to teach God's Word.

NOT ADDICTED TO WINE: An elder must be above reproach in his use of alcohol. Paul uses strong language here that means not preoccupied or overindulgent with wine. Drunkenness is sin, and persistently drunken people require church discipline (see 1 Cor. 5:11; 6:9,10; Gal. 5:21; Eph. 5:18; 1 Peter 4:3). So a person in a position of trust and authority over other people can't have a drinking problem.

The Bible contains many warnings against the potential dangers of wine and strong drink (Isa. 5:11,22; Prov. 20:1; 23:30-35; Hos. 4:11). It specifically warns leaders about the dangers of alcohol:

It is not for kings, O Lemuel,
It is not for kings to drink wine,
Or for rulers to desire strong drink,
Lest they drink and forget what is decreed,
And pervert the rights of all the afflicted
(Prov. 31:4,5; cf. Lev. 10:8,9; Isa. 28:1,7,8; 56:9-12).

Drunkenness has ruined countless lives. It is reported that nearly half of the murders, suicides, and accidental deaths in America are related to alcohol. One in four families has some problem with alcohol, making alcohol one of the largest health problems in America.[13] The misery and heartbreak that alcoholism has caused multitudes of families is beyond imagination. No one who has worked with the people or families who are its victims jokes about its destructive power. Alcoholism reduces life expectancy, breaks up families, and destroys people financially. It's a moral and spiritual problem of the greatest magnitude.

Elders work with people, often those who are troubled. If an elder has a drinking problem, he will lead people astray and bring reproach upon the church. His overindulgence will interfere with spiritual growth and service, and it may well lead to more degrading sins.

Note, however, that Paul says, "not addicted to wine." He is not presenting an absolute prohibition against drinking wine. He is prohibiting the abuse of wine (or any other substance) that would damage a man's testimony and work for God.

NOT PUGNACIOUS: A pugnacious man is a fighter, a bad-tempered, irritable, out-of-control individual. The Greek word is derived from the verb "to strike" and suggests a violent person who is prone to physical assault on others. Wives and children especially feel the blows of a pugnacious man, and anyone who seriously frustrates a pugnacious man is a potential target for verbal, even physical, assault.

Elders must handle highly emotional interpersonal conflicts and deeply felt doctrinal disagreements between believers. Elders are often at the center of very tense situations, so a bad-tempered, pugnacious person is not going to solve issues and problems. He will, in fact, create worse explosions. Because a pugnacious man will treat the sheep roughly and even hurt them, he cannot be one of Christ's undershepherds.

GENTLE: "Gentle" is one of the most attractive and needed virtues required of an elder. No English word adequately conveys the fullness of this word's beauty and richness. "Forbearing," "kind," "gentle," "magnanimous," "equitable," and "gracious" all help capture the full range of its meaning. Forbearance comes from God and is a chief source of peace and healing among His people. So in his letter to the Philippian Christians, who were experiencing internal as well as external conflict, Paul says, "Let your forbearing spirit be known to all men" (Phil. 4:5).

The gentle man stands in vivid contrast to the pugnacious man. A gentle man exhibits a willingness to yield and patiently makes allowances for the weakness and ignorance of the fallen human condition. One who is gentle refuses to retaliate in kind for wrongs done by others and does not insist upon the letter of the law or his personal rights. "Graciously amenable," says one commentator, "yielding wherever yielding is possible rather than standing up for one's rights."[14]

Forbearance is a characteristic of God: "For Thou, Lord, art good, and ready to forgive [the same Greek word used in the LXX meaning forbearing or gentle], and abundant in lovingkindness to all who call upon Thee" (Ps. 86:5). Gentleness also characterized the life of Jesus on earth: "Now I Paul myself urge you by the meekness and gentleness of Christ" (2 Cor. 10:1). God fully expects His undershepherds to shepherd His people in the same way He does. He will not let His people be driven, beaten, condemned, or divided. Thus the shepherd must be patient, gracious, and understanding with the erring—and at times, exasperating—sheep. So many wrongs, disagreements, faults, hurts, and injustices exist in this sinful world that one would be forced to live in perpetual division, anger, and conflict were it not for forbearance. So elders must be "gentle" and "forbearing" like Christ.

UNCONTENTIOUS: Along with being gentle, it is important that an elder be uncontentious or peaceable. Since the day Cain killed Abel, his brother, men have been fighting and killing one another (Gen. 4:5-8). This is one of the wretched consequences of man's sinful nature. Christians, however, are commanded to be different, "to malign no one, to be uncontentious, gentle, showing every consideration for all men" (Titus 3:2).

God hates division and fighting among His people: "There are six things which the Lord hates...A false witness who utters lies, and one who spreads strife among brothers" (Prov. 6:16-19). Yet fighting paralyzes and kills many local churches. It may be the single, most distressing problem Christian leaders face. Therefore, a Christian elder is required to be "uncontentious," which means "not fighting" or "not quarrelsome." Positively stated, an elder must be a peaceable man. As Paul writes, "And the Lord's bond-servant must not be quarrelsome, but be kind to all, able to teach, patient when wronged, with gentleness correcting those who are in opposition" (2 Tim. 2:24,25*a*).

FREE FROM THE LOVE OF MONEY: An elder must not love money or be greedy. So this qualification prohibits a base, mercenary interest that uses Christian ministry and people for personal profit. Both Paul and Peter condemn what we would call "being in it for the money" (1 Peter 5:2; Titus 1:7). False teachers, Paul points out, are overly interested in money and in personal financial gain (1 Tim. 6:5; Titus 1:11). The Pharisees were lovers of money who devoured widow's houses (Luke 16:14; Mark 12:40). The chief religious leaders of Jesus' day turned the temple into a merchandise mart for their own profit (Mark 11:15-17).

Like a powerful drug, the love of money can delude the judgment of even the best men. Scripture sternly warns against the love of money: "For the love of money is a root of all sorts of evil, and some by longing for it have wandered away from the faith, and pierced themselves with many a pang" (1 Tim. 6:10). Elders, then, cannot be the kind of men who are always interested in money. They cannot be men who need to control the church's funds and who refuse financial accountability. Such men have distorted spiritual values and set the wrong example for the church. They will inevitably fall into unethical financial dealings that will publicly disgrace the Lord's name.

In stark contrast, an elder should be content with God's provision. In Hebrews 13:5 the writer exhorts his readers, "Let your character be free from the love of money, being content with what you have; for He Himself has said, 'I will never desert you, nor will I ever forsake you.'" Paul states the matter this way: "For we have brought nothing into the world, so we cannot take anything out of it either. And if we have food and covering, with these we shall be content. But those who want to get rich fall into temptation and a snare and many foolish and harmful desires which plunge men into ruin and destruction" (1 Tim. 6:7-9). Elders, then, must model godly contentment and faith in Christ's loving provision for them.

In summarizing verse 3, George Knight observes, "In short, the bishop's life is not to be dominated or controlled by wine or money, nor may it be one of strife, but rather it must be one of peace and gentleness."[15] In contrast, a man who is controlled by money or alcohol is not controlled by the Holy Spirit. He is not stable, self-controlled, sound-minded, or respectable. He is controlled by base desires that will inevitably lead to other sins and public reproach.

A MAN WHO MANAGES HIS HOUSEHOLD WELL: A prospective elder must be able to manage (*prohistēmi*: lead and care for; see 1 Thess. 5:12) his household "well." The key measurement when evaluating a man's management of his household is his children's behavior. So Paul requires that he keep "his children under control with all dignity." This means he must be a responsible Christian father, husband, and household manager. He must have a reputation for providing for his family, financially, emotionally, and spiritually. Concerning this qualification, Donald Guthrie, former professor at London Bible College, remarks, "A most important principle, which has not always had the prominence it deserves.... Any man unable to govern his children graciously and gravely by maintaining good discipline, is no man for government in the Church."[16]

A well-managed family means that the children obey and submit to the father's leadership. The way in which that relationship is manifested is especially important: it is to be "with all dignity." The father is not to be a spirit-crushing tyrant who gains submission by harsh punishment. Elsewhere Paul writes, "Fathers, do not provoke your children to anger; but bring them up in the discipline and instruction of the Lord" (Eph. 6:4). Thus a Christian father must control his children in an honorable, respectful, and dignified way. Of course there are no perfect, problem-free children in this world. Even the best Christian fathers and mothers have child-rearing problems, but these parents resolve the problems and are involved with their children in responsible, caring ways. They guide their children through the many storms of life.

We must note that the children referred to in verse 4 are children who live at home, under their father's authority: "keeping [present tense] his children under control with all dignity." In the Titus 1:6 passage, the verb in the phrase "having children who believe" also indicates that the children are presently in the home and under the father's authority.[17] I mention this because some people believe that a man is not a viable candidate for eldership until all his children have reached adulthood. But this is not what the passage says. Some men still father children at the age of forty or forty-five, and God does not intend for them to wait until they are nearly seventy years of age before they are qualified to serve as elders. Furthermore, we must note that the passage doesn't teach that an elder must have children. This instruction simply applies to men who do have children.

The critical importance of this requirement is immediately underscored by the rhetorical question Paul asks in verse 5: "But if a man does not know how to manage his own household, how will he take care of the church of God?" The answer to that question is a resounding negative—he can't care for the church of God if he doesn't know how to manage his own household. The Greek word rendered "care for" (*epimelēsetai*) stresses the loving, personal attention of meeting the church's various needs. It doesn't, however, eliminate the idea of leading or directing, which is an essential part of caring for the church.

NOT A NEW CONVERT: Scripture prohibits a "new convert" from serving as an elder. A new convert is a beginner in the faith, a baby Christian, a recent convert. No matter how spiritual, zealous, knowledgeable, or talented a new convert may be, he is not spiritually mature. Maturity requires time and experience for which there is no substitute, so a new convert is simply not ready for the arduous task of shepherding God's flock.

There is nothing wrong with being "a new convert." All Christians begin life in Christ as babies and grow to maturity. An elder, however, must be mature and know his own heart. A new Christian does not know his own heart or understand the craftiness of the enemy, so he is vulnerable to pride—the most subtle of all temptations and most destructive of all sins. Pride caused the devil's ruin (Ezek. 28:11-19; Gen. 3:5, 14,15). Like the devil, the prideful elder will inevitably fall. "Pride goes before destruction," the Bible says, "And a haughty spirit before stumbling" (Prov. 16:18; cf. 11:2; 18:1; 29:23). Biblical history shows that pride has destroyed the greatest of men (2 Chron. 26:16; 32:25).

The position of elder (especially in a large, well-established church such as the one in Ephesus) carries considerable honor and authority. For a recent convert, the temptation of pride would be too great. Pride would destroy the man, causing personal disgrace, loss, exposure, divine chastisement, and possibly wrecking his faith. It would also hurt the church. So Paul warns against appointing a new convert as an elder, "lest he become conceited and fall into the condemnation incurred by the devil."

As to why this qualification is not listed in the Titus catalog of qualifications, we can only guess. It may have been that leadership by new converts was a real problem in the church at Ephesus. Perhaps new converts were deceived about their giftedness and spiritual intelligence and stirred up confusion in the church.

A MAN WITH A GOOD REPUTATION AMONG NONBELIEVERS: Finally, and of significant importance, an elder "must have a good reputation with those outside the church." Both the apostles Paul and Peter express deep concern that Christians have a good reputation before a watching, nonbelieving world (1 Cor. 10:32; Phil. 2:15; Col. 4:5,6; 1 Thess. 4:11,12; 1 Tim. 2:1,2; 5:14; 6:1; Titus 2:5,8,10; 3:1-2; 1 Peter 2:12,15; 3:1,16). If all believers are required to have a good testimony before nonChristians, then it is imperative that the leaders have a good reputation with unbelievers. The church's evangelistic credibility and witness is tied to the moral reputation of its leaders.

In reality, the nonChristians may know more about the character and conduct of the prospective elder than the church. Quite often the prospective elder's nonChristian fellow workers or relatives actually have more daily contact with the church leader than do the people in church. So "Paul is concerned," writes George Knight, "that those who may judge less sympathetically but perhaps also more realistically and knowledgeably will render a 'good'...verdict both from the perspective of their own consciences...and also from their awareness of the particular man's commitment and consistency in terms of his Christian faith."[18]

An outsider's opinion of a Christian leader's character cannot be dismissed, for it affects the evangelistic witness of the entire church, "the pillar and support of the truth." That is why Paul emphatically states "he must have a good reputation." The verb "must," the same verb used in verse 2, again stresses the absolute necessity and importance of this matter.

The reason for emphatically insisting on this qualification is that an elder with an unfavorable or sinful reputation among nonChristians will "fall into reproach and the snare of the devil" in a far more destructive way than those he leads. If a pastor elder has a reputation among nonbelievers as a dishonest businessman, womanizer, or adulterer, the unbelieving community will take special note of his hypocrisy. NonChristians will say, "He acts that way, and he's a church elder!" They will ridicule and mock him. They will scoff at the people of God. They will talk about him and will generate plenty of sinister gossip. They will raise tough, embarrassing questions. He will be discredited as a Christian leader and suffer disgrace and insults. His influence for good will be ruined and he will endanger the church's evangelistic mission. The elder will certainly become a liability to the church, not a spiritual asset.

But that is not all. Fully aware of the devil's ways (2 Cor. 2:11), Paul adds that the defamed elder will also fall into "the snare of the devil." The devil is pictured as a cunning hunter (1 Peter 5:8). Using public criticism and the elder's own inconsistencies, the devil will entrap the unwary Christian into more serious sin—uncontrolled bitterness, angry retaliation, lying, further hypocrisy, and stubbornness of heart. What may begin as a small offense can become something far more destructive and evil. Therefore, an elder must have a good reputation with those outside the Christian community.

Qualifications Demand Examination

Thus far we have talked about the elders' qualifications, but following the list of qualifications Paul presents an equally important subject—the examination of elders. The fifteen qualifications for elders presented in 1 Timothy 3:1-7 are just empty words without the requirement (v. 10) to examine a candidate's qualifications for office. The text insists that no one can serve as an elder until he is first tested (examined) and approved:

> And let these [deacons] also [like the overseers] first be tested; then let them serve as deacons if they are beyond reproach (1 Tim. 3:10).

Starting in verse 8, Paul lists the qualifications for deacons, just as he has just done for elders. In the middle of the deacon's list of qualifications, Paul interjects an essential requirement that makes all the other requirements meaningful: "And let these also first be tested; then let them serve as deacons." The words "and...these also" are important to the development of Paul's thought in this section (1 Tim. 3:8-13). They alert us to something slightly different from, but essential to, the five character requirements listed for deacons (1 Tim. 3:8,9). Through these words, Paul emphasizes that deacons must be tested in the same way that elders must be tested. Thus, "and...these also," refers back to the overseer mentioned in the previous section (1 Tim. 3:1-7).[19]

It is essential that we do not overlook this key point. In fact, translators of the *New English Bible* took the liberty to add the term "bishops" (overseers) to the translation in order to make this point perfectly clear. This translation reads, "No less than bishops, they must first undergo a scrutiny, and if there is no mark against them, they may serve."

The reason Paul places this injunction in the middle of the list of qualifications for deacons is that there would be a tendency to think that the biblical standards for deacons require less enforcement than the standards for overseers. Paul has already assumed that his readers recognize the need to examine overseers as to their qualification for office but recognizes that the requirement to examine deacons may not be as highly regarded. Thus Paul demands that deacons also be examined in a similar manner.

The passive imperative form of the verb that is rendered "let these...be tested" stresses the necessity for testing a prospective deacon or elder. Testing is not an option. Every prospective elder or deacon must be evaluated by others.

The word "tested" is derived from the Greek word *dokimazō*. Anglican Archbishop Richard Trench (1807-1886), in his classic work *Synonyms of the New Testament*, claims that "in *dokimazein*...lies ever the notion of proving a thing whether it be worthy *to be received* or not."[20] In ancient Greek literature, this word was sometimes used in relation to testing a person's credentials for public office.[21] In our present context, it means "the examination of candidates for the diaconate."[22] The idea here is for others to officially examine, evaluate, and scrutinize the prospective elder's or deacon's character. Just as medical doctors must be officially examined before they are licensed, prospective elders and deacons are to be examined in light of God's requirements before they take office.

The proper examination of deacons and elders is precisely where many churches fail. The examination process takes time and effort, and many churches are too busy with other matters to make that effort. Perhaps the church in Ephesus was also too busy to examine thoroughly its deacons and elders.

THE ELDERS LAY HANDS ON TIMOTHY

In 1 Timothy 4:6-16, Paul reminds Timothy of how he should faithfully execute his duties, and in verse 14, he specifically warns Timothy about neglecting his spiritual gift. Paul had personal knowledge of Timothy's spiritual gift and the unique circumstances accompanying the reception of his gift. Paul was the human channel through whom God conveyed Timothy's spiritual gift (2 Tim. 1:6):

> Do not neglect the spiritual gift within you, which was bestowed upon you through prophetic utterance with the laying on of hands by the presbytery (1 Tim. 4:14).

Timothy was converted during Paul's first missionary journey (A.D. 49). Thus he was Paul's true child in the faith. At the beginning of the second missionary journey, Luke records that Timothy joined with Paul to assist him in his gospel mission (Acts 16:1-3). Three significant things happened to Timothy on that occasion.

First, Timothy and Paul learned of Timothy's unique commission in the gospel through a series of Spirit-given, prophetic utterances: "This command I entrust to you, Timothy, my son, in accordance with the prophecies previously made concerning you, that by them you may fight the good fight" (1 Tim. 1:18; cf. Acts 16:6-10 for other supernatural utterances accompanying the second missionary journey). Timothy had been singled out by the prophetic word for a specific task, just as Paul and Barnabas had been singled out in Antioch (Acts 13:1-3).

Second, in complete accordance with the prophetic word, Paul placed his hands on Timothy in order to convey a gift, that is, a *charisma* or special endowment for service: "And for this reason I remind you to kindle afresh the gift of God which is in you through the laying on of my hands" (2 Tim. 1:6). By the laying on of Paul's hands and the impartation of a spiritual gift through Paul's hands, Timothy was officially set aside to share as a helper in Paul's commission in the gospel. The laying on of hands did not make Timothy the minister or bishop of a church or body of churches. Most likely, Timothy was unmarried and totally devoted to spreading and guarding the gospel as Paul's special assistant (Acts 19:22). He was an evangelist (2 Tim. 4:5), a co-worker, and partner with Paul in the work of the gospel.

Third, and closely associated with the prophecies and the laying on of Paul's hands, was "the laying on of hands by the presbytery." The significance of the elders' action differed from that of Paul's action. Paul and the prophetic word were the channels "through" (Greek, *dia*) which God conferred the "spiritual gift." The laying on of the elders' hands, Scripture shows, was done *in association with* (Greek, *meta*) Paul's laying on of hands and the prophecies. Precisely what the laying on of the elders' hands signified, however, is not explained. If we assume the act was similar in significance to that recorded in Acts 13:1-3, then the laying on of the elders' hands was a public commissioning by which the church entrusted Timothy to God's care and to the work to which God had called him. By doing this, the elders identified themselves as partners with him and expressed full agreement with his special task. In accordance with the "prophetic utterance," the elders, as public witnesses to that word and representatives of the church(es), placed their hands upon him. Timothy was to remember this act and not allow men to despise his labor or his youth.

The word "presbytery" is a transliteration of the Greek word *presbyterion*, the collective noun for elders (*presbyteroi*). It would have been better if the *New American Standard Bible* had translated *presbyterion* as "eldership," "council of elders," or "body of elders," since it renders the other two occurrences of *presbyterion* as *council of elders* (Luke 22:66; Acts 22:5). By using the collective noun *eldership*, Paul stresses the elders' official role and the significance of their act: the official body of church elders laid hands upon Timothy, publicly affirming his special commission in the gospel, a fact he was never to forget.

The elders referred to in this account were the elders Paul and Barnabas appointed on their first missionary journey. Again, not one elder, but the entire body of elders laid hands on Timothy. As community leaders, their function was to represent the church in the communication of its approval and fellowship. Whether these elders were from one local church or several, the text doesn't indicate.

Honor Due the Elders

The entire section of 1 Timothy from 5:1 to 6:2 addresses the proper treatment of various groups of people within the church: older men (5:1),[23] younger men (5:1), older women (5:2), younger women (5:2), widows (5:3-16), elders (5:17-25), nonChristian employers (6:1), and Christian employers (6:2). Following a rather lengthy and emotionally charged section on the Christian's duty to honor godly widows (5:3-16), Paul next addresses the congregation's duty to honor the church elders. That is, he gives further instruction on how Christians must treat one another in God's household (1 Tim. 3:14,15). It is impossible to fully understand biblical eldership without grasping this highly instructive passage:

> Let the elders who rule well be considered worthy of double honor, especially those who work hard at preaching and teaching. For the Scripture says, "You shall not muzzle the ox while he is threshing," and "The laborer is worthy of his wages." Do not receive an accusation against an elder except on the basis of two or three witnesses. Those who continue in sin, rebuke in the presence of all, so that the rest also may be fearful of sinning. I solemnly charge you in the presence of God and of Christ Jesus and of His chosen angels, to maintain these principles without bias, doing nothing in a spirit of partiality. Do not lay hands upon anyone too hastily and thus share responsibility for the sins of others; keep yourself free from sin. No longer drink water exclusively, but use a little wine for the sake of your stomach and your frequent ailments. The sins of some men are quite evident, going before them to judgment; for others, their sins follow after. Likewise also, deeds that are good are quite evident, and those which are otherwise cannot be concealed (1 Tim. 5:17-25).

Honoring Elders Who Rule Well and Labor at Preaching and Teaching

In verses 17 and 18, Paul instructs the congregation to care for the economic welfare of elders who rule well, particularly those who labor at preaching and teaching. In the same way that needy widows had been abandoned by family members and fellow believers as a result of self-centered living caused by false teaching (1 Tim. 5:3-16), it appears that the church's spiritual leaders had been neglected. So Paul exhorts the church saying, "Let the elders who rule well be considered worthy of double honor, especially those who work hard at preaching and teaching."

The elders to whom Paul refers are identified by two qualifying clauses: "who rule well" and "those who work hard at preaching and teaching." There are two ways to understand how these clauses relate to one another, and they depend on how one translates the Greek adverb *malista*. Most commentators render *malista* by its standard meaning: "especially," "above all," or "particularly," and the *New American Standard Bible* here renders *malista* as "especially." If this rendering is correct, Paul has two groups of elders in focus: those who exercise pastoral leadership well and those who give special attention to teaching as well as ruling. Elders who lead well deserve "double honor," but "above all" those who work hard at preaching and teaching.

The other interpretation contends that in certain contexts *malista* means "that is," "in other words," or "to be precise."[24] In this sense, the term is used when a general statement needs to be more precisely defined. It is possible that this is how *malista* should be read in 1 Timothy 4:10; 2 Timothy 4:13; and Titus 1:10. If this is how *malista* is used in 1 Timothy 5:17, the text should read: "Let the elders who rule well be considered worthy of double honor, *that is*, those who work hard at preaching and teaching." If this is the case, the clause "those who work hard at preaching and teaching" defines more precisely the general clause, "the elders who rule well." Both clauses refer to one and the same group: those who labor at preaching and teaching.

Although both interpretations fit the context, the first interpretation is preferable because Paul could have stated directly that teaching elders deserve double honor without the mention of ruling well. The fact that he mentions both ruling well and laboring at teaching, however, suggests he has in mind all elders who deserve double honor because of their work, but chiefly those who labor at teaching. Regardless of the interpretation favored, Paul's uppermost concern is that the congregation properly honor those elders who labor at preaching and teaching. On this point there should be little disagreement.

Although all elders rule, certain elders deserve financial support because they "rule well." The word "rule" translates the Greek word *prohistēmi.* As we have already noted in 1 Thessalonians 5, the word *prohistemi* means "lead," "care for," "manage," or "direct." The *New American Standard Bible's* translation of *prohistēmi* as "rule" is a bit strong, and the translation "care for," which some scholars prefer, is too weak unless one clearly understands that the care involved is that of leading and teaching people. The idea conveyed here is that these elders exercise effective pastoral leadership. Such elders are natural leaders, visionaries, planners, organizers, and motivators. They are the kind of men who get things done and can effectively care for people. Moreover, they are willing and able to give a good deal of their time, skill, and energy to the spiritual care of the local congregation.

In addition, the elders who particularly deserve double honor are those who "work hard" at preaching and teaching. Paul uses the same term for "work" (*kopiaō*) here that he uses in 1 Thessalonians 5:12 where he refers to the Thessalonian church leaders who worked hard at leading and instructing the people. "With this verb," writes George Knight, "he is self-consciously designating the work of these elders as a vigorous and laborious work."[25] Because these elders diligently lead and teach the congregation, Paul exhorts, "Let them be considered worthy," which means "rightfully deserving" or "entitled to." Because of their skills and strenuous labor, such elders are rightfully entitled to double honor.

Good teachers "work hard" at long hours of study, preparation, and demanding teaching situations. Teaching is absorbing work. It is mentally strenuous, time-consuming work that demands a great deal of strength and self-discipline. Commenting on "the expenditure of energy" in teaching and preaching, the well-known author and Christian apologist R.C. Sproul writes:

> Though preachers differ in the expenditure of energy given in a sermon, it has been estimated that a half-hour address can use as much physical energy as eight hours of manual labor. Billy Graham, for example, has been cautioned by physicians against the danger of physical exhaustion due to preaching.... Dynamic preaching requires physical strength and stamina. When the preacher's body goes out of shape, it will invariably affect the quality of his speaking.[26]

The precise meaning of the phrase, "at preaching and teaching," is difficult to understand, although the general thought is clear. The word "preaching" in the original text is *en logō. Logos* is the Greek word for "word" or "speech." The context, which is the primary consideration for translating a term with such a broad range of meaning, demands the rendering "preaching," in the general sense of exhorting, admonishing, or evangelizing. Linked with preaching, yet distinct, is "teaching" (*didaskalia*). It is hard to decide if "teaching" is used here in the active sense of the act of teaching and instructing or in the passive sense of doctrine. The active sense seems to fit the context better. If so, *preaching* is the broader term, which would include proclaiming the gospel and exhorting believers, and *teaching* is the more specialized term, meaning authoritative instruction in doctrine for believers. By using "preaching and teaching," Paul covers all dimensions of public discourse.

The big question that arises when discussing this passage is, Who are these elders? Since *all* elders are required to be "able to teach" (1 Tim. 3:2), but only *some* elders labor at teaching, what is the difference between these elders? The answer is found in the participle "those who work hard" (*kopiōntes*). The reason these elders "work hard" at teaching is because they are spiritually gifted to do so. They are driven to study Scripture and to work fully at teaching. Nothing else satisfies them like teaching and preaching God's Word. They are skilled at communicating divine truth, and there is a marked effectiveness to their teaching. They have a wide appeal among people, and the people have confidence that they are knowledgeable in Scripture. Their teaching bears consistent fruit. Although all elders must be able to teach, not all elders are Spirit-gifted teachers and shepherds who labor in the Word.

To understand the difference between elders who teach and elders who labor at teaching, consider the following. Every Christian is instructed to be able to defend the faith (1 Peter 3:15) and to seize opportunities to witness to nonChristians (Col. 4:5,6). Although all Christians must be ready and able to witness for Christ, only some are Spirit-gifted evangelists. Even among Spirit-gifted evangelists, there are differences and degrees of evangelistic gift and effectiveness. Not every evangelist, for example, is a Billy Graham.

The same is true of teaching. All mature Christians should be able to teach and defend the faith (Col. 3:16; Heb. 5:12). Thus all elders, as mature, exemplary Christians, are required to be able to teach, exhort in sound doctrine, and defend the truth from false teachers (1 Tim. 3:2; Titus 1:9). Even if the qualification "able to teach" implies the spiritual gift of teaching, as some commentators think, not every elder would have the same level of skill or interest in teaching (Rom. 12:6). However, because the catalog of elder qualifications can fit any mature Christian man, and all mature Christians should be able to teach the truth to others, the requirement "able to teach" doesn't necessarily require the spiritual gift of teaching. First Timothy 5:17 helps to confirm this viewpoint by asserting that only some elders labor at teaching. Of course 1 Timothy 5:17 doesn't limit other elders from teaching, it merely states the fact that some labor in the Word.

The kind of spiritual gift envisioned in 1 Timothy 5:17 parallels what we find in Ephesians 4:11, which states that the risen Christ gives to the Church gifted shepherds and teachers to equip His people for better service on behalf of the body: "And He gave some as apostles, and some as prophets, and some as evangelists, and *some as pastors [shepherds] and teachers*, for the equipping of the saints for the work of service, to the building up of the body of Christ" (Eph. 4:11,12; italics and brackets added). According to the grammatical structure of the phrase, "and some as pastors [shepherds] and teachers," shepherds and teachers are closely linked together but not identical. Shepherds are included in the category of teachers, but not all teachers are included in the category of shepherds. The shepherd gift, then, uniquely combines teaching and governance.[27] It is this kind of gift that would enable an elder to "rule well" and "work hard" at teaching.

A great deal of flexibility exists as to how teachers operate. They may function locally or as itinerant teachers. They may or may not be elders. Shepherds, on the other hand, are more than teachers because they teach, govern, protect, and care for the flock in practical ways. Shepherds may be itinerant, but their gift is most often used in caring for the needs of one local flock. Thus elders who have the spiritual gift of shepherding are extremely vital to the local church and to the eldership.

Differences in spiritual giftedness must not be allowed to create jealousy or division within the eldership. By stating God's approval of such elders and their entitlement to double honor, Paul emphasizes that these elders ought to be viewed by the congregation and their fellow elders as a source of blessing, joy, and profit, rather than as a threat. Furthermore, we should not overlook the fact that Paul envisions a plurality of elders who are entitled to double honor, not just one man who receives double honor. He doesn't say, "Let the *elder* who rules well be considered worthy of double honor." In a large church like that in the city of Ephesus, one person would be totally inadequate to teach and manage the church (Acts 13:1; 15:35).

As critically important as the teaching and shepherding gifts are to the local church, the New Testament does not elevate those who possess these gifts to a special priestly or clerical status. Nor does it create a distinct office separate from the eldership. Nor does it give to any party exclusive rights to preach, baptize, lead in worship, or administer the Lord's supper. [28] In fact, the New Testament doesn't assign a special title or name for these elders even though their giftedness and full- or part-time working status for the church distinguishes them from the other elders.

From the New Testament's perspective, it is difficult even to define the difference between those who evangelize, teach, and shepherd in a full-time capacity and those who serve in the manner in which the Bible charges all Christians to serve (Rom. 12:11; 1 Cor. 15:58; 16:15,16; Col. 3:23,24; 1 Peter 2:16; 4:10). Precisely defined divisions such as priest and people, clergy and laity—so much a part of most religious practice—do not exist in the New Testament Christian brotherhood. Paul was the chief enigma of all, for he supported himself by manual labor and at the same time evangelized and taught (Acts 18:3; 20:34; 1 Cor. 4:12; 9:6) without diminishing his divine commission as the apostle to the Gentiles. The elders, then, who labor in the Word and exercise good leadership are in the words of Scripture, "leading men among the brethren" (Acts 15:22).

GIVING DOUBLE HONOR

According to Paul, all elders should be honored, but elders who rule well and work hard at preaching and teaching are entitled to "double honor." By using the expression, "double honor," Paul wisely avoids slighting other elders of their due honor and is able to call special attention to those who rule well and those who labor at teaching. So "double honor" refers to honor for an elder of the church and honor for his extra labor.

The word "*honor*" (*timē*) means "respect," "consideration," or "high regard," and in certain instances includes the idea of monetary aid. This latter sense appears to be predominant in 1 Timothy 5. Consider the following points:

- Although the word "*honor*" (*timē*) itself doesn't necessarily mean material assistance (2 Chron. 32:33; Prov. 26:1; Eph. 6:2; 1 Tim. 6:1), it includes in certain contexts the sense of material aid (Matt. 15:3-6; cf. Num. 22:17,37; 24:11; Prov. 3:9; 14:31; 27:18; Dan. 11:38; Acts 28:10).

- First Timothy 5:3 states, "Honor widows who are widows indeed." The "widow indeed" is a truly destitute Christian widow. The instruction that follows (vv. 4-16) demonstrates that honoring these widows primarily involves monetary assistance (vv. 4,8,16). A church honors a destitute Christian widow by providing for her material livelihood.

- The biblical quotations in verse 18 show that material provision is uppermost in Paul's thought. The immediate context, therefore, indicates that "honor" involves material maintenance. Biblical commentator J.E. Huther best summarizes the strength of this point:

  > The 18th verse makes it evident that, if the word *timēs* (v. 17) does not distinctly mean *reward* or *remuneration*, this idea was prominent in the Apostle's mind as connected with the honor of which these presbyters were to be accounted worthy. The quotation from the O.T. in the first clause as united with the words...of the second, and as used and applied in 1 Cor. 9:9, scarcely admits of any other explanation.[29]

- Using "honor" rather than a more tangible term like "money" is in harmony with Paul's choice of expression for financial matters. Paul favors terms that express grace, liberality, love, and partnership: service (Rom. 15:25,27; 2 Cor. 8:4; 9:1,12,13); fellowship (2 Cor. 8:4; Gal. 6:6; Phil. 1:5); grace (1 Cor. 16:3; 2 Cor. 8:6,7); liberality (2 Cor. 8-9); bounty (2 Cor. 8:20); blessing (2 Cor. 9:5); good work (2 Cor. 9:8); good things (Gal. 6:6); a fragrant aroma, an acceptable sacrifice (Phil. 4:18); seed (2 Cor.

9:10); harvest of your righteousness (2 Cor. 9:10); gift (Phil. 4:17); honor (1 Tim. 5:3,17).

- The word "honor" expresses financial compensation in a thoroughly Christian manner. Financial provision for elders is really honor due the elders, and such honor conveys the congregation's esteem, thoughtfulness, and loving concern. We should not be like the people whom Hendriksen describes as thinking "that if any honor is to be bestowed it should be by means of the funeral sermon."[30] Or in the words of the well-known Lutheran commentator Richard C.H. Lenski (1864-1936), "Wreaths are not to be laid on their graves after they are dead; flowers are to be given to them now in order to cheer them in their work."[31]

- The rights of some in the brotherhood to receive financial support is in full agreement with other passages of Scripture. Jesus was a full-time teacher and preacher who was financially supported by the believing community (Luke 8:3). He called certain disciples to leave their employment and follow Him so that they could preach the gospel and teach believers (Luke 5:4-11; Matt. 28:19,20). Like their Master, they, too, depended on the loving financial support of others for their livelihood. Furthermore, Jesus taught that those who labor in the Word "get their living from the gospel" (1 Cor. 9:14; Matt. 10:10). Paul also affirmed the right of those who preach and teach to receive financial provision from others (1 Cor. 9:4-14; 2 Cor. 11:8,9; Gal. 6:6; Phil. 4:16; 1 Thess. 2:5,6; 2 Thess. 3:8,9; Titus 3:13). In our present passage, Paul instructs the congregation to support congregational elders who preach and teach.

Paul feels very strongly about the congregation's duty to care for elders who labor in the Word. He wants no misunderstanding as to the meaning or necessity of his instruction, so in verse 18 he adds scriptural support and clarification to his charge. Quoting from both the Old and New Testaments, Paul writes: "For the Scripture says, 'You shall not muzzle the ox while he is threshing,' and 'The laborer is worthy of his wages.'"

Paul introduces both quotes by saying, "For the Scripture says." For the believer, just the mention of the word "Scripture" signals the ultimate voice of authority—God's Word (John 10:35). By using this qualifying phrase, Paul is saying that complete unity exists between the Old and New Testaments—both Moses and Jesus agree that a laboring man "is worthy of his wages."

Paul's Old Testament quotation is from Deuteronomy 25:4, "You shall not muzzle the ox while he is threshing." The context of Deuteronomy concerns equity and justice in daily life—even the right of an animal to enjoy the fruit of its labor while working for its owner. The full intent of Deuteronomy 25:4 is explained in 1 Corinthians 9:6-14:

> Or do only Barnabas and I not have a right to refrain from working? Who at any time serves as a soldier at his own expense? Who plants a vineyard, and does not eat the fruit of it? Or who tends a flock and does not use the milk of the flock? I am not speaking these things according to human judgment, am I? Or does not the Law also say these things? For it is written in the Law of Moses, "You shall not muzzle the ox while he is threshing." God is not concerned about oxen, is He? Or is He speaking altogether for our sake? Yes, for our sake it was written, because the plowman ought to plow in hope, and the thresher to thresh in hope of sharing the crops. If we sowed spiritual things in you, is it too much if we should reap material things from you? If others share the right over you, do we not more? Nevertheless, we did not use this right, but we endure all things, that we may cause no hindrance to the gospel of Christ. Do you not know that those who perform sacred services eat the food of the temple, and those who attend regularly to the altar have their share with the altar? So also the Lord directed those who proclaim the gospel to get their living from the gospel.

Twice in the New Testament, Deuteronomy 25:4 is quoted to support the right of teachers and preachers to receive material sustenance for their labors (1 Cor. 9:9; 1 Tim. 5:18). To refuse to support hard-working teachers of the Word is as unjust, heartless, and selfish as muzzling an animal while it is working, which was a common practice among greedy, ancient farmers. The passage thus implies the provision of adequate living support, not merely token gifts, for the worker.

Paul's New Testament quotation, "the laborer is worthy of his wages," is from Luke 10:7. Jesus originally spoke these words to the seventy before He sent them out to preach. Paul applied His words to all who teach and preach the gospel (1 Cor. 9:14). Here, in 1 Timothy 5:17,18, Paul applies the same words to elders who labor in the Word.

No matter how poor a local congregation is, it must exercise faith and liberality before the Lord (2 Cor. 8:1-5) in giving to those who labor in the Word. In short, God's people must honor their elders. "For what could be more unkind," writes Calvin, "than to have no care for those who have the care of the whole Church."[32]

Today we desperately need to capture Paul's passion and vision for the centrality of preaching and teaching the Word in the power of the Holy Spirit. If we do, we will gladly render double honor to elders who labor in the Word. If we don't, we are doomed to wander far off course into forbidden waters, just as the church at Ephesus did.

PROTECTING AN ELDER

Honoring elders also includes protecting them from malicious people and false accusations. The Scripture says, "Do not receive an accusation against an elder except on the basis of two or three witnesses" (v. 19). We must not be naive about the fact that there are plenty of hateful, unstable people who aim to ruin people in authority. Godly men like Joseph, Moses, David, Jeremiah, Nehemiah, and Paul all experienced the bitter sting of false accusation. David, for example, pleaded with King Saul not to listen to false reports about his intentions toward him: "And David said to Saul, 'Why do you listen to the words of men, saying, "Behold, David seeks to harm you?"'" (1 Sam. 24:9; cf. Neh. 6:5-9).

Discontent, rancorous members of the infant China Inland Mission nearly destroyed the mission by their false reports and complaints about their saintly leader, Hudson Taylor. Hudson's wife, Maria, indignantly wrote to the wife of one of her husband's accusers, reminding her of 1 Timothy 5:19:

> I am aware that (your husband) has received...serious misrepresentations—to call them nothing worse. Would it not have been the right course, before allowing these to affect his *conduct*, to have endeavored to ascertain the other side of the

> question? "Against an elder"—and such my dear Husband surely is to the rest of our party—"receive not an accusation but before two or three witnesses." I am more intimately acquainted than anyone else with the whole tenor of my beloved Husband's private and social walk, and...that walk is in all *meekness* and *forbearance*, in all *purity*, in all *sincerity of purpose*, and all *singleness of eye.*[33]

Unfortunately, Maria's scriptural admonition was not heeded until considerable pain and damage was inflicted on the Taylor family.

If an elder stands between a husband and wife in conflict or disciplines a prominent church member, accusations will fly. Amos (ca. 755 B.C.), the Old Testament farmer-turned-prophet, wrote: "They hate him who reproves in the gate, and they abhor him who speaks with integrity" (Amos 5:10). The more diligently and conscientiously an elder becomes involved in others' problems, the greater the risk of facing angry, false accusations.

When people become angry at their leaders, they think they have the right to strike out at them and say whatever they want to say. So Scripture provides protection for elders by stating, "do not receive an accusation against an elder except on the basis of two or three witnesses." This means: don't listen to unsubstantiated charges, and don't automatically accept as true an accusation made against an elder.

At heart, we all love to hear rumors and scandals. Proverbs 18:8 says, "The words of a whisperer are like dainty morsels, and they go down into the innermost parts of the body." But Christians are to be people of truth, love, and light. Therefore, we should hate scandalous tales and unsupported rumors. We should silence them whenever we hear them because they are destructive and harmful to individual people and to the life of the community. Good people have been ruined by unfounded accusations, and we should not allow this to happen in the Christian community.

Love always tries to see others in the best possible light, not the worst (Prov. 17:9). Our judgments, then, are to be governed by facts, evidence, and witnesses—not rumors. We should live by the principle, "No judgment without the facts." We shouldn't believe any story, even from our most trusted friends, until we have all the facts from all the people involved.

However, fair, reasonable protection from accusation doesn't imply immunity. So Paul adds the condition, "except on the basis [on the evidence of] of two or three witnesses." This means that an accusation brought by two or three people who have witnessed the sin, or by two or three people who have verified another's accusation, must be investigated and properly judged. George Knight aptly explains this condition:

> In effect, Paul is urging Timothy to follow...Matthew 18 and the O.T. before the church accepts or acknowledges as correct an accusation against an elder. The process may consist of two or three witnesses bringing an accusation, but normally it would consist of two or three witnesses verifying an accusation that may come from only one individual before it is considered further.[34]

The legal principle on which this directive is based is Deuteronomy 19:15: "A single witness shall not rise up against a man on account of any iniquity or any sin which he has committed; on the evidence of two or three witnesses a matter shall be confirmed" (Deut. 19:15; cf. John 8:17; Deut. 17:6; Heb. 10:28). An accusation of sin that is substantiated by witnesses must be heard; it cannot be brushed aside. As unpleasant and time-consuming as a fair investigation into an accusation might be, it must be done. Sin must not be hidden, nor can an innocent person remain falsely accused.

DISCIPLINING AN ELDER

How should an elder be treated if an accusation of sin is found to be true? Verse 20 provides the answer: "Those who continue in sin, rebuke in the presence of all." Some expositors think that verse 20 begins a new subject regarding the treatment of sinners in general, but this view is incorrect. Such a break in thought would be too abrupt and unexpected. Furthermore, it is clear that verses 19-25 deal with the topic of elders, particularly the sin of elders.

The clause, "those who continue in sin," translates a present active participle (*tous hamartanontas*). The *New American Standard Bible* rendering stresses the persistent nature of the sinning. There is disagreement among commentators, however, as to what is implied by this present tense participle.

Some commentators believe that only those elders who stubbornly persist in sin after private warnings are to be publicly rebuked and that repentant elders need not be rebuked publicly. This interpretation, however, misconstrues the point of the passage. A more accurate interpretation recognizes that the contrast is made between elders who are innocent (v. 19) and elders who sin (v. 20). The elders to be publicly rebuked are those who are found guilty of sin as proven by witnesses (v. 19).

The elder's disposition toward his sin is not the issue here. The issue is: an elder's sin demands public exposure. Paul gives no consideration as to whether or not the elder is repentant. The present tense participle should be rendered "the ones who sin," not "those who continue in sin." The participle describes the "present guilt"[35] which has been substantiated by witnesses (v. 19). To add the condition that a one-time-occurrence of sin or the sin of a repentant elder is not to be publicly rebuked is to distort Paul's instruction. The passage teaches that a proven, public accusation against an elder who has sinned (or is still sinning) must be publicly exposed and rebuked.

Furthermore, 1 Timothy 5:20 is not simply an example of Matthew 18:15-17 (Christ's teaching on discipline) in action. First Timothy 5:20 provides additional biblical instruction on church discipline, specifically the matter of a church leader's sin. Of course, if an elder refuses to repent, he would be disfellowshiped from the congregation according to Matthew 18.

Paul's instructions go on to add that an elder who has been proven to be guilty of sin by witnesses is to be rebuked before the church. The imperative verb "rebuke" translates the Greek word *elenchō*, which is a rich term conveying the ideas of "exposing," "proving guilt," "correcting," and "reproving." In this context, "rebuke" includes the ideas of public exposure, correction, and reproof. After Timothy's departure from Ephesus, the elders would be responsible to rebuke any sinning elders.

The context indicates that the sin to which Paul refers is serious. It is "sin" that is the problem, not merely a leadership blunder or minor shortcoming. Witnesses are required to verify the truth of the charges (vv. 19,20) and a public rebuke is demanded, which would not be required of minor offenses. Since verse 20 is written in very general terms, Paul's instruction covers various degrees of sin, circumstances, and consequences. Godly wisdom, counsel, and prayer will guide the local church and its spiritual leaders in implementing this instruction in individual cases.

Paul specifically requires the guilty elder to be rebuked in "the presence of all." This means public exposure before the entire congregation, not just the council of elders. The major point is that an elder's sin must be publicly exposed, not hidden or swept under the carpet. A spiritual leader's sin must be treated with great concern because it has grave ramifications; it can lead more people astray and can cause the unbelieving world to mock God, the church, and the gospel. If the world sees that local churches take sin seriously, especially in the discipline of sinful leaders, then it will believe that Christians mean what they preach. Furthermore, only when the discipline of an erring church leader is made public is there any chance of controlling one of the most divisive forces in a church: rumormongering, gossip, and misinformation.

Public rebuke of an elder who sins fulfills another important purpose: "that the rest also may be fearful of sinning." Not only is the public discipline for the correction of the sinning elder, it is also for deterring others from sin. "The rest" seems to refer to the other elders, but the entire congregation would also experience some measure of fear (Acts 5:11). The phrase "of sinning" is not in the original text, which reads, "so that the rest also may have fear." The fear the elders would experience includes not only the fear of sinning, but the shame of public exposure. To see the sin of a fellow elder publicly exposed before the church would produce a fear of sinning and of its shameful consequences (Deut. 13:11). God uses such fear as a powerful deterrent to keep people, especially church leaders, from sinning.

A Call to Courageous Obedience and Justice

No part of Christian ministry is more difficult than investigating and disciplining sin, especially the sin of a church leader. One can easily think of a thousand clever excuses for evading the discipline of a church leader. This is particularly true if the leader is rich or a prominent member of a powerful or large family within the church. At heart we are cowards, afraid to take action, afraid to disturb the balance of church politics. We're afraid people will leave the church or that the offerings will decrease if we follow through with discipline.

Knowing the human propensity to avoid such harsh realities, Paul dramatically charges Timothy (and the church) to comply with his instructions in verses 19 and 20. The absolute seriousness "to maintain these principles" is underscored by Paul's use of the first person singular verb, "I solemnly charge," and the mention of "God" Himself, the Mediator "Christ Jesus," and the elect "angels" of God—all who see and will someday judge. Furthermore, Timothy is to execute "these principles" justly and righteously. There is to be no discrimination or favoritism shown when dealing with accusations or sin.

"Without bias" means without "prejudgment" or "discrimination," that is, without judging someone guilty or innocent before the facts are known. "Without bias" seems to refer particularly to verse 19. It is possible to be prejudiced toward those who accuse an elder of sin, or toward certain elders, so we are to guard ourselves against such prejudices. The second term, "partiality," may refer primarily to verse 20. Showing "partiality," that is, "favoritism" or "preferential treatment," to prominent leaders is a common practice in the world. So when listening to an accuser or rebuking the guilty, all proceedings are to be done "without bias" and without "partiality." This is an important requirement because God, Christ, and the angels see and will someday judge the proceedings.

Despite this forceful appeal to act, the public discipline of church leaders has been, until recently, almost unheard of in most churches. The practice of covering up church officials' sins and the trick of quietly moving the offending official to another church is not uncommon.[36] Sadly, the predominant reason churches are beginning to discipline sinful pastors is not because they fear and honor God, but because of the proliferation of multi-million dollar lawsuits against churches by people who have been hurt and abused by sinning pastors.

The failure to publicly discipline church leaders demonstrates a grievous lack of love for God and His Word. It reveals that we do not fear and serve God, but want to play church games. No matter how difficult or unpleasant such discipline may be, we must "maintain these principles" in obedience to God. The fear of God's judgment and assessment of our stewardship is to be our constant motivation and encouragement in all such difficult matters.

Assessing Prospective Elders

Investigating accusations of sin and disciplining leaders are always emotionally traumatic experiences. So in verses 22-25, Paul counsels

Timothy about how to best avoid further problems with church leaders. His counsel, "Do not lay hands upon any one too hastily," shows that prevention is still the best cure.

The laying on of hands is a biblical expression for appointment to office or a specific task (Num. 27:18-23; Acts 6:6). So in verse 22, Paul charges Timothy not to appoint elders (or anyone) too "hastily" or "quickly." Because of the crying need for church leaders, there is always pressure to make hasty appointments, but such appointments create more serious, long-lasting problems. Time and testing are still the best principles to follow when appointing church leaders.

Paul's warning not to "lay hands upon anyone too hastily" indicates that elders were appointed by the laying on of hands. Although the New Testament provides no specific example of the laying on of hands at the time of an elder's appointment, it was probably the common procedure used by Paul and the first Christians (Acts 6:6; 13:3; 1 Tim. 4:14).

The warning not to appoint prospective elders too quickly can be applied in two ways: to the initial appointment of an elder to office or to the restoration of a disciplined elder to office. In numerous cases of leadership failure (but certainly not all), the real problem is that unfit, unproven men were appointed too quickly to positions of spiritual leadership. So Paul advises Timothy that one way to prevent unworthy men from becoming spiritual leaders is to avoid rash, hasty appointments.

The same principle applies, particularly in this context, to a disciplined elder who seeks restoration to his position after being removed from office because of sin. It is not uncommon for an ambitious leader to press the church for restoration to office. A problem with such dynamic men is that they are often so consumed by personal ambition and "the ministry" that they don't have a clue as to the damage they do to the Lord's people or to the Lord's name. They don't understand that even when it is possible, healing and restoration take a considerable period of time. J. Carl Laney, author of *A Guide to Church Discipline*, remarks:

> Restoration takes *time*. If the service station attendant gives me directions which result in my getting lost, it will be a long time before I trust his directions again. If a husband commits adultery, it will require a long period of faithfulness to restore his wife's

> trust. Similarly, sufficient time must pass for a disciplined Christian worker to be tried and proven. The leader who has fallen must once again earn the reputation of being "above reproach." It took years of faithful Christian living to qualify the first time. It may take that long to re-qualify for leadership after a fall.[37]

The local church and its leaders, therefore, must remember not to lay hands too quickly on a fallen leader or a new, prospective elder. The possible consequence of such rash, hasty appointments by Timothy (or the elders) could mean participating in "the sins of others."

The mention of "sins" in verse 22 carries forward the idea of sin that is presented in verse 20—the sin of the elder who was found guilty and required public discipline. The laying on of hands creates a bond between two parties. The one (or ones) who appoints by the laying on of hands "shares" (*koinoneō*, "participate") in the sins or success of the one appointed. If an unfit person is appointed to leadership and sins by creating division, teaching false doctrine, or acting immorally, those who appointed the leader "share responsibility" for those sins (2 John 11). The more we understand the solemn, personal responsibility of appointing people to positions of leadership in the church, the more we will exercise reservation, thoughtfulness, and prayerfulness in our appointments. One good reason to encourage the practice of the laying on of hands is that it creates an observable, personal, and tangible sense of responsibility and fellowship between the parties involved.

Fully aware of the seriousness of his charge to Timothy, Paul adds the warning, "keep yourself free from sin [literally, "keep yourself pure"]." The unwise appointment of an unqualified elder could stain Timothy's character and reputation. It could cause him to "share responsibility" in that person's sins and failure. So Paul reminds Timothy to keep himself pure from participating in the sins of unfit elders by carefully and prayerfully examining all candidates to church office (1 Tim. 3:10; 5:24,25).

Verse 23 is a short digression, sparked by the word "pure," that requires clarification. Knowing about the situation at Ephesus (1 Tim. 4:1- 5) and Timothy's personal habits and frequent health problems, Paul encourages him to drink "a little wine for the sake of your stomach." "A little wine" will not defile, although using much wine would. Hence, Timothy could take some wine and remain pure before those he leads. This brief, personal digression expressing regard for Timothy's personal health is a clear example of the true-to-life nature of this letter and is an affirmation of its Pauline authorship.

Help for Assessing Prospective Elders

Paul's warning against sharing in other's sins could easily frighten those who must appoint people to responsible positions in the church. To counter this fear, Paul picks up where he left off in verse 22 and cites two brief maxims:

> The sins of some men are quite evident, going before them to judgment; for others, their sins follow after. Likewise also, deeds that are good are quite evident, and those which are otherwise cannot be concealed (1 Tim. 5:24,25).

"As far as avoiding mistakes is concerned," writes Lenski, "and thus possibly making the wrong man an elder, Timothy need not worry, for the difficulty as to judging is not great. This is said for Timothy's comfort."[38] E.K. Simpson comments, "Timothy has been called on to diagnose character, and Paul supplies him with a clue for the task, and the verdicts he has to pass."[39]

The first maxim refers to two categories of unfit candidates: those who are obviously unfit and those who upon careful examination are found to be unfit. The second maxim refers to two categories of fit candidates: those who are obviously fit and those who upon careful examination are found to be fit. Let us consider each category of candidate.

Some men's sins are so obvious that no one would think of appointing them to office, thus no evaluation for appointment to leadership is necessary: "The sins of some men are quite evident, going before them to judgment." Their "sins" precede them, that is, they show in advance of any formal examination that the man is utterly unfit for a position of spiritual leadership. The "judgment" Paul refers to is human assessment (Matt. 5:21; John 7:24), not God's judgment. God is not the subject here because all sins are evident to Him (1 Cor. 4:5).

The sins of some men are not easily seen, so action must be suspended until the man's character and conduct are examined: "For others, their sins follow after." Paul assures Timothy that the "sins" of these men will be exposed at the time of their examination. God is not the only one who can see sin—men can too, if they take the time to investigate. Like the first category of unfit men, these men, although their sins are more subtle, must be refused eldership because they are not above reproach.

If an unworthy man is appointed to office after careful examination, those in charge cannot be accused of sin because they did all they humanly could to assess the candidate's character. "'In exceptional cases of deception and hypocrisy,' writes Lenski, quoting another commentator, 'which only [God] who is able to see the heart could detect, evidently no sin can be charged against the conscientious judge who has nevertheless been deceived'...In such rare cases Timothy will *not* be fellowshiping the sins of such men; he will still be pure."[40]

The form of the second maxim is similar to the first. The good works of some men are obvious before any examination is made: "Likewise also, deeds that are good are quite evident." These men are easily identified as men who are fit for church eldership.

Some men's good works are not obvious, but upon examination their good deeds become apparent: "and those which are otherwise cannot be concealed." The good works of these men cannot be hidden, and it will become obvious that they are fit candidates for appointment to eldership.

Paul is assuring Timothy that as long as he does not act hastily in appointing elders and carefully examines the candidates, that he will find the right men. Armed with these words of encouragement, Timothy and the church leaders are prepared to accomplish the challenging task before them.

CHAPTER 10

Paul's Instruction to Titus

"The overseer must be above reproach as God's steward."
Titus 1:7

Titus was one of Paul's most gifted co-workers. Like Timothy, Titus faithfully devoted himself to assisting Paul in his apostolic mission of proclaiming the gospel and strengthening the churches. Shortly after Paul's release from his Roman imprisonment (A.D. 62), Paul and Titus (and probably others) visited the island of Crete. When he left Crete, Paul left Titus behind to finish organizing and teaching the churches. Titus was Paul's special deputy to fulfill a temporary assignment, a role he had filled many times before for Paul. Titus was soon replaced by Arteman or Tychicus (Titus 3:12).

Although it is possible, as some claim, that Paul had recently planted churches on the island of Crete, there is no compelling evidence to support this view. The presence of false teachers who infiltrated Christian homes (Titus 1:10-16; 3:9-11) and Paul's lengthy introduction regarding his apostleship (Titus 1:1-3) seem to indicate that the churches on Crete were established prior to Paul's arrival. The fact that there were no official elders in these churches doesn't imply that Paul founded the churches. Rather, the absence of elders means that the churches were weak and in urgent need of apostolic direction and care. Perhaps Paul felt the same way about the Cretans as he did about the Roman Christians: "I long to see you in order that I may impart some spiritual gift to you, that you may be established" (Rom. 1:11).

Shortly after his departure from Crete, Paul wrote to Titus to restate his verbal instructions in official, written form. In no sense is the letter to Titus strictly private correspondence (Titus 3:15*c*). This letter, as well as his other letters, was a significant part of Paul's missionary work and strategy. The letter was meant to authorize Titus, who was not an apostle, to act with apostolic authority: "These things speak and exhort and reprove with all authority. Let no one disregard you" (Titus 2:15). The letter was also to provide continual, permanent directives for the churches long after Titus was gone. Paul fully expected the churches to obey his letter and his personal envoy, Titus.

SET CHURCHES IN ORDER AND APPOINT ELDERS

After his formal introduction stating his apostleship and its purposes (Titus 1:1-4), Paul reminds Titus that there is unfinished business to complete. The churches of Crete lack proper organizational structure and order, so Titus must "set right" what is deficient in these churches:

> For this reason I left you in Crete, that you might set in order what remains, and appoint elders in every city as I directed you (Titus 1:5).

The first order of business and chief priority for Titus was to appoint qualified elders for every church: "appoint elders in every city as I directed you." For Paul, setting churches in order meant, among other things, establishing a council of qualified elders. Churches can exist without elders (see Acts 14:23), but qualified, functioning elders must be established for the protection and proper ordering of a church.

The Greek word for "appoint" is *kathistēmi*. This verb often is used to express the act of appointing a person to an official position, such as the appointment of a judge or governor (Acts 7:10). The same verb is used in Acts 6:3 in reference to the twelve apostles who appointed the Seven to care for the poor in the Jerusalem church. In that situation, the people selected seven men, and the apostles officially placed those men in charge of the administration of the church's care for the poor. The verb can also express appointment in an unofficial sense. Either way, as biblical commentator R.J. Knowling says, "The verb implies at all events an exercise of authority."[1]

The verb *kathistēmi*, however, conveys no special religious or clerical connotations. It is the common word used for appointing judges, governors, or anyone to an official position. Thus to translate the verb as "ordained," which some scholars do, communicates wrong concepts.

Titus was instructed to designate qualified brothers from within the local churches as elders, not to ordain sacred priests or clerics. Elders are not priests. They have no sacred ordination status, such as that of the Old Testament priests (see chapter 14). Moreover, *kathistēmi* suggests nothing about the actual procedures leading up to the installation of elders. The appointment by Titus was the final act in the process and thus summarizes the whole process.

The phrase "in every city" is another way of saying "in every church." As the New Testament writers consistently record, the local church embraced all believers within a particular city (see Acts 20:17). The New Testament never speaks of *churches* within a city, only *the church*. Thus, in each city, that is, each church, Titus was to designate a plurality of elders. "Thus Titus," writes F.J.A. Hort, "was in this respect to do what Paul and Barnabas had done in the cities of Southern Asia Minor on their return from the first missionary journey."[2]

A key point of emphasis is that Titus is to make his appointments according to Paul's guidelines: "as I directed you." The "I" is emphatic in the original language, so it is an authoritative directive from the apostle himself. The verb "directed" (*diatassō*) means "command," "ordered," or "charged." Paul gave specific, apostolic directives on this vital matter so that neither Titus nor the local Christians could do as they pleased. These apostolic directives remain universally binding for local churches today.

The Qualifications for Elders

What exactly were Paul's directives for appointing elders? Our translation reads: "Namely, if any man be above reproach." In order to better grasp what Paul is saying, we need to expand his words a bit: "Appoint elders as I had directed you, that is, consider only the kind of man who is above reproach in moral character for appointment to eldership." F.F. Bruce's paraphrase conveys Paul's meaning quite well:

> The reason I left you behind in Crete was this: I wanted you to set right the things that remained to be dealt with, and in particular to appoint elders in each city, in accordance with my directions.
>
> You remember those directions of mine about the kind of man who is fit to be appointed as an elder—one who is beyond reproach.... The man who exercises pastoral leadership must be beyond reproach because that befits a steward in God's house.[3]

As in 1 Timothy 3:1-7, the apostolic qualifications are the basis for appointment to eldership. These qualifications represent God's standards that no man or organization has the right to change. Christian elders must be qualified according to God's criteria:

> ...[5*b*] appoint elders in every city as I directed you, [6] namely, if any man be above reproach, the husband of one wife, having children who believe, not accused of dissipation or rebellion. [7] For the overseer must be above reproach as God's steward, not self-willed, not quick-tempered, not addicted to wine, not pugnacious, not fond of sordid gain, [8] but hospitable, loving what is good, sensible, just, devout, self-controlled, [9] holding fast the faithful word which is in accordance with the teaching, that he may be able both to exhort in sound doctrine and to refute those who contradict. [10] For there are many rebellious men, empty talkers and deceivers, especially those of the circumcision, [11] who must be silenced because they are upsetting whole families, teaching things they should not teach, for the sake of sordid gain (Titus 1:5*b*-11; verse references added).

Note that Paul does not change subjects in verse 6, although he does change from the plural, "elders" (v. 5), to the singular, "any man [whoever]" (v. 6). So in verse 6, Paul is still speaking about elders, although he uses the singular term "any man." Paul uses the same singular construction, "if any man aspires to the office of overseer," in 1 Timothy 3:1.

ABOVE REPROACH: The term "above reproach" (*anegklētos*, a synonym of *anepilēmptos*, 1 Tim. 3:2) means "unaccused," that is, one whose character or conduct is free from any damaging moral or spiritual accusations. This first qualification, as in 1 Timothy, stands out as the fundamental qualification under which all other qualifications are subsumed. John Calvin's summary of this overarching qualification is worth repeating: "By *anegklēton*, blameless, he does not mean someone who is free from every fault, for no such man could ever be found, but one marred by no disgrace that could diminish his authority—he should be a man of unblemished reputation."[4]

Paul immediately lists two critical areas of the prospective elder's life that especially must be above reproach: the elder's marital-sexual life and the management of his children.

THE HUSBAND OF ONE WIFE: See comments on 1 Timothy 3:2.

HAVING CHILDREN WHO BELIEVE: Not only is an elder to be maritally faithful, "a one woman man," he must also have proper control of his children. The translation, "having children who believe," is better rendered as "having faithful children," which is the choice in the *Authorized King James Version.* The Greek word for "believe" is *pistos*, which can be translated either actively as "believing" (1 Tim. 6:2) or passively as "faithful," "trustworthy," or "dutiful" (2 Tim. 2:2).

The contrast made is not between believing and unbelieving children, but between obedient, respectful children and lawless, uncontrolled children. The strong terms "dissipation or rebellion" stress the children's behavior, not their eternal state. A faithful child is obedient and submissive to the father. The concept is similar to that of the "faithful servant" who is considered to be faithful because he or she obeys the Master and does what the Master says (Matt. 24:45-51).

The parallel passage in 1 Timothy 3:4 states that the prospective elder must keep "his children under control with all dignity." Since 1 Timothy 3:4 is the clearer passage, it should be allowed to help interpret the ambiguity of Titus 1:6. "Under control with all dignity" is closely parallel with "having trustworthy children." In the Titus passage, however, the qualification is stated in a positive form—the elder must have children who are trustworthy and dutiful.

Those who interpret this qualification to mean that an elder must have believing, Christian children place an impossible burden upon a father. Even the best Christian fathers cannot guarantee that their children will believe. Salvation is a supernatural act of God. God, not good parents (although they are certainly used of God), ultimately brings salvation (John 1:12,13).

In striking contrast to faithful children are those who are wild or insubordinate: "not accused of dissipation or rebellion." These are very strong words. "Dissipation" means "debauchery," "profligacy," or "wild, disorderly living" (cf. 1 Peter 4:3,4; Luke 15:13). "Rebellion" means to be "disobedient," "unruly," or "insubordinate." Wild, insubordinate children are a terrible reflection on the home, particularly on the father's ability to guide and care for others. A man who aspires to eldership but has profligate children is not a viable candidate for church leadership.

The unquestionable necessity for a prospective elder to be above reproach as a husband and father is reinforced in verse 7*a*: "For the overseer must be above reproach as God's steward." Paul's repetition of the idea that an elder must be "above reproach" shows the intensity of his feelings on this matter. The conjunction "for" in verse 7*a* shows the close, logical connection in thought with verse 6. Verse 7*a* illuminates a profound reason for the necessity of the qualifications that appear in verse 6: an elder is God's household manager. Since an elder must manage God's household, it logically follows that he must be able to manage his own family. This is the same reasoning Paul uses in 1 Timothy 3:5: "if a man does not know how to manage his own household, how will he take care of the church of God?

In verse 7*a*, Paul switches to the title "overseer" (*episkopos*): "For the overseer must be above reproach." Some scholars try to assert that the change in terminology indicates a change of subject. They claim that Paul is no longer talking about the elders but about the church overseer. They say that the church overseer is selected from among the elders, who comprise an informal body of senior members. The overseer is then the official leader of the church.[5] Thus, they conclude, Titus was instructed to appoint from among the elders an "overseer" for each city.

This interpretation, however, violates the natural reading of the passage. The text does not say that the overseer is chosen from the body of elders. Furthermore, if verse 7 begins a list of qualifications for someone other than the elders of verses 5 and 6—someone superior to the elders—it is a most confusing and awkward subject change. Such a change makes complete nonsense out of the transitional word "for" that connects verses 6 and 7. The clear message of verse 5 is that Paul left Titus in Crete to appoint "elders," not to appoint elders and an overseer or an overseer from among the elders. It is best to affirm the standard interpretation that "overseer" is an interchangeable term for *elder*, and that there is no change of subject between verses 6 and 7.

The term *overseer* stresses function more than honor, and in this case is better suited to the image of the household manager than the term *elder*. The singular form "overseer" can be explained as a generic singular just as is the case in 1 Timothy 3:2. Paul has already switched from the plural "elders" in verse 5 to the singular "any man" [any elder] in verse 6, so we should not be surprised by his use of the singular "overseer," which agrees with the singular "any man" in verse 6 and focuses the reader's attention on the individual character of the overseer.

An overseer must be above reproach because he is "God's steward" (*oikonomos*). The Greek word *oikonomos* means house manager (*oikos* is the Greek word for "house" or "household"). Thus a steward is a manager, administrator, or trustee of someone else's household, property, or business (Luke 12:42; 16:1-8: Gal. 4:2). A steward acts on behalf of another's interests or possessions. He is accountable and responsible to another for what is entrusted to his care.

"Steward" is an appropriate description for an elder. Since the local church is called the household of God (1 Tim. 3:15), an elder who manages it can be rightfully called a steward. Paul's point in using the household steward imagery is simple and profound: since an elder is God's household steward, he must be morally and spiritually above reproach. E.F. Scott succinctly expresses Paul's logic: "In an ordinary household the most trusty servant was chosen as steward, and the same rule must obtain in the household of God."[6]

We should also note that Paul's emphasis is on God as the steward's Master and owner. The steward is *God's* household manager, not the church's. Thus the household belongs to God, not to the elders. God demands that those to whom His precious children are entrusted be morally and spiritually fit. He will not have unfit, untrustworthy stewards caring for His children and the truth of the gospel.

After masterfully demonstrating why an elder must be above reproach in verse 7*a*, Paul continues his list of qualifications in verse 7*b*, where he enumerates five sinful vices. When any one of these vices controls a person's life, it renders that person "reproachful" and disqualifies him from being a steward of God's household:

- "self-willed"
- "quick-tempered"
- "addicted to wine"
- "pugnacious"
- "fond of sordid gain"

We would not want a person who is controlled by any one of these vices to manage our family or our possessions, and neither does God.

SELF-WILLED: To be self-willed or arrogant is the opposite of being "gentle" [forbearing], which is one of the qualifications listed in 1 Timothy 3:3. A self-willed man wants his own way. He is stubborn, arrogant, and inconsiderate of others' opinions, feelings, or desires. A self-willed man is headstrong, independent, self-assertive, and ungracious, particularly toward those who have a different opinion. A self-willed man is not a team player, and the ability to work as a team is essential to eldership.

We must remember that the local congregation belongs to God, not to the overseer. The overseer is God's servant, not a master or owner, thus he has no right to be self-willed when caring for God's precious people. A self-willed man will scatter God's sheep because he is unyielding, overbearing, and blind to the feelings and opinions of others (2 Peter 2:10).

QUICK-TEMPERED: One of God's attributes is that He is slow to anger, so His stewards must also be slow to anger. Man's anger is a hindrance to the work of God, "for the anger of a man does not achieve the righteousness of God" (James 1:20). Since an elder must deal with people and their problems, a "hothead" will quickly find much material to fuel his anger. Proverbs warns against the perils of an angry man: "An angry man stirs up strife, And a hot-tempered man abounds in transgression" (Prov. 29:22). With his ugly, angry words, a quick-tempered man will destroy the peace and unity of God's family. The fierce looks and harsh words of the quick-tempered man will tear people apart emotionally, leaving people sick and destroyed in spirit. So a man who desires to be a church shepherd must be patient and self-controlled.

Of course, everyone experiences anger, and leaders who must deal with contentious situations often may experience a great deal of anger.

Hudson Taylor, for example, confessed his own struggle with anger: "My greatest temptation is to lose my temper over the slackness and inefficiency so disappointing in those on whom I depended. It is no use to lose my temper—only kindness. But oh, it is such a trial."[7] The issue is whether or not an individual who aspires to pastoral eldership recognizes and controls his anger. If he isn't controlled, he's a powder keg ready to go off in the midst of the next problem.

ADDICTED TO WINE AND PUGNACIOUS: Both of these qualifications are covered in 1 Timothy 3:3.

FOND OF SORDID GAIN: The Greek word, *aischrokerdēs*, used here is very similar in meaning to *aphilargyros* ("free from the love of money") used in 1 Timothy 3:3. See comments on 1 Timothy 3:3.

After listing five vices, Paul next lists seven virtues. Verse 8 begins with "but," which contrasts the five vices of verse 7 with the seven virtues of verses 8 and 9. God requires His stewards to be characterized by these virtues.

HOSPITABLE: See comments on 1 Timothy 3:2.

LOVING WHAT IS GOOD: Closely associated with hospitality, "loving what is good" is a positive virtue that is required of those who seek to help people and live as Christlike examples. The Greek word used here is *philagathos*, which one Greek lexicon defines as "one who willingly and *with self-denial* does good, or is kind."[8] William Hendriksen explains the word as "ready to do what is beneficial to others."[9] The *Theological Dictionary of the New Testament* states: "According to the interpretation of the early Church it relates to the unwearying activity of love."[10]

King David was a lover of goodness. He spared his enemy Saul, who had to reluctantly admit: "And you have declared today that you have done good to me, that the Lord delivered me into your hand and yet you did not kill me. For if a man finds his enemy, will he let him go away safely?" (1 Sam. 24:18,19*a*). David sought to show kindness to his deceased friend Jonathan, Saul's son, by taking Jonathan's crippled son, Mephibosheth, into his own house (2 Sam. 9).

Job's friends had to admit that he was a lover of goodness: "Behold, you have admonished many, And you have strengthened weak hands.

Your words have helped the tottering to stand, And you have strengthened feeble knees" (Job 4:3,4). But the greatest example of one who loved goodness is our Lord Jesus Christ, who "went about doing good" (Acts 10:38*b*).

An elder who loves goodness seeks to do helpful, kind things for people. He will be loving, generous, and kind toward all and will never sink to evil, retaliatory behavior (Acts 11:24; Rom. 12:21; 15:2; Gal. 6:10; 1 Thess. 5:15; 1 Peter 3:13). In contrast, Paul prophesied that in the last days more people will be "lovers of self, lovers of money...without self-control...haters of good." (2 Tim. 3:3). A society that is led by lovers of good rather than haters of good is truly blessed.

SENSIBLE: For some unexplainable reason, the *New American Standard Bible* translates the same Greek term, *sōphrōn*, as "prudent" in 1 Timothy 3:2, and "sensible" in Titus 1:8. *Sensible* is the better choice of the two English translations. See comments on the word "prudent" in 1 Timothy 3:2.

JUST: "Just" (*dikaios*) means "righteous" or "upright." To be righteous is to live in accordance with God's righteous standards, to be law-abiding. John writes that "the one who practices righteousness is righteous, just as He is righteous" (1 John 3:7).

An elder who is righteous can be counted on to be a principled man and to make fair, just, and righteous decisions for the church (Prov. 29:7). Job is a good example of a just man:

> There was a man in the land of Uz, whose name was Job, and that man was blameless, upright, fearing God, and turning away from evil (Job 1:1).
>
> "I put on righteousness, and it clothed me;
> My justice was like a robe and a turban.
> I was eyes to the blind,
> And feet to the lame.
> I was a father to the needy,
> And I investigated the case which I did not know.
> And I broke the jaws of the wicked,
> And snatched the prey from his teeth" (Job 29:14-17).

God's steward, then, must be like Job. He must live a morally upright life and be clothed in practical righteousness.

DEVOUT: To be "devout" (*hosios*) is to be firmly committed to God and His Word. It is to be separated unto God and pleasing to God. Despite the changing winds of culture and circumstances, the devout person faithfully clings to God and His Word.

One of the terrible facts of Israel's history is that many of its leaders were not "just" and "devout," so the people were led astray. An elder must not lead people astray! He must model godly commitment, character, and conduct, and thereby lead people in righteousness and devotion to God.

SELF-CONTROLLED: God's steward must be characterized by self-control and self-discipline in every aspect of life, particularly in his physical desires (Acts 24:25; 1 Cor. 7:9; 9:25). An undisciplined man has little resistance to sexual lust, anger, slothfulness, a critical spirit, or other base desires. He is easy prey for the devil.

Solomon warns against the undisciplined man's vulnerability to all the enemies of his soul: "Like a city that is broken into and without walls is a man who has no control over his spirit" (Prov. 25:28). In Solomon's time, walls were a strategic part of a city's defense system. A strong and secure city fortified its walls. Solomon likens a person's power of self-control to the walled fortifications of a city. Without self-control, a person is exposed to attack and becomes easy prey for any enemy.

Self-control is an essential part of the Spirit-controlled life (Gal. 5:23). Leaders who lack discipline frustrate their fellow workers as well as those they lead. Not only are they poor examples, but they cannot accomplish what needs to be done. Consequently, their flock is poorly managed and lacks adequate spiritual care.

HOLDING FAST THE FAITHFUL WORD...ABLE BOTH TO EXHORT IN SOUND DOCTRINE AND TO REFUTE THOSE WHO CONTRADICT: Verse 9 presents the final and crucial point in the Pauline catalog of elder qualifications. This is the heart of Paul's concern. The verses following this qualification elaborate on why this qualification is so indispensable to an elder and to the local churches of Crete (Titus 1:10-16). This last requirement is more than just another personal character quality, it is a specific task the elder must be able to do: to teach correct doctrine and reprove false teachers.

In order for an elder to exhort in sound doctrine and reprove false teachers, he must first be wholeheartedly committed to sound doctrine. So Paul begins by saying that an elder must "[hold] fast the faithful word which is in accordance with the teaching." By "word" (*logos*), Paul means the original preaching or oral proclamation of the gospel message which they heard and received. It is God's message of salvation and life in Christ. This "word" is described as (1) "faithful" (trustworthy) and as (2) "in accordance with the teaching." The "word" is "faithful" because it is in full agreement with "the teaching." "The teaching" refers to the apostolic message, that is, the authentic, authoritative, fixed body of doctrine taught by Christ and communicated by His holy apostles. There is only one apostolic doctrine (Acts 2:42; Eph. 4:5), one standard, and one teaching, and it is absolutely "faithful." Any teaching that contradicts the apostles' teaching as recorded in the New Testament is false, untrustworthy, and from the devil (Titus 1:10 ff; Gal. 1:8,9).

God requires that an elder be "holding fast" to His Word. "Holding fast" (*antechō*) means "cling firmly to," "be devoted to," or "adhere wholeheartedly to." "Paul…calls for the overseer's firm acceptance of [the faithful word],"[11] writes George Knight. This term implies unshakable, fervent conviction and commitment. Newport White says that this requirement for elders suggests "the notion of withstanding opposition."[12] A man who doesn't tenaciously adhere to orthodox, biblical doctrine doesn't qualify to lead God's household because he, who is himself in error and unbelief, will mislead God's people. Such a man is no match for "deceitful spirits and doctrines of demons" (1 Tim. 4:1). The priests, kings, and leaders of the Old Testament who did not hold firmly to God's law were swept away by the pressures of idolatrous religion. So, too, an elder who rejects or is uncertain about biblical doctrine will, along with the flock, be devoured by wolves.

The reason an elder is required to adhere firmly to the Word is so that he "may be able," that is, "equipped" to perform two specific tasks: (1) exhort believers and (2) refute opponents. "A pastor needs two voices," writes Calvin, "one for gathering the sheep and the other for driving away wolves and thieves. The Scripture supplies him with the means for doing both."[13]

Without question, Paul requires *all* elders, not just some, to be able to exhort in sound doctrine and rebuke false teachers. In 1 Timothy 3:2, Paul requires all elders to be "able to teach." Titus 1:9 expands on 1 Timothy 3:2 by adding that an elder must "be able both to exhort in sound doctrine and to refute" false teachers. We must require the same from *all* our elders.

Exhortation is closely associated with teaching (1 Tim. 4:13; 6:2), but while teaching primarily relates to the intellect, exhortation chiefly influences the conscience, heart, will, and actions of the hearer. Exhortation urges people to receive and to apply the truth that has been taught.

Specifically, elders are to exhort believers "in sound doctrine." The word "sound" means healthy or physically whole (Luke 5:31; 3 John 2). Here it is used metaphorically to describe teaching, so it means "correct," "wholesome," or "sound" teaching. "Sound doctrine" is in direct contrast to false teaching, which is diseased, corrupted, and defiled. Diseased doctrine ruins the lives of its adherents (1 Tim. 6:3-5), while sound doctrine produces godly, clean, wholesome, healthy lives (Titus 1:13; 2:1). The congregation's health and well-being depends upon elders who continually "exhort in sound doctrine." No man qualifies for eldership unless he is able to use God's Word in such a manner.

As in Acts 20:28-31, an elder's duty is to protect the church from false teachers—those who speak against "sound doctrine." Thus an elder must be able "to refute those who contradict" sound doctrine. A more accurate translation of the word "refute" (*elenchō*) in this context is "rebuke" or "reprove," which is used in verse 13. Verse 13 is actually a concrete application of verse 9, so the purpose of rebuking a false teacher would be "that they may be sound in the faith." To qualify for eldership, then, one must be able to detect false teaching and confront it with sound doctrine.

The climactic significance of this last qualification is made clear in verses 10-16: "For there are many rebellious men, empty talkers and deceivers, especially those of the circumcision, who must be silenced because they are upsetting whole families, teaching things they should not teach, for the sake of sordid gain" (Titus 1:10,11). The situation in Crete was alarming. There were "many rebellious men, empty talkers and deceivers." In such a threatening environment the churches' greatest need was for shepherd elders who maintained unwavering allegiance to God's Word and had the ability to exhort, teach, and reprove.

Without the appointment of qualified elders, the churches of Crete were destined to remain weak and disorderly. With Titus' effort to appoint qualified elders, however, there was every reason to believe that the churches would flourish despite the surrounding dangers.

CHAPTER 11

Peter's Instruction to the Asian Elders

"And when the Chief Shepherd appears, you will receive the unfading crown of glory."

1 Peter 5:4

Peter sent the letter known to us as 1 Peter to suffering Christians who were scattered throughout the Roman provinces of Pontus, Galatia, Cappadocia, Asia, and Bithynia (1 Peter 1:1). He most likely wrote this letter from Rome in approximately A.D. 63. In it, he directly addresses the elders of the churches of northwestern Asia Minor. The fact that Peter can address in one letter the elders of churches in five Roman provinces demonstrates that the elder system of government was standard practice. It is also noteworthy that Peter uses the designation, *elder*, rather than *overseer* in writing to these predominately Gentile churches. *Elder* was probably the more common term used to describe the members of the church leadership body:

> Therefore, I exhort the elders among you, as your fellow elder and witness of the sufferings of Christ, and a partaker also of the glory that is to be revealed, shepherd the flock of God among you, exercising oversight not under compulsion, but voluntarily, according to the will of God; and not for sordid gain, but with eagerness; nor yet as lording it over those allotted to your charge, but proving to be examples to the flock. And when the Chief Shepherd appears, you will receive the unfading crown of glory.

> You younger men, likewise, be subject to your elders; and all of you, clothe yourselves with humility toward one another, for God is opposed to the proud, but gives grace to the humble (1 Peter 5:1-5).

First Peter 5 singles out the elders from the rest of the congregation for direct exhortation and encouragement. The other major example of direct exhortation to elders in the New Testament is found in Paul's farewell speech to the Ephesian elders (Acts 20:17-38), which is strikingly similar to 1 Peter 5. In fact, we could consider 1 Peter 5 to be Peter's farewell message to the elders of Asia Minor because many scholars believe that a year or two after he wrote 1 and 2 Peter, Peter was martyred in Rome during Nero's persecution against the Roman Christians (ca. A.D. 65).

There is a deep sense of personal concern and urgency in Peter's exhortation. The word, "therefore," links the exhortation to the elders (1 Peter 5:1-4) with the preceding instructions to the entire church (1 Peter 4:12-19). These instructions relate to the inevitability of fiery trials, persecution, suffering, and the ominous warning of purifying judgment that begins with God's house: "but if anyone suffers as a Christian, let him not feel ashamed, but in that name let him glorify God. For it is time for judgment to begin with the household of God; and if it begins with us first, what will be the outcome for those who do not obey the gospel of God?" (1 Peter 4:16,17).

Peter's point is that if purifying judgment is to begin with the house of God, then, as the prophet Ezekiel illustrates, it must start with the elders (Ezek. 9:1-6). Furthermore, when churches experience persecution and suffering, it falls primarily on the church leaders to provide help, comfort, strength, and guidance. So the spiritual well-being of the house of God depends significantly on the elders; they must do their shepherding duty and do it with the proper Christian spirit.

Peter's fervent desire to communicate his heartfelt burden to the Asian elders is evidenced by his lengthy, threefold self-description as "your fellow elder," a "witness of Christ's sufferings," and "a partaker also of the glory that is to be revealed" (1 Peter 5:1). This is the first time since the opening verse that Peter personally identifies himself in the letter. Since no other group of people addressed in the letter receives such a persuasive, personal appeal, both shepherds and flock should pay close attention to these instructions.

By identifying himself as a "fellow elder," Peter establishes a special bond of affection with the church elders. He creates a sense of colleagueship and mutual regard. By placing himself on the same level with them, he secures their attention. Calling himself a "fellow elder" is more than a convenient metaphor, however. At one time Peter was a local church elder. He served with eleven other men during turbulent times in the church in Jerusalem. Even though the twelve apostles weren't called *elders*, they were the infant community's acting elders. At the time he wrote 1 Peter, Peter was an active shepherd caring for many churches. Hence, Peter has every right to call himself a "fellow elder."

As a fellow elder, Peter fully sympathizes with the problems and dangers the Asian elders face. He is not an armchair pastor or a heady author dispensing theoretical advice; he is a well-seasoned, veteran shepherd elder. Like his fellow elders, he serves daily on the front lines of battle. He knows how difficult the work is and is well-acquainted with the many pitfalls, abuses, and temptations of leadership. He, too, feels the daily pressures and strains of pastoral responsibility. His instruction wells up from a deep spring of life experiences gained by shepherding God's people for more than thirty years.

Peter next states that he shares with his fellow elders both in suffering and in future glory. The "sufferings of Christ" to which Peter testifies are the sufferings common to all believers as a result of confessing Christ and living in a Christlike manner in an unjust, sinful world (1 Peter 2:12,19-21; 4:1,4,14,16). In the words of New Testament commentator J. Ramsey Michaels: "Christians share in Christ's sufferings neither sacramentally in baptism nor in mystical union with him, but simply by following the example of his behavior when facing similar circumstances."[1] The future glory that Peter shares with the Asian elders is the joyous anticipation of the glory that will be revealed when Christ returns. In the same way they have shared in Christ's sufferings, so, too, they will share in the glory to come. In light of these shared experiences, Peter is eminently qualified to speak to the Asian elders.

BE SHEPHERDS TO GOD'S FLOCK

After tactfully winning the elders' confidence, Peter appeals to them to do their duty: "Therefore, I exhort the elders among you...shepherd the flock of God." Peter's exhortation demands urgent attention. He uses the aorist imperative verb *poimanate* (from *poimainō*), which means "shepherd" or "tend." In effect, he exhorts the elders to be what good shepherds should be, or, as R.C.H. Lenski says, to "do everything that shepherding requires."[2] King Solomon expressed a similar understanding of the shepherding task in these words: "Know well the condition of your flocks, And pay attention to your herds" (Prov. 27:23).

Peter's charge encompasses the full shepherding responsibility of feeding, folding, protecting, and leading. Biblical commentator Charles E.B. Cranfield succinctly summarizes: "The chief functions of the shepherd, as they are depicted in the Bible, are to seek out the lost, gather the scattered, watch over and defend against wild beasts and robbers, to feed and water, to lead."[3]

Some thirty-five years before Peter wrote these words, in an unforgettable scene on the shore of the Sea of Galilee, Jesus charged Peter to shepherd His sheep:

> So when they had finished breakfast, Jesus said to Simon Peter, "Simon, son of John, do you love Me more than these?" He said to Him, "Yes, Lord; You know that I love You." He said to him, "*Tend My lambs*."
>
> He said to him again a second time, "Simon, son of John, do you love Me?" He said to Him, "Yes, Lord; You know that I love You." He said to him, "*Shepherd My sheep*."
>
> He said to him the third time, "Simon, son of John, do you love Me?"...And he said to Him, "Lord, You know all things; You know that I love You." Jesus said to him, "*Tend My sheep*" (John 21:15-17; italics added).

Peter now passes on the same commission to the Asian elders. The mandate for elders to shepherd the flock of God is vitally important to the local church. The Bible teaches that people are like sheep (1 Peter 2:25), and sheep cannot be left unattended. Their well-being depends on a great deal of care and attention. As God's sheep, Christian people need to be fed God's Word and to be protected from wolves in sheep's clothing. They need continuous encouragement, comfort, guidance, prayer, and correction. Thus the elder's life is one of devoted work for the welfare of the flock. At times it is even a life of danger, which was true for the Asian elders.

Since the elders are to "shepherd" the local church, those they tend are figuratively called "the flock [*poimnion*] of God among you." What makes this flock special is that it is *God's* flock. It is His precious possession—the sheep He owns, cares for, and loves. As Paul reminded the Ephesian elders, this flock is the one "He purchased with His own blood" (Acts 20:28). So elders must never forget that the flock is not their own, and they should never be indifferent toward a single one of His sheep. Cranfield draws out the implications of this truth when he writes, "A church that could be ours would be only a false church. So the sheep are not ours for us to use or misuse as we like. If we lose one, we lose another's property, not our own; and He is not indifferent to what becomes of His flock."[4]

The flock metaphor signifies the Church's true ownership and recognizes its dependence and need for feeding, protection, and care. Other images that describe the Church, however, express the Church's strength and splendor. So the image of the Church as a flock must not be isolated from other biblical images such as pillar and support of the truth, holy priesthood, the temple of God, household of God, body of Christ, holy nation, etc. To isolate one image from the others is to misrepresent the biblical message. Misuse of the shepherd-flock metaphor, for example, has resulted in tragic abuse of people. It has been used to justify the imperial pastor and to limit God's people nearly to the status of dumb sheep who are totally dependent on the pastor. This is not what Scripture intends. Each metaphor emphasizes a particular aspect of God's Church and, of course, is limited in its ability to portray all dimensions of the Church. When these diverse images are placed together, however, they set forth a balanced and glorious picture of the Church's multidimensional nature.

Following the imperative command to shepherd God's flock, Peter further describes the elders' duty: "Shepherd the flock of God among you, exercising oversight." He uses the participle *episkopountes,* which means "exercising oversight." This participle comes from the Greek verb, *episkopeō*, which corresponds to the noun *episkopos*, meaning "overseer."[5]

The terms *shepherding* and *overseeing* are often closely associated because they are similar in concept.[6] In this passage, *overseeing* is equivalent to *shepherding*. *Shepherding* is the figurative expression for governance, while *overseeing* is the literal term, which can be used to clarify the first. To shepherd the flock entails oversight—the overall supervision and watchful care of the flock. Of the two terms, *shepherding* conveys a richer, more vivid image than *overseeing*. There is an amazing likeness between real shepherds and sheep, and God's shepherds and His people. The shepherd-flock vocabulary communicates the skillful, loving, sacrificial image of the type of leader-follower relationship that befits the Christian community.

SHEPHERD GOD'S FLOCK IN GOD'S WAY

Concerning the responsibility of the church elders, Paul and Peter are in full agreement. The kind of overseers they have in mind are shepherd overseers. In Acts 20:28, Paul reminds the Ephesian elders that the Holy Spirit placed them in the flock as "overseers." Their purpose was "to shepherd the church of God." Peter also charges the elders to "shepherd the flock of God," adding that they must "serve as overseers" with the proper spirit. So the elders' basic responsibility can best be described as providing pastoral oversight for the flock of God.

Peter is greatly concerned about how the elders shepherd and oversee God's flock. God is preeminently concerned about the motives, attitudes, and methods of those who lead His people, so Peter considers the attitudes or motives that should or should not characterize the elders to be very important. Therefore, he carefully describes how the elders are to serve: "exercising oversight not under compulsion, but voluntarily, according to the will of God; and not for sordid gain, but with eagerness; nor yet as lording it over those allotted to your charge, but proving to be examples to the flock" (1 Peter 5:2-3).

This emphasis on the proper motivation and attitude for shepherd elders perfectly complements the theme of holy living found in 1 Peter:

> As obedient children, do not be conformed to the former lusts which were yours in your ignorance, but like the Holy One who called you, be holy yourselves also in all your behavior; because it is written, "You shall be holy, for I am holy" (1 Peter 1:15,16).

> Beloved, I urge you as aliens and strangers to abstain from fleshly lusts, which wage war against the soul. Keep your behavior excellent among the Gentiles, so that in the things in which they slander you as evildoers, they may on account of your good deeds,

as they observe them, glorify God in the day of visitation (1 Peter 2:11,12).

If all Christians are to be holy as God is holy, it is particularly important that church leaders be holy. If the elders function with greedy hands or unholy egos, the flock will be defiled and will stray from its holy path.

Jesus repeatedly taught His disciples to act toward one another in a humble, loving, sacrificial, and servantlike manner. He rebuked prideful ambition, covetousness, and half-hearted devotion. Since elders must shepherd God's flock in a distinctly Christlike way, Peter reiterates some of Jesus' teaching—even using some of the same terminology found in the Gospels (Mark 10:42). The following three adverbial contrasts indicate the wrong and right ways to shepherd God's flock.

NOT UNDER COMPULSION, BUT VOLUNTARILY: God doesn't want reluctant, unwilling shepherds to care for His people, so Peter warns against an elder serving "under compulsion." Peter doesn't deny Paul's teaching that divine compulsion in service for God is necessary (1 Cor. 9:16). However, in this instance, he uses the word "compulsion" in a negative sense, meaning without God-given motivation (2 Cor. 9:7; Philem. 14). If a man serves as an elder because his wife or friends pressure him to serve, or because he is trapped by circumstances, or because no one else will do the work, he is serving "under compulsion." Lenski captures the spirit of Peter's thought well when he says elders are not to serve "like drafted soldiers but like volunteers."[7]

In contrast to serving under compulsion, Peter emphatically says that elders are to shepherd the flock "freely," "willingly," and "voluntarily." Those who oversee the church "voluntarily" do so because they freely choose to serve. It is what they want to do. John Henry Jowett (1863-1923), the famous British preacher and former minister of Westminster Chapel in London, masterfully expresses Peter's point: "One volunteer is worth two pressed men. I am not quite sure whether the proverbial saying is pertinent.... On the high planes of spiritual service no number of pressed men can take the place of a volunteer."[8]

The willing spirit that Peter speaks of is "according to the will of God" (literally, "according to God"). Glad, voluntary service is God's standard. It is the way God expects things to be done. God is not a reluctant, unwilling shepherd. He cares for His sheep gladly, willingly, freely, and graciously. In the same way that "God loves a cheerful giver" (2 Cor. 9:7), He loves cheerful, willing elders.

NOT FOR MONEY, BUT WITH EAGERNESS: Peter next addresses what Cranfield terms "the spirit of hirelings."[9] Peter uses the Greek word *aischrokerdōs*, "sordid gain," the adverb form of the same word Paul uses in reference to elders in Titus 1:7. (See comments on 1 Timothy 3:3 and Titus 1:7.)

In contrast, Peter describes the right spirit in which to shepherd God's flock as "with eagerness," which means "readily," "zealously," and "enthusiastically." "Eagerness" emphasizes, even more than the term "voluntarily," personal desire and passion. It is this kind of eagerness—a strong desire and motivation—that is endorsed by the "trustworthy statement" of 1 Timothy 3:1: "if any man aspires to the office of overseer, it is a fine work he desires to do."

Eager elders are driven to care for the sheep. The sheep are their life, their chief concern. Hence, they are not concerned about the personal sacrifice they make or their own financial gain. Like Paul, who at times provided his own income through tent making, they gladly serve without pay or recognition. They go beyond minimal duty, self-interest, and money. They love to shepherd God's people.

NOT AS AUTOCRATIC LEADERS, BUT AS EXAMPLES: Peter saves the worst and the best for last. The third unworthy motive for an elder is a far more subtle and widespread temptation than that of greed. This unworthy motive is the abuse of authority, the desire for power and control over others. Jowett remarks about the subtlety of autocratic leadership: "Pride ever lurks just at the heels of power. Even a little authority is prone to turn the seemly walk into a most offensive strut."[10] In a similar observation, Cranfield perceptively notes: "how extensively does the worldly view of power penetrate and permeate the life of the Church! The truth of the saying that 'power corrupts' is far too often confirmed in the Church, and when spiritual leadership is abused in this way, 'the corruption of the best is worst!'"[11]

The verb for "lording it over" (*katakyrieuō*) conveys the idea of forcefully gaining mastery over others. It describes an authoritarian attitude. Autocratic leadership has long been a temptation to church leaders:

- The prophet Ezekiel describes the lordly, autocratic shepherds of Israel when he writes: "with force and with severity you have dominated them [the sheep]" (Ezek. 34:4).

- Jesus especially forbids any individual or group within the family of God to treat brothers and sisters like subjects to be ruled, which is what the leaders of this world often do: "Jesus said to them, 'You know that those who are recognized as rulers of the Gentiles lord it over them [*katakyrieuō*]; and their great men exercise authority over them. But it is not so among you, but whosoever wishes to become great among you shall be your servant and whoever wishes to be first among you shall be slave of all'" (Mark 10:42-44).

- Following our Lord's instruction, John, the apostle, denounces a man named Diotrephes, the first-known dictatorial pastor, for lording his authority over a Christian congregation. John writes: "I wrote something to the church; but Diotrephes, *who loves to be first among them*, does not accept what we say…neither does he himself receive the brethren, and he forbids those who desire to do so, and puts them out of the church" (3 John 9,10*b*; italics added).

There is no place for dominating, lordly leaders in a family that is to be marked by mutual love (1 Peter 1:22; 3:8; 4:8; 5:14), brotherhood, submission, and humility (1 Peter 2:13,14,18; 3:1; 5:5). The elders are not to shepherd the church like "little popes or petty tyrants."[12] In fact, in verse 5, Peter tells all Christians how to dress for success: to clothe themselves with "humility." Even more important, there is only one Lord and Master in God's Church: the Lord Jesus Christ. All others are His servants.

The clause, "those allotted to your charge," further strengthens the concept that the people are not the elders' possessions. The people do not belong to the elders; they belong to the One who assigned them to the elders' care, that is, to God. This clause represents the definite article and the plural form of the noun, *klēros*, which literally rendered is: "the lots," "the portions," or "the allotments." So the Greek text reads, "nor as exercising lordship over the portions."

Lots were used by the apostles to determine God's choice for

Judas' replacement: "And they drew lots [*klērous*] for them, and the lot [*klēros*] fell to Matthias; and he was numbered with the eleven apostles" (Acts 1:26). But *klēros* also means an "allotment" or "portion assigned to someone" (Acts 1:17; 8:21).[13] *Klēros*, then, is something given, not earned. In this context, it is not land, money, or responsibility that is allotted, it is God's people. Thus the elders are prohibited from dominating people.

Peter is saying that God has allotted portions of the whole flock of God to various groups of elders (John 10:16; 1 Peter 5:9). In a similar way, Peter refers to the specific flock of God in which the respective elders function as "the flock of God *among you* [*in your care*]" (1 Peter 5:2; italics added). The elders, then, are not to lord it over their allotted portions of God's flock. Peter's strong warning against lording it over others certainly demonstrates that elders had authority to govern.

In contrast to lording it over others, elders are to be examples or models of godly living. "Being an example," says commentator Peter Davids, "fits well with the image of 'flock,' for the ancient shepherd did not drive his sheep, but walked in front of them and called them to follow."[14] The Spirit of God places in the hearts of obedient believers a desire to seek godly examples to follow. Much of the Bible is biographical, demonstrating by example how and how not to live for God. Jesus is the greatest example of all and the chief example to follow (1 Peter 2:21). So in the church, the elders' primary style of leadership is to model Christ.

Throughout this epistle, Peter emphasizes the importance of humility and submission (1 Peter 2:13-3:12; 5:5). If elders are petty tyrants who lord their authority over the local church, others will follow their example, abusing and fighting one another to gain power and recognition. If the elders are examples of uncompromising fidelity to Scripture, then the congregation will be loyal to Scripture. If the elders trust God, the people will trust God. If the elders love God and His people, the people will love. If the elders are peaceful, gentle, loving, and prayerful, the church (for the most part) will emulate their pattern. If the elders are humble, the people will be humble, avoiding much contention. If the elders are servant leaders, the church will be marked by Christlike, humble servanthood. "What a blessed influence," writes Scottish pastor and commentator John Brown (1807-1858), "is the holy character and conduct of Christian elders calculated to diffuse through the church."[15]

THE FUTURE REWARD FOR CHRIST'S UNDERSHEPHERDS

Peter concludes his appeal to the Asian elders by reminding them of that triumphant, glorious day "when the Chief Shepherd appears" and when they "will receive the unfading crown of glory." Victory day is ahead! Reward day is coming! On that day all the labors, sacrifices, and hardships of pastoral life will be fully recognized and lavishly rewarded.

Peter appropriately calls Jesus Christ the "Chief Shepherd." According to the New Testament there is only "one flock with one shepherd" (John 10:16) and Jesus Christ is that one, incomparable, irreplaceable Shepherd. In chapter 2, Peter states, "For you were continually straying like sheep, but now you have returned to the Shepherd and Guardian of your souls" (1 Peter 2:25). Indeed, Jesus Christ is "the great Shepherd" (Heb. 13:20) and "the good shepherd" (John 10:11,14). As the good Shepherd, He loves the sheep. He laid down His life for the sheep. He calls the sheep by name. Someday He will return in all His glory to take His flock to be with Him forever: He "shall be their shepherd, and shall guide them to springs of the water of life" (Rev. 7:17). At that time, the "Chief Shepherd" will fully reward His undershepherds.

The imagery of the "Chief Shepherd" or "Arch Shepherd" (*archipoimenos*) emphasizes Christ's relationship to all other shepherds. Because He is "Chief," all other shepherds are His undershepherds. As undershepherds, all elders are under the authority and rule of the Chief Shepherd. Thus, the elders' shepherding work must be done in complete agreement with His ways and teaching. Like their loving Chief Shepherd, shepherding elders must shepherd the flock eagerly and willingly, as models of godly disposition. Shepherding elders are not free to speak or lead the people in any way they wish, for they must answer to the Chief Shepherd. Everything the elders do will be judged on the basis of faithfulness to Him. In the words of commentator and professor I. Howards Marshall, "Christian leadership is thus a sharing in the leadership of Christ under His direction."[16]

What could be more encouraging to faithful shepherds who face many heartaches, problems, trials, and persecutions than to look forward to Christ's return as the "Chief Shepherd" and to share in His divine glory? When elders think of Christ as "Chief Shepherd," their present work is enhanced and His return becomes even more personal.

Peter states that upon Christ's return the faithful elders will receive an "unfading crown of glory." In this context, "crown" is used symbolically to represent reward or special honor. The reward is for faithful, honorable achievement as undershepherds of God's flock. This crown is unlike any earthly crown made of precious metal or ivy because it is "unfading." It will never wither like a laurel wreath or tarnish like gold. "Joys of royal pomp, marriages and feasts," writes Archbishop Robert Leighton (1611-1684), "how soon do they vanish as a dream…! But this day begins a triumph and a feast, that shall never either end or weary, affording still fresh, ever new delights."[17]

The reason for this crown's unfading quality is that the material used to make this crown is divine, heavenly glory. The adjective "glory" tells us of what the crown consists. In Greek, "glory" is in the genitive case, here a genitive of apposition, meaning that the crown consists of glory. The glory is the reality, and the crown is the metaphor. This glory is Christ's glory that will be displayed at His appearing. He will give the "crown of glory" to His undershepherds.

What a time of victory, vindication, and joy Christ's appearance will bring to lowly, unnoticed elders who have faithfully shepherded God's flock! Hard-working, selfless shepherds may not have many earthly goods to show for a lifetime of toil, but some day the Chief Shepherd will come and fully reward His undershepherds. Their work will no longer go unnoticed or unappreciated, for He will reward them publicly before the hosts of heaven. He will bestow on them heavenly honor and glory. All elders are to keep their eyes steadfastly fixed on His appearing, for reward day is coming!

THE NEED FOR YOUNG MEN TO SUBMIT TO THE ELDERS

Following his exhortation to elders, Peter adds a brief word of counsel for the younger men of the church: "You younger men, likewise, be subject to your elders." Many commentators think that verse 5 refers to "younger men" submitting to "older men." If so, this is simply a general statement (similar to 1 Timothy 5:1,2) regarding proper Christian relationships between age groups. However, because of the use of *presbyteroi* in verse 1 as an official title of office; the connective word "likewise" in verse 5, which can mean a continuation of the same topic (cf. 3:6,7); and the call to "subjection," suggesting authority rather than just respect, it seems more probable that Peter is referring to the official elders of the church. Peter has just exhorted the elders not to lord it over the flock. Now he feels compelled to instruct the younger men to subject themselves to the elders.

The "younger men" who are diligently working—eager for change and further service—are the ones who are most likely to conflict with the church elders. Polycarp, in his letter to the Philippian congregation, also encouraged the younger men to submit to the elders: "In like manner also the younger men must be blameless in all things...submitting yourselves to the presbyters and deacons as to God and Christ."[18] If the eldership is stagnant or ineffective, the younger men are the ones who are most likely to be discontent. Peter Davids's vivid portrayal of the natural tension between young people and the church elders bears repeating:

> It appears best, therefore, to see the "younger" here as the youthful people in the church.... Such younger people are often (but not necessarily) junior leaders, ready to learn from and assist those directing the church...but their very readiness for service and commitment can make them impatient with the leaders, who either due to pastoral wisdom or the conservatism that often comes with age (the two are not to be equated) are not ready to move as quickly or as radically as they are. It would be quite fitting to address such people with an admonition to be subject to their elders. Indeed, particularly in a time of persecution their willingness to take radical stands without considering the consequences could endanger the church.[19]

The best training a Christian young man can have in preparation for church leadership is to first learn to submit to those in spiritual leadership. A spiritually keen young man can gain invaluable wisdom and leadership skills through the experience of older, godly men, even if they are not paragons of leadership excellence (which most are not).

Knowing the ever-lurking potential for disagreement, fighting, and division between all parties within the local church that is accentuated by the pressures of a hostile society, Peter offers the best possible counsel: "all of you, clothe yourselves with humility toward one another, for God is opposed to the proud, but gives grace to the humble." Only when everyone wears the garments of humility—elders, young men, women, and deacons—will peace and unity prevail.

CHAPTER 12

James' Instruction to the Sick

"Let him call for the elders of the church, and let them pray."
James 5:14*a*

The author of the Epistle of James is James "the Lord's brother" (Gal. 1:19). This is the same James mentioned in Acts 21:18. Along with Peter and John, James was one of the most prominent and highly respected leaders of the church in Jerusalem (Gal. 1:9).

James, a master teacher like his brother, addresses his epistle "to the twelve tribes who are dispersed abroad" (James 1:1). It seems best to understand this statement to mean that James was writing to Christian Jews who lived outside Palestine. These Jewish Christians were scattered abroad possibly because of persecution (see Acts 11:19) and had formed local Christian congregations (James 2:2; 5:14). What is of special interest to us is the fact that these early Jewish Christian churches had elders. If we are correct in assuming that the Epistle of James was written between A.D. 45-48, then James provides the earliest recorded mention of Christian elders.[1]

According to James, the elders were to be called upon in times of sickness for prayer and anointing with oil. Writing in a bold, sermonic style, James states:

> Is anyone among you suffering? Let him pray. Is anyone cheerful? Let him sing praises. Is anyone among you sick? Let

him call for the elders of the church, and let them pray over him, anointing him with oil in the name of the Lord; and the prayer offered in faith will restore the one who is sick, and the Lord will raise him up, and if he has committed sins, they will be forgiven him (James 5:13-15).

CALL FOR THE ELDERS

James' letter begins and ends with prayer (James 1:5-7; 5:13-18). He insists that believing prayer is one of the primary solutions to life's trials and adversities. James declares that "the effective prayer of a righteous man can accomplish much," or as one commentator translates, "the prayer of a righteous man is very powerful in its operation" (James 5:16*b*).[2] So for all of life's afflictions and joys, James prescribes prayer and praise: "Is anyone among you suffering? Let him pray. Is anyone cheerful? Let him sing praise. Is anyone among you sick? Let him call for the elders of the church, and let them pray over him." It is this third category, the sick, on which James elaborates in verses 14*b*-16.

Sickness is a specific kind of suffering that often requires the help and prayers of others. In this passage, James envisions a bedridden Christian whose weakened condition requires special prayer and attention. Hence he urges the sick person to call for the elders of the church.

The Puritan preacher Thomas Manton (1620-1677) reminds us that "Christ's worshippers are not exempted from sickness, no more than any other affliction…Those that are dear to God have their share of miseries."[3] When a child of God is faced with debilitating sickness, James instructs him or her to take the initiative and call for the church elders. The verb "call" is an aorist imperative that implies urgent action.

Some Christians do not call for the elders because they doubt God's power to heal sickness. Still others may be harboring sin and are in rebellion against God. For example, King Asa was very angry with God and wouldn't seek God's forgiveness or healing when he became sick. Rather, he consulted with doctors only: "And in the thirty-ninth year of his reign Asa became diseased in his feet. His disease was severe, yet even in his disease he did not seek the Lord, but the physicians" (2 Chron. 16:12). The predominate reason people don't call for the elders of the church when they are sick, however, is that they have never been taught to do so. They have never seen it done. S.J. Kistemaker, coauthor of the *New Testament Commentary* series, assesses the situation accurately: "the practice of calling the elders of the church to pray over the sick seems to belong to a bygone age."[4]

James specifies that the sick are to "call for the elders of the church," not for deacons, friends, or miracle workers. He clearly assumes that all congregations have an official, recognized body of elders. It is also noteworthy that a plurality of elders is required, not a single elder. In the same way the elders governed jointly, they visited and prayed for the sick jointly. James states that no less than two elders ought to be present at the sick person's bedside. This important point, which is easily missed or ignored because it is inconvenient, is an essential element of the biblical instruction.

The church elders are to be called to the sick person's bedside not because they are particularly gifted as healers, but because they are the official representatives of the church whose task is to shepherd the flock. Visiting the sick and praying for healing are essential responsibilities of the shepherding task. For example, Ezekiel denounces Israel's shepherds because they callously refuse to care for the sick: "Those who are sickly you have not strengthened, the diseased you have not healed, the broken you have not bound up"(Ezek. 34:4; cf. Zech. 11:16). Every compassionate, knowledgeable shepherd knows that caring for sick people is a particularly significant and intimate part of the shepherding task.

LET THE ELDERS PRAY AND ANOINT WITH OIL

It is perfectly clear from these verses that the sick should summon the church elders and that the elders should pray. What James depicts is an official, church prayer gathering at the sick person's bedside at which the elders serve as the official representatives of the church. What a deeply moving experience such a gathering would be—for both the one who is ill and for the elders!

James' primary instruction to the elders is to pray for the sick person. Prayer is the chief subject of this entire passage, in which the word prayer is used seven times (James 5:13-18). The sick need prayer, and the issue of anointing with oil must not be allowed to overshadow the prayer, which is the main point.

The phrase "over him" in verse 14 doesn't imply the laying on of hands, although that certainly may have been done. The prepositional phrase "over him" depicts the actual situation, in which the sick person lies on the bed and the elders stand or kneel close by. The elders and the sick person are face to face. This kind of flesh-and-blood contact fuels the soul's fire in prayer. Prayer in the presence of suffering comes alive and is endowed with a great deal more vitality. Manton comments that "prayer must be made…over them [the sick], that their sight may the more work upon us [the elders], and our prayers may work upon them."[5] R.V.G. Tasker, biblical translator, commentator, and former professor at the University of London, develops this idea even further:

> While it is true that they [the elders] could intercede for the sick man without being present at his bedside, nevertheless, by coming to the actual scene of suffering and by praying within sight and hearing of the sufferer himself, not only is their prayer likely to be more heart-felt and fervid, but the stricken man may well become more conscious of the effective power of prayer uttered in faith, by which, even in moments of the most acute physical weakness, communion with God can be maintained.[6]

C.L. Mitton's comments on this point also deserve repeating:

> Could not prayer have been offered just as effectively in the church gathering? Did they need to be physically present with the sick man? If our religion were a matter of theory, these questions would be justified. But we are dealing with men and women in need of help. Our Lord Himself did not decline to go to people in need, when invited, though He could heal from a distance with a word, when it was appropriate to do so. In fact, prayer offered in our presence and for our precise needs by Christian friends has a power and efficacy that may be lacking in prayers offered in our absence. We are creatures of flesh and blood, as well as spirit, and when love for us is proved by the readiness of Christian friends to give their time to come to our home in our need, we are more immediately aware of that love.

> Its effectiveness in prayer is increased by the fact that we have been made aware of it.[7]

Accompanying the elders' prayer for healing, James calls for the anointing with oil.[8] James doesn't explain the significance of the oil, so it is difficult to be certain about its exact meaning. We can assume that if the use of oil had a new or obscure meaning, James would have had to explain himself to his readers. Hence, in a letter directed to a Jewish audience regarding special prayer by the church officials for the sick, it is likely that the anointing with oil was meant to aid the prayer for the sick by tangibly dedicating the sick person to the Lord's special attention and care.

Throughout the Old Testament, one of the primary ideas underlying the use of oil was to set people or things apart for a special purpose, particularly for God's use. The first example of this in the Bible occurs when Jacob pours oil over a rock pillar he had set up to dedicate the special place where God first spoke to him: "So Jacob rose early in the morning, and took the stone that he had put under his head and set it up as a pillar, and poured oil on its top. And he called the name of that place Bethel" (Gen. 28:18,19*a*). Oil was used to consecrate ("set apart" or "dedicate") the priests, their garments, the tabernacle, and all that was in it to God's service (Ex. 29:21; 30:30; 40:9). Kings also were set apart by an anointing with oil (1 Sam. 10:1; 16:13; 1 Kings 1:39; 2 Kings 9:6).

The use of oil for setting apart a sick person for special attention fits well with our passage in James. The sick person has summoned the elders for prayer. The elders, as the official representatives of the church, meet around the person's bed to pray for healing. The anointing with oil in the name of the Lord aids their prayers by visually and physically dedicating the sick person to the Lord's care and healing. The oil, applied in the name of the Lord, helps the sick person remember that he or she is the special object of prayer and the Lord's care.

Medicinal vs. Symbolic Use of Oil

Some commentators think James indicates that oil is to be used for medicinal purposes only (Luke 10:34; Isa. 1:6). They conclude that his message is that medicine and prayer work together. This of course is true, but it is unlikely that James intends to comment on medicine or to encourage elders to act as physicians. James certainly is not naive enough to believe that oil is curative for all diseases. We can assume that if oil were needed for medicinal purposes, it would have been applied long before the elders' visit. It is because medicine did not work that the elders are called. The elders' task is to pray for healing, and according to verse 15, it is the prayer of faith—not the oil—that restores the sick. No matter what the sickness is, the elders' prayer accompanied by oil is the scriptural prescription.

In the only other passage in which anointing the sick with oil appears (Mark 6:13), the anointing suggests a symbolic significance only. According to the Gospel record, anointing the sick with oil was practiced by the apostles during our Lord's earthly ministry, presumably at His instruction. Mark 6:13 provides help in interpreting the use of oil mentioned in James 5:14: "And they went out and preached that men should repent. And they were casting out many demons and were anointing with oil many sick people and healing them" (Mark 5:12,13).

According to the Gospel accounts, Jesus sent out the Twelve in twos to preach, cast out demons, and heal the sick (Mark 6:7,12; Matt. 10:1; Luke 9:1,2). Mark alone adds that the Twelve anointed (*aleiphō*) the sick with oil. Some commentators believe that the apostles anointed people with oil for medicinal purposes (Luke 10:34), but that is doubtful. Applying oil for medicinal purposes would have seriously weakened and confounded the apostles' unique, miracle-working ministry which was intended to supernaturally confirm their Messianic message (Luke 10:9). Christ gave the Twelve the power "to heal every kind of disease and every kind of sickness," so they didn't need medicine (Matt. 10:1; cf. Luke 9:2). The oil, therefore, must have had a symbolic significance.

Those who hold the medicinal anointing view also claim that if James meant to say that elders anoint with oil for spiritual and symbolic reasons, then he would have used the more sacred Greek term for anointing, *chriō*, rather than *aleiphō*. The distinction between *aleiphō* and *chriō*, however, is not hard and fast. Although *chriō* is the more common term used in the Greek Old Testament (LXX) for the ceremonial anointing of priests or kings, *aleiphō* is also used (at least three times) for anointing priests. "And you shall bring his sons and put tunics on them; and you shall anoint [*aleiphō*] them even as you have anointed [*aleiphō*] their father, that they may minister as priest to Me; and their anointing shall qualify them for a perpetual priesthood throughout their generations" (Ex. 40:14,15). The Jewish historian Josephus also uses *aleiphō* interchangeably with *chriō* (compare *Antiquities* 6.165 with 6.157). So James' use of *aleiphō* is insufficient evidence for adopting the medicinal viewpoint.

Finally, the clause, "in the name of the Lord," suggests a spiritual significance to the anointing rather than a medicinal one.

James further specifies that the physical symbol of oil is applied "in the name of the Lord." There is no magical, curative power in the oil, or in the elders. All power and authority is in Jesus Christ exalted in heaven. Within His sovereign will lies the power to heal; nothing is too great for Him to do. So the elders act and the sick are healed in Christ's name alone (Acts 4:7-10; Luke 10:17). All trust is placed in the Lord. All glory goes to Him.

THE PRAYER OF FAITH

In verse 15, James adds the marvelous promise that "the prayer offered in faith will restore the one who is sick, and the Lord will raise him up." Here, as in a number of Gospel accounts, the prayers and faith of the individuals trying to effect healing (not those being healed) actually bring about healing (Matt. 8:5-13; 9:18-26; 15:21-28; 17:14-21; Mark 2:5). What makes the difference in healing the sick is not the oil, but the kind of prayer the elders offer to God (James 1:6,7; 4:3).

The prayer of faith is prayer inspired by sincere, unwavering confidence in God (Matt. 21:21,22; 17:20). Indeed, the prayer itself is an expression of deep faith in God. Prayerless, worldly-minded, and spiritually impotent elders cannot offer such a prayer (James 1:5-8; 4:3). This places a solemn responsibility, then, upon the elders to be men of living, vital faith and prayer.

James' unqualified promise of recovery is similar to other unconditional statements about prayer found in the Gospels. The prayer of faith is so powerful that James, like our Lord, states its effectiveness in limitless terms: "And all things you ask in prayer, believing, you shall receive" (Matt. 21:22; cf. Mark 9:23; 11:22-26; Luke 11:5-13; John 15:7,16; 16:24). These absolute, unrestricted statements teach the power of faith and prayer. Such absolute expressions are part of a rich diversity of images[9] used by our Lord to vividly and dramatically teach people who by nature are dull to spiritual matters (Rom. 6:19).

James rightly expects his listeners to understand that there are legitimate, unexpressed qualifications to such statements. As one commentator says of James' provocative style of teaching, "It is an aspect of James' style to say things bluntly and not to spell out details or make refinements."[10] This is why he does not say when or how the Lord will restore the one who is sick. Without an understanding of the qualifications to such statements, one is faced with contradictions and absurdities. For example, although he prayed three times for relief from "a thorn in the flesh," Paul did not receive what he prayed for (2 Cor. 12:8,9). That didn't mean Paul lacked faith. God, however, had His perfect reasons for answering in a different way (2 Cor. 12:9).

God has many ways to cure people's ills, as demonstrated by the case of Epaphroditus in Philippians 2. Epaphroditus was extremely ill, almost to the point of death, and Paul seemed powerless to prevent it. Why didn't Paul pray and receive immediate, miraculous healing for Epaphroditus? How could a deathbed experience involving two such mighty men of faith occur? The answer is that even apostles could not heal indiscriminately (Gal. 4:13,14; 1 Tim. 5:23; 2 Tim. 4:20). Consequently, Paul writes that God had mercy on Epaphroditus (Phil. 2:27). God certainly cares for His own. Epaphroditus recovered but not, it seems, by the spectacular means we might have expected. The means of healing is not revealed. What is revealed is God, the ultimate source of healing.

James' teaching does not mean that a spectacular miracle of healing must take place. He writes in a general manner that says nothing specific about how the Lord will heal. James' instruction, therefore, cannot be brushed aside as a unique, temporary, first-century practice.

"Love toward sick members
should have a special place in the
Christian congregation.
Christ comes near to us in the sick.
The pastor who neglects
the visitation of the sick must ask
whether or not he can exercise
his office on the whole."

(Dietrich Bonhoeffer, *Spiritual Care*, 56)

DEAL WITH SIN

James adds a second promise to his instruction: "and if he has committed sins, they will be forgiven him." James leaves open the possibility that sin may have caused the sick person's illness. God does, indeed, chasten His erring children with the rod of physical sickness. Petty fighting and boastful divisions in the church at Corinth brought God's disciplining hand down upon the transgressors in the form of sickness, and even death. Paul writes: "For this reason many among you are weak and sick, and a number sleep. But if we judged ourselves rightly, we should not be judged. But when we are judged, we are disciplined by the Lord in order that we may not be condemned along with the world" (1 Cor. 11:30-32).

Among James' readers we find "jealousy and selfish ambition" (James 3:14); "quarrels and conflicts" (James 4:1); "lust" for worldly comforts and possessions (James 4:1-3,13,16); discrimination against the poor (James 2:1-13); complaining against one another (4:11; 5:9); and a lack of practical Christian unity, faith, and love (James 1:22-27; 2:14-26). Thus James is acutely aware that in some cases sin may be the underlying cause of physical sickness (James 5:12).

When visiting the sick, elders also must be aware of the possibility that sin may be the cause of the sickness. A person who is willing to call on the church elders is more inclined to confess sin and receive total physical and spiritual healing. Assuming that a genuine confession has been made, James promises that the sick person's sins will be forgiven. So the visiting elders may need to deal with far more than sickness. Their visit may turn out to be a time for spiritual counsel, confession, encouragement, or restoration.

Although sickness may occur because of sin, we should emphatically state that not all sickness is a result of personal sin. The book of Job makes this point crystal clear. James also makes this plain by adding the qualifier, "if he has committed sin." Many devout men and women of faith and prayer have suffered from illness for reasons other than personal sin. Paul himself suffered from some infirmity that became a means of guidance for him (Gal. 4:13,14). If his "thorn in the flesh" refers to a bodily infirmity, his bodily infirmity also became a means of spiritual development and protection (2 Cor. 12:7-10). However, if a suffering member's sickness is due to sin, elders must be prepared to deal with the situation accordingly.

Although there are unresolved questions related to the anointing with oil and the nature of illness in this passage, they must not be allowed to detract from its clear message: the sick are to call for the elders and the elders are to pray. What blessing, help, and comfort is denied God's people when this portion of Scripture is not taught faithfully to them.

CHAPTER 13

Hebrews: Obey Your Leaders

"for they keep watch over your souls."

Hebrews 13:17*b*

The identity of the writer of the Epistle to the Hebrews is unknown to us, although he was well known to his readers (Heb. 13:18-24). It seems probable that this letter was written shortly before the destruction of the temple in Jerusalem in A.D. 70. It was written to a predominately Jewish Christian community, possibly located in Rome (Heb. 13:23,24). Of interest to our study is the writer's closing, in which he exhorts his readers to obey their "leaders" and to greet them all:

> Obey your leaders, and submit to them; for they keep watch over your souls, as those who will give an account. Let them do this with joy and not with grief, for this would be unprofitable for you (Heb. 13:17).
>
> Greet all of your leaders and all the saints (Heb. 13:24).

Although the exact identity of these leaders is not disclosed, they would certainly have included the local elders, if they existed, and there are sound reasons for believing they did exist. There is disagreement over the geographic location of the congregation addressed by the writer of Hebrews. If the letter was written to a Jewish Christian community in Palestine, which is a well-recognized view, then elders definitely would be included under the designation "leaders." If the letter was written to Rome, which is the majority opinion among scholars today, elders should still be considered as a part of the designated leadership of the church. There is ample, compelling evidence supporting the existence of congregational leadership by elders in Rome at the time Hebrews was written:

- We know from the book *Shepherd of Hermas* (ca. A.D. 140), the so-called *Pilgrim's Progress* of early Christianity, that represents well the state of Roman Christianity in the first quarter of the second century, that a body of elders—not a single overseer—presided over the church in Rome. Hermas states: "And afterwards I saw a vision in my house. The aged woman came, and asked me, if I had already given the book to the elders.... But thou shalt read (the book) to this city [Rome] along with the elders that preside over the Church."[1] In addition, the term *overseer* is used twice by Hermas, but it is synonymous with elders and is always used in the plural.[2]

- In Ignatius's letter to the church in Rome in A.D. 115, he makes no mention of a Roman overseer (bishop). This is a radical departure from his other six letters in which he refers to a single overseer.

- In A.D. 96, the church in Rome wrote a letter to the church in Corinth, which is erroneously entitled, *The Epistle of S. Clement to the Corinthians* (also called *1 Clement*). The letter demonstrates that there had been a close relationship between the two churches. What is of paramount significance to us is that the letter of *1 Clement* exhorts the Corinthians to submit to their elders because the elders had been established by the apostles and prescribed by the Old Testament Scriptures:

  > The Apostles received the Gospel for us from the Lord Jesus Christ; Jesus Christ was sent forth from God. So then Christ is from God, and the Apostles are from Christ.... So preaching everywhere in country and town, they appointed their first-fruits, when they had proved them by the Spirit, to be bishops

> [elders] and deacons unto them that should believe. And this they did in no new fashion; for indeed it had been written concerning bishops and deacons from very ancient times; for thus said the scripture in a certain place, *I will appoint their bishops in righteousness and their deacons in faith.*[3]
>
> And our Apostles knew through our Lord Jesus Christ that there would be strife over the name of the bishop's [elder's] office. For this cause therefore, having received the complete foreknowledge, they appointed the aforesaid persons [elders], and afterwards they [the apostles] provided a continuance, that if these [elders] should fall asleep, other approved men [elders] should succeed to their [elders'] ministration. Those therefore who were appointed by them [the apostles], or afterward by other men of repute [elders] with the consent of the whole Church, and have ministered unblameably to the flock of Christ in lowliness of mind, peacefully and with all modesty, and for long time have borne a good report with all—these men we consider to be unjustly thrust out from their ministration.[4]

Although *1 Clement* says nothing about the presence of elders in Rome, the assertion that it was the apostles' regular practice to appoint a plurality of overseers (elders) implies that the Roman Christians agreed with and followed the same pattern.

- The Epistle to the Hebrews, written thirty years earlier than *1 Clement*, refers to a plurality of leaders only, not to a single leader. The joint function of these leaders, described as keeping watch over the spiritual welfare of the readers, suggests the work of the church elders that we have observed throughout the New Testament (James. 5:14,15; Acts 20:28; 1 Peter 5:2).

- The first Christian community in Rome was comprised of "Jews and proselyte members" who had heard the gospel in Jerusalem on the day of Pentecost (Acts 2:10). Jewish Christian communities outside Jerusalem would most likely pattern themselves after the mother church in Jerusalem (James 5:14), and the Roman Christians would have known that elders were established among the Christian Jews in Jerusalem.

Based on this evidence, we have good reason to believe that elders existed in Rome at the time the Epistle to the Hebrews was written. Thus we include Hebrews 13:17 as part of our study on elders.

OBEY AND SUBMIT TO SPIRITUAL LEADERS

The inspired writer points his readers to their responsibility to remember and obey their spiritual leaders because this will significantly help them in their battle against sin. In verse 7 of Hebrews 13, the writer urges his readers to mentally ponder their former leaders' outstanding examples of godly fidelity: "Remember those who led you, who spoke the word of God to you; and considering the result of their conduct, imitate their faith." In verse 17, the writer exhorts his readers to obey and submit to their present leaders. The purpose of these exhortations is twofold. First, by contemplating the life examples of their former leaders, the readers will be inspired to greater faithfulness to Christ. Second, by obeying their present leaders, they will be spiritually protected and nourished.

It is tremendously important that Christians understand God's will regarding submission and obedience to their spiritual guides. More than any other New Testament passage, Hebrews 13:17 addresses the believer's duty to obey the church shepherds. By using two imperative verbs, "obey" and "submit," the inspired writer intensifies his exhortation. His charge is of utmost importance. Although it is difficult to distinguish the precise differences in meaning between these two verbs, "submit" is the stronger and broader of the two. Christians are not only to "obey" their leaders (*peithō*, meaning "obey," "to listen to," "follow") but are to "submit" to them (*hypeikō*, meaning "yield," "give way," "defer to"). This means Christians are to be responsive to their leaders, yield to their authority, and subordinate themselves to them even when they have a difference of opinion.

Submission to authority is necessary for the proper ordering of society, and the church of God is no exception. "Anarchy then is an evil, and a cause of ruin," states the ancient churchman, John Chrysostom, "but no less an evil also is the disobedience to rulers. For it comes again to the same. For a people not obeying a ruler, is like one which has none; and perhaps even worse."[5]

A spirit of obedience and submission to authority is fundamental to

Christian living (Rom. 16:19; 2 Cor. 2:9; Phil. 2:12; Philem. 21; 1 Peter 1:2,14). Submission is the fruit of genuine humility and faith. It is a mark of the Spirit-filled life (Eph. 5:18-6:9). The Bible says, first and foremost, "Submit therefore to God..." (James 4:7*a*). True submission to God naturally expresses itself in obedience and submission to earthly authority. Thus genuine submission to God and His Word expresses itself in obedience and submission in the home, in marriage, at work, in society, and in the local assembly of believers.

The effectiveness of any body of church leaders is measurably affected by the response of the people they lead. People who are stubborn and unsubmissive are unteachable and incapable of changing for their own good. Consider the nation of Israel: because of continual disobedience, the nation as a whole did not enter the Promised Land (Heb. 3:16-4:16). The same is true today. When God's people act independently and in self-will, there is little growth, peace, or joy in the ministry of the local church. Only when believers properly submit to their spiritual leaders does the local church have any chance to be the growing, loving, joyous family God intends it to be. William Kelly admirably summarizes for us the importance of this subject when he writes: "Christ Himself led the way here below in this path of invariable and unswerving obedience...[believers] are only blessed as they walk in obedience and submission, instead of a vain clamor for their own rights, which if realized would be Satan's slavery."[6]

We should not overlook the fact that the inspired writer calls upon his readers to submit to a plurality of leaders. He doesn't say, "obey your leader, and submit to him;" he says, "obey your leaders." As we have observed throughout our study, a team of shepherd leaders, not one person, is responsible to guard the spiritual welfare of a local congregation of believers.

The Greek word for "leaders" used here is *hēgoumenoi*, from the verb *hēgeomai*, which is a generic term like our English word *leader*. It can be used to describe military, political, or religious leaders. In the Greek Old Testament, *hēgoumenos* was used to describe the heads of tribes (Deut. 5:23), a commander of an army (Judg. 11:11), the ruler of the nation Israel (2 Sam. 5:2; 7:8), a superintendent of the treasury (1 Chron. 26:24), and the chief priest (2 Chron. 19:11). In Acts, Silas and Judas are called "leading [*hēgoumenous*] men among the brethren" (Acts 15:22). In a paradoxical statement about leadership, Jesus says, "let him who is the greatest among you become as the youngest, and the leader [*hēgoumenos*] as the servant" (Luke 22:26). The writer's use of the word *hēgoumenoi* in Hebrews 13:7,17,24 may serve to cover a broad spectrum of leaders from apostles to elders. The work of the leaders in verse 17, which is described as keeping "watch over your souls," certainly sounds like the work of local church elders (Acts 11:30; 15:6,22; James 5:14,15). Although the term *elder* does not appear here, the exhortation to obey and submit to church leaders would certainly include elders who keep watch over the church.[7]

THEY KEEP WATCH OVER YOUR SOULS

Knowing that submission to authority is often resisted or resented, even by God's children, the writer bolsters his exhortation by adding important reasons for submission and obedience. Spiritual leaders should be obeyed because "they keep watch over [for] your souls." The verb "keep watch" (*agrypneō*) literally means "keep oneself awake," but here it is used metaphorically for watching, guarding, or caring for people. Like the ancient city watchmen or shepherds of a flock, spiritual leaders must always be keenly alert, conscientious, and diligent. Watchfulness demands tireless effort, self-discipline, and selfless concern for the safety of others.

These leaders are involved in spiritual care. They are keeping watch for "your souls." The Greek term for *soul* is *psychē*. In many instances, *psychē* is used as the equivalent of "person" or "oneself," thus we could render *psychē* by the personal pronoun *you*, which some translations do: "They keep watch over you" (NIV). However, in this context, *psychē* seems to have a deeper meaning that relates to the inward, spiritual dimension of life (cf. Heb.10:39; 3 John 2). Above all else, these leaders keep watch for the spiritual welfare of the congregation. Their task, if taken lightly, could result in serious harm to the spiritual lives of God's children.

Bible commentator R.C.H. Lenski points out that keeping watch implies potential danger: "Watching implies keeping oneself and others safe where danger is known to exist or where one fears its existence. Where no danger exists watching is not needed.... All this applies to the church in the highest degree where the safety of souls is to be guarded."[8] Since false teachers and spiritual pitfalls abound, since all Christians start out as newborn babes in Christ, and since some Christians are perpetually weak in faith, watching over the spiritual development of God's people is indispensable, continuous work.

Hebrews itself is an illustration of spiritual watchmen in action and reveals the critical need for spiritual watchmen. Serious problems existed among some believers: spiritual apathy and immaturity, neglect of the truth, compromise with Judaism's old ways, fear of hardship, bitterness of soul, backsliding, and disregard for God's shepherds. The leaders responsible for this needy community faced problems that required vigilant attention and action.

If the leaders referred to in verse 17 were the ones who alerted the writer of Hebrews to the congregation's problems, they are an excellent example of spiritual watchfulness. It appears that these leaders were stable, mature Christians in whom the author had complete confidence. Indeed, as one commentator points out, "The clause ['they keep watch'] offers a commendation of the leaders as men with divinely given pastoral authority and responsibility."[9] However, their good, pastoral efforts would be of little success if the believers did not submit to their wise, loving leadership.

Not only do spiritual leaders deserve to be obeyed because they keep watch for God's people, but their greater responsibility requires a stricter scrutiny and standard of accountability before God. All spiritual leaders are watchmen and shepherds "who will give an account." Jesus said, "and from everyone who has been given much shall much be required; and to whom they entrusted much, of him they will ask all the more" (Luke 12:48*b*; cf. Mark 12:40). If these spiritual leaders fail at their task, God's people will be hurt. Thus they, like the watchmen of a city, are keenly aware that they will have to render an account to God for the critical task entrusted to them. Lenski well reminds us: "Whoever assumes or is given responsibility over the souls of any others, *even of only one other*, is fully accountable" (italics added).[10]

According to the Old Testament, God promised that He would call the watchmen into account regarding their holy responsibility:

> When I say to the wicked, "You shall surely die"; and you do not warn him or speak out to warn the wicked from his wicked way that he may live, that wicked man shall die in his iniquity, but his blood I will require at your hand.
>
> Yet if you have warned the wicked, and he does not turn from

his wickedness or from his wicked way, he shall die in his iniquity; but you have delivered yourself (Ezek. 3:18,19).

In a similar way, Paul viewed himself as a watchman who was accountable to God for those entrusted to his care: "Therefore I testify to you this day, that I am innocent of the blood of all men. For I did not shrink from declaring to you the whole purpose of God" (Acts 20:26,27). Because Paul knew the certainty of God's evaluation of his labor, he diligently sought God's approval for all his work (1 Cor. 4:1-5; 9:27; 2 Cor. 5:9-11; 2 Tim. 2:15; 4:7,8).

The Bible says that teachers will receive more severe judgment because of their influence and responsibility (James 3:1). Since positions of teaching and leadership require greater responsibility and accountability, a wise individual will never rush into leadership. The knowledge that a leader must give an account to God should greatly affect the leader's quality of spiritual leadership. Furthermore, when God's people understand that their leaders must give an account to God, they will be much more tolerant, understanding, and sensitive toward their leaders' actions and decisions. They will be more willing to obey and submit to their leaders.

MAKE THEIR WORK JOY, NOT GRIEF

The result of submission on the part of those who are led is deep, satisfying joy on the part of those who lead. Every shepherd knows the inexpressible joy of seeing lives transformed by the power of the gospel, watching people grow as a result of teaching the Word, and seeing the flock prosper. John, the apostle, expressed this joy: "I have no greater joy than this, to hear of my children walking in the truth" (3 John 4). This joy, which every leader has a right to expect (2 Cor. 2:3), is possible only when the people obey and submit to their leaders.

When God's people disobey, complain, and fight, however, the joys of shepherding vanish. When Christians refuse to heed the shepherds' warning, the shepherds feel "grief." So the writer states, "let them do this with joy, and not with grief." The word "grief" can also be rendered "groan," "sigh," or "moan." *Grief* expresses a strong inward emotion—an emotion that words are unable to articulate (Mark 7:34;

Rom. 8:23,26). Here the word expresses a deep sorrow and longing for better conditions.

Godly leaders sigh over a brother or sister who willfully wanders after false teaching. They groan in sorrow over those who refuse to grow, learn, change, or receive correction. Moses grieved many times because of the people's disobedience and stubbornness. At one time in his life, the people's complaining became so intolerable that Moses called on God to take his life: "I alone am not able to carry all this people, because it is too burdensome for me. So if Thou art going to deal thus with me, please kill me at once, if I have found favor in Thy sight, and do not let me see my wretchedness" (Num. 11:14,15). Paul also suffered many heartaches because of his converts' disobedience. Rebellious behavior takes its toll on the shepherds. Sometimes good shepherds give up because of the painful kicks and deep bites of disobedient sheep. When that occurs, everyone in the congregation suffers.

While disobedience distresses the church shepherds, it has an even more serious impact on the wayward believer. This is a final reason why the readers ought to obey and submit to their spiritual leaders. By means of an intentional understatement, "this would be unprofitable for you," the writer to the Hebrews warns the disobedient believer against grieving their spiritual leaders. This statement is a literary device, called a *litotes*, in which a milder, negative statement is used instead of a strong, affirmative statement. It is the opposite of a hyperbole. (For example, instead of saying "really great work," we might say, "not bad work.") The expression causes the reader to stop, think, and fill in the fuller meaning. Stated positively, this clause would read, "that is harmful to you," or "that is disastrous for you."

To cut oneself off from God's watchmen or to run away from the shepherds' care is dangerous business. God may severely chastise the disobedient believer (1 Cor. 11:29-34), the devil may delude the mind (2 Cor. 11:3), or a bitter spirit may set in, halting all growth and maturity. Certainly all the God-given blessings of the shepherding ministry are lost to those who refuse to heed the cries and pleas of the church shepherds. So the concluding clause is, as biblical commentator William Lane remarks, "a sober reminder that the welfare of the community is tied to the quality of their response to their current leaders."[11]

Part Four

RELATED TOPICS

Chapter 14

Appointment of Elders

"And when they had appointed elders for them in every church, having prayed with fasting, they commended them to the Lord in whom they had believed."

Acts 14:23

Another misunderstood and sorely neglected aspect of biblical eldership relates to the process of appointing elders. It is in this area that many churches fail, with the sad result that unfit men are appointed as pastor elders, and/or qualified men are never developed or properly recognized. Most churches have two separate standards for the appointment process: one for the professional class, which is very demanding and thorough, and another for the so-called lay class or board elder, which is quite abbreviated. But this dual standard is without scriptural warrant. All pastor elders are to be fully qualified, formally examined, and publicly installed into office.

In order to understand what is involved in the biblical process of appointing elders, we must first look at those who initiate and guide the appointment process, and then consider the major elements in the appointment process: desire, qualification, selection, examination, installation, and prayer.

Initiating and Guiding the Appointment Process

According to 1 Timothy 3:1 and Titus 1:7, a local church should have overseers. By definition, overseers supervise the activities of the church. In 1 Timothy 5:17, the elders are the ones who "rule" the local church. The word "rule" is the Greek word *prohistēmi*, which means lead, manage, or direct. So in vitally important matters such as selecting, examining, approving, and installing prospective elders or deacons, the overseers should direct the entire process. (In all New Testament cases of initial elder or deacon appointment, the apostles or an apostolic delegate initiated and supervised the appointment process. See Acts 6:1-6; 14:24; Titus 1:5.) If the elders do not oversee the appointment process, disorder and mismanagement will ensue, and people will be hurt. Moreover, if the elders do not take the initiative, the process will stagnate. The elders have the authority, position, and knowledge to move the whole church to action. They know its needs, and they know its people. So they can, intentionally or not, stifle or encourage the development of new elders. The reason some churches can't find new elders is that no one is really looking for them.

Although the New Testament provides no example of elders appointing elders, perpetuation of the eldership is implied in the elders' role as congregational shepherds, stewards, and overseers. Perpetuating the eldership is a major aspect of church leadership responsibility. It is absolutely vital to the ongoing life of the church that the elders recognize the Spirit-given desire of others to shepherd the flock. If a brother desires to shepherd the church and truly exhibits that desire through appropriate action, and if he is morally qualified, then the elders are obligated to see that such a person is not frustrated in his desire. Such a brother needs to be officially made a member of the church eldership team.

For this reason, a good eldership will be praying and looking for capable men to join them and will be conscientiously training and preparing men for future leadership. What Paul told Timothy applies to the eldership: "And the things which you have heard from me in the presence of many witnesses, these entrust to faithful men, who will be able to teach others also" (2 Tim. 2:2). Ideally, long before the church examines a prospective elder, he will have prepared himself and been trained by the elders and watched by the congregation. When this has occurred, the process of examining and approving the candidate moves quickly and in an orderly fashion.

Kenneth O. Gangel, professor and chairman of the department of Christian education at Dallas Theological Seminary, is right on target when he says, "The key to reproducing leadership is to clearly plan for it."[1] "Church leaders," exhorts Gangel, "need to produce leaders who will reproduce leaders precisely as it is done in the family—through experience, instruction, and modeling."[2] In related comments on the necessity for discipling men for church leadership, Bruce Stabbert says:

> Most churches, however, find the majority of their men sadly stunted spiritually and with little knowledge of the Bible. If this is the case, such men would probably be very reticent to view themselves as prospective pastors. This is where the plan [to train elders] becomes work.
>
> We might imagine Peter being informed upon his first encounter with Christ that within three years he would be an apostle and preach to thousands of people at one time. He would probably have said, "Who me?" How did Jesus prepare Peter and the other apostles for church leadership? He discipled them. He spent time with them. He taught them. He prayed with them and for them.
>
> And that is the primary way that true elders will be developed in a local church. Somebody is going to have to disciple some men. We may not have much more than a bunch of fishermen in our congregation, but they should be discipled. Someone must spend time with them. Someone must teach them. Someone must pray with them and for them. But they can be discipled![3]

The church elders (or founding missionary) should take the initiative and supervise the appointment process. As the Scripture says, "but let all things be done properly and in an orderly manner (1 Cor. 14:40).

Elements in the Appointment Process: Desire, Qualification, Selection, Examination, Installation, and Prayer

It is commonly thought that Acts 6:1-6 provides the model for all the stages in the process of appointing deacons or elders. Acts 6, however, is the account of the original establishment of the Seven; it doesn't tell us how the group perpetuated itself, assuming it continued to exist after the great persecution of Acts 8. If the group did continue to function (and the need for it certainly didn't disappear), did the Seven ask the congregation to select new members and have the apostles lay hands on them, or did they simply replace themselves? Was the group always required to have seven members, or could there be six or ten? Was there a fixed time each year when the church selected new replacements for the Seven? We don't know the answers to these questions, and the same is true concerning the elders. Even if, in Acts 14:23, Paul and Barnabas followed the model of Acts 6, we still don't know exactly how the Galatian elders perpetuated themselves after the apostles left.

The New Testament says very little concerning such detailed procedures as appointing elders. In the same way, the New Testament is amazingly silent regarding specific procedures for administering the Lord's Supper and baptism. Exact procedures for these activities are left to the discretion of the local church. Even under the Mosaic law, which prescribed detailed regulations for every area of life, matters such as the appointment and organization of elders were left to the people's discretion. God expects His saints to use the creativity and wisdom He has given to organize all such matters within the revealed guidelines of His Word. He expects His people to do so in a way that exemplifies the gospel's truth and the true nature of the Church. I concur with Neil Summerton, who captures the biblical spirit when he writes:

> It is characteristic of Technological Man of the twentieth century to worry abnormally about the precise mechanism of selection. But biblically of much greater importance is its manner and spirit. Be we ever so precise about the *modus operandi*, it will be of no avail if the mechanism still succeeds in choosing the wrong people. For this reason it may not matter much whether selection of elders is by church planters, the existing elders, or the congregation as a whole, so long as all are certain that the outcome is the choice of God.[4]

Although the New Testament doesn't provide a blueprint for the process of elder appointment, it specifies certain key elements. Let us consider the elements of desire, qualifications, selection, examination, installation, and prayer.

PERSONAL DESIRE

The Bible says, "if any man aspires to the office of overseer [eldership], it is a fine work he desires to do" (1 Tim. 3:1*b*). The first matter to consider in appointing elders is the candidate's personal desire. The desire to be an elder is not sinful or self-promoting, if it is generated by God's Spirit. Paul reminded the Ephesian elders that it was the Holy Spirit who had placed them in the church as elders (Acts 20:28). This means, among other things, that the Holy Spirit planted in the hearts of the elders the desire and motivation to be shepherd elders. In a similar way, Peter addresses the need for an elder to shepherd God's flock with a willing heart (1 Peter 5:2). So the starting point is a Spirit-given desire to be a shepherd of God's people.

A Spirit-given desire for pastoral eldership will naturally demonstrate itself in action. It cannot be held in. A man who desires to be a shepherd elder will let others know of his desire. That is one way in which the congregation and elders can know of a prospective elder. The knowledge of this desire will prompt the elders to pray and to encourage such desire through appropriate training and leadership development. More important, the person with a Spirit-created motivation for the work of eldership will devote much time, thought, and energy to caring for people and studying the Scriptures. There is no such thing as a Spirit-given desire for eldership without the corresponding evidence of sacrificial, loving service and love for God's Word. Eldership is a strenuous task, not just another position on a decision-making board. In fact, the stronger a man's desire for eldership, the stronger will be his leadership and love for people and the Word.

So before a man is appointed to eldership, he is already proving himself by leading, teaching, and bearing responsibility in the church. In 1 Thessalonians 5:12, Paul reminds the congregation of its responsibility to acknowledge and recognize those in the congregation who work hard at leading and instructing others: "But we request of you, brethren, that you appreciate those who diligently labor among you, and have charge over you in the Lord and give you instruction." One way the congregation and elders acknowledge a man's diligent labors is to recommend and encourage him to prepare for eldership. So it ought to be clearly known in the church that "if any man aspires to the office of overseer, it is a fine work he desires to do."

MORAL AND SPIRITUAL QUALIFICATIONS

The New Testament is positively emphatic that only morally and spiritually qualified men can serve as elders. So, in addition to his subjective desire to be a shepherd elder, Scripture demands that a candidate for eldership meet certain objective qualifications (1 Tim. 3:1-7; Titus 1:5-9). Since we have previously explored in detail the biblical qualifications for elders, I refer you back to chapters 4, 9, 10, and 11.

SELECTION AND EXAMINATION

The actual selection of elders can be done by the congregation, especially in the case of a new church (Acts 6:3), or it can be done by the existing elders, or by a combination of both.

Exactly how the congregation in Jerusalem selected seven of its men for the task of distributing funds to its widows is not explained (Acts 6:3). It would not have been difficult for the congregation to organize itself for such selection, however. From its earliest days, the nation of Israel was organized into precisely defined, manageable groups for the purpose of expediting communication, war, service, and travel (Ex. 13:18; 18:13-27; 36:6; Num. 2:2 ff; 7:2; 1 Kings 4:7). Congregational decisions and operations were conducted primarily through representatives or heads of clans and towns (compare Lev. 4:13 with 4:15; Ex. 3:15,16; compare Ex. 4:29 with 4:31; Ex. 19:7,8; Deut. 21:1,2,6-9). So it is possible that the Jewish congregation in Jerusalem was already organized into manageable units (Acts 12:12,17; 15:4,6,22; 21:17,18). Such organization would enable issues to be decided and information to be passed along quickly. We should not conclude that this account proves that each member had one equal vote in selecting the Seven. These were Jews, not Gentiles, so they were accustomed to having representative leaders, such as elders, act on their behalf (Acts 15:6-22; 21:18).

Closely associated with selecting prospective elders is the examination of their moral and spiritual fitness for office. Since the qualifications for eldership are to be taken seriously by the local congregation, it follows that a formal, public examination of a prospective elder's qualifications is necessary. This is exactly what 1 Timothy 3:10 states: "And let these [deacons] also [like the elders] first be tested;

then let them serve as deacons if they are beyond reproach." First Timothy 5:24,25 also teaches that an assessment of character and deeds is necessary in order to avoid appointing the wrong people as elders or overlooking qualified men: "The sins of some men [prospective elders] are quite evident, going before them to judgment [human examination]; for others, their sins follow after. Likewise also, deeds that are good are quite evident, and those which are otherwise cannot be concealed."

Although the elders are to take the lead in all church procedures, this does not mean that the congregation is passive. Biblical elders want an informed, involved congregation. Biblical elders eagerly desire to listen to, consult with, and seek the wisdom of their fellow believers. The prospective elder or deacon will serve the congregation, so the people must have a voice in examining and approving their prospective elders and deacons. The context in which 1 Timothy 3:10 appears lays out general instructions for the whole church (1 Tim 2:1-3:16), not just for the elders. Therefore, everyone in the church is to know the biblical qualifications for church elders and is obligated to see that the elders meet those qualifications. Some people in the congregation may have information about a prospective elder or deacon that the elders do not have, so their input in the evaluation process is absolutely essential, regardless of how that process is carried out in detail.

If objections or accusations are voiced as to a candidate's character, the elders should investigate to determine if the accusations are scripturally based. If not, the objections or accusations should be dismissed. No candidate should be refused office because of someone's personal bias. Members of the congregation must give scriptural reasons for their objections. This examination process is not a popularity contest or church election. It is an assessment of a candidate's character according to the light of Scripture. If even one person in the congregation has a verified scriptural objection, the prospective elder should be declared unfit for office—even if everyone else approves. *God's standards alone, not group popularity, govern God's house.*

During a meeting (or several meetings) with the prospective elder, the elders and the congregation should inquire about the candidate's doctrinal beliefs, personal giftedness, ministry interests, family unity, moral integrity, and commitment of time. Remember, one of the qualifications for eldership is "that he may be able to exhort in sound doctrine and to refute those who contradict" (Titus 1:9*b*), so time needs to be allotted to examine the prospective elder regarding his knowledge and ability to use his Bible to counsel people and direct the church. For example, the candidate should be able to open the Bible and answer questions such as "What does the Bible teach about divorce and remarriage?" "Where in the Bible does it teach Christ's divine nature?" "What is the gospel message?" "What does the Bible say about male-female roles?" "What does the Bible say about church discipline?" and many more.

Opportunity must be provided for members of the congregation, either verbally or in written form such as through an elder-evaluation survey, to express freely their questions, doubts, or approval of a candidate for eldership. Since God's Word provides an objective, public standard, everyone is responsible to see that God's requirements for eldership are followed.

Finally, the elders, acting as the chief representatives and stewards of God's household, will formally state, in full consultation with the church, their approval, rejection, reservations, or counsel concerning the prospective elder.

INSTALLATION

After the examination process and the elders' final approval, the candidate should be publicly installed into office. The word "first" in 1 Timothy 3:10 informs us that there is an order to observe when appointing elders or deacons. The text reads, "And let these also *first* be tested; *then* let them serve as deacons" (italics added). A prospective elder's or deacon's character must first be examined. Only after he is shown to be biblically qualified can he be installed into office.

The New Testament provides little detailed instruction about the elder's public installation into office, and the Old Testament says nothing about it. In contrast, there was an elaborate and detailed ceremonial procedure for installing the Old Testament priest. There were special sacrifices to be offered, special washings, ceremonial garments, prescribed actions on certain days, and anointing with holy oil (Ex. 28:40-29:41). No one could deviate even slightly from these prescribed laws.

New Testament elders and deacons, however, are not anointed priests like Aaron and his sons (Lev. 8:12). Elders and deacons are not appointed to a special priestly office or holy clerical order. Instead, they are assuming offices of leadership or service among God's people. *We should be careful not to sacralize these positions more than the writers of Scripture do.*[5] The New Testament never shrouds the installation of elders in mystery or sacred ritual. There is no holy rite to perform or special ceremony to observe. Appointment to eldership is not a holy sacrament. Appointment confers no special grace or empowerment, nor does one become a priest, cleric, or holy man at the moment of installation. The vocabulary of the New Testament is carefully chosen to communicate certain concepts and beliefs, and its writers chose to express simple appointment to office. Therefore, to speak of ordaining elders or deacons is as confusing as speaking of ordaining judges or politicians.

Appointment Terminology

Luke records that Paul and Barnabas "appointed" elders for their newly founded churches: "And when they had appointed elders for them in every church, having prayed with fasting, they commended them to the Lord in whom they had believed" (Acts 14:23). The Greek word Luke uses for "appointed" is *cheirotoneō*, which here means "appoint," or "designate." Although the term *cheirotoneō* later became a technical term for church ordination and the laying on of hands, it simply meant "appoint" at the time Luke wrote Acts. (see chapter 7, page 136).

Paul writes to Titus, his personal delegate on the island of Crete, instructing him to "appoint" elders: "For this reason I left you in Crete, that you might set in order what remains, and appoint elders in every city as I directed you" (Titus 1:5). The Greek term Paul uses for "appoint" is *kathistēmi*, which is a common term for appointing to office or a specific task. *Kathistēmi* has no special religious connotations (see chapter 10, page 227).

When referring to appointment to specific tasks or positions, the New Testament writers use common words for appointment (*poieō*, *tithēmi*, *kathistēmi*, *cheirotoneō*). These terms do not express or imply modern, ecclesiastical ordination concepts. Even well-known Bible scholars who support clerical ordination and are themselves clergymen admit that the New Testament's vocabulary speaks of general appointment only. For example, Leon Morris, an Anglican clergyman and one of the most prolific biblical commentators of the twentieth century, writes: "Considering the role played by the ministry throughout the history of the church, references to ordination are surprisingly few in the N.T. Indeed, the word 'ordination' does not occur, and the verb 'to ordain' in the technical sense does not occur either. A number of verbs are translated 'ordain' in AV, but these all have meanings like 'appoint.'"[6] In similar fashion, Alfred Plummer, another Anglican clergyman and biblical commentator, makes the following remarkable comments on the Greek verbs for *appoint* in Titus 1:5 and other similar passages:

> In these passages [Titus 1:5; Mark 3:14; John 15:16; 1 Tim. 2:7; Heb. 5:1; 8:3] three different Greek words (*poieō, tithēmi, kathistēmi*) are used in the original; but not one of them has the special ecclesiastical meaning which we so frequently associate with the word "ordain"; not one of them implies, as "ordain" in such context almost of necessity implies, a rite of ordination, a special ceremonial, such as the laying on of hands. When in English we say, "He ordained twelve,"...the mind almost inevitably thinks of ordination in the common sense of the word; and this is foisting upon the language of the New Testament a meaning which the words there used do not rightly bear.... The Greek words used in the passages quoted might equally well be used of the appointment of a magistrate or a steward. And as we should avoid speaking of ordaining a magistrate or a steward, we ought to avoid using "ordain" to translate words which would be thoroughly in place in such a connexion. The Greek words for "ordain" and "ordination," in the sense of imposition of hands in order to admit to an ecclesiastical office (*cheipotheti, cheipothesia*), do not occur in the New Testament at all.[7]

So, to translate the New Testament words *poieō* (Mark 3:14), *kathistēmi* (Acts 6:3; Titus 1:5), or *cheirotoneō* (Acts 14:23) as "ordain" imposes unscriptural priestly or clerical connotations in people's minds. Surprisingly, not only is ordination not found in the New Testament, it is not found in the writings of the early second century church writers. One can be sure that Ignatius would have used the rite of ordination to bolster his arguments for the overseer's supremacy over the local congregation if he found any basis for it. But no such practice existed in the early second century.

In a detailed study on ordination, Warkentin makes the following observation about the postapostolic period: "Installation into office in the early postapostolic period apparently involved little in the way of ceremony or protocol....we see the simple vocabulary of the New Testament still being used for appointment to office."[8] For the Christian community, in which all members are priests, holy ones, humble ministers, and family members, the simple word *appoint* best expresses the placement of elders and deacons into office. In the New Testament, no exclusive class of men is admitted into ministerial office by the rite of ordination. No one needs to be ordained to preach Christ or administer the ordinances. All such concepts are foreign to the New Testament apostolic churches.

The New Testament indicates that elders were formally installed into office by the laying on of hands and prayer. Within the context of his instructions on elders (1 Tim. 5:17-25), Paul's reference to the laying on of hands must mean appointment to office: "Do not lay hands upon anyone too hastily and thus share responsibility for the sins of others" (1 Tim. 5:22). Thus Paul thought of Timothy as formally appointing new elders for the church in Ephesus by the laying on of hands. If the term "appointed" in Acts 14:23 is a summary description of the full process that is explained in Acts 6, then hands were laid on the Galatian elders by Paul and Barnabas. Certainly the laying on of hands was practiced frequently by Paul (Acts 9:17; 13:3; 14:3; 19:6,11; 28:8; 2 Tim. 1:6), and from 1 Timothy 4:14 we know that the church elders laid their hands on Timothy as he was about to begin his travels and work with Paul.

The first Christians were not adverse to simple, public ceremony for appointing or commissioning fellow members to special positions or tasks (Acts 6:6; 13:3; 1 Tim. 4:14). For important events such as the appointment of elders, some kind of public, official recognition of new elders would be necessary. The formal installation of an elder before the congregation by the laying on of hands and prayer (or any other means) would signal the start of the new elder's ministry. It would say to the new elder, "You now officially begin your responsibilities. You are now a member of the church's eldership team. The pastoral care of the flock rests on your shoulders and on the shoulders of fellow elders." It would say to the people, "Here is a new pastor elder to care for you and your family." So formal installation is an official starting point. Furthermore, the formal installation of an elder by the laying on of hands would communicate to the new elder the approval, blessing, prayers, recognition, and fellowship of the church.

Regarding the laying on of hands, the New Testament provides few instructions (1 Tim. 5:22). It is not a prescribed practice such as baptism or the Lord's Supper, nor is it restricted to a particular person or group within the church (Acts 9:12; 13:3). So the precise significance of the laying on of hands in specific situations is difficult to determine. We do know that the imposition of hands, like fasting, was practiced by the first Christians because it was useful and a blessing to all. Because of the confusion and superstition surrounding the laying on of hands, many churches avoid its use entirely. This is tragic because the laying on of hands can be a meaningful, precious expression of blessing, approval, and partnership.[9] Christians are free, then, to use the laying on of hands if they desire, or to refrain from practicing it if it creates misunderstanding or division.

PRAYER

Finally, all procedures concerning this important decision must be bathed in patient prayer. The church and its leaders must pray for spiritual insight, guidance, and unbiased judgment. They must desire God's will and God's choice, not their own. God said, of Israel "They have set up kings, but not by Me; They have appointed princes, but I did not know it" (Hos. 8:4*a*). May God not say the same of us.

Sadly, too many churches expend the least amount of time and effort possible when selecting and examining prospective elders or deacons. A friend told me that in his church the pastor invites all the members to assemble in the church basement once a year, after a Sunday-evening service, to select and elect deacons. After everyone gathers in front of a blackboard, the chairman of the deacons asks for nominations to the diaconate. Several names are suggested and quickly voted on. The new deacons are then installed, and the pastor closes the meeting in prayer. The entire process takes half an hour. There is no consideration of scriptural qualifications, no prayer, and no time to fully examine the nominated deacons. For many, it is a simple matter of, "We have to replace outgoing members of the board. We have a quota to maintain."

Thoughtless, lazy, and prayerless procedures such as those described above weaken our churches and demean the eldership and deaconship. Evaluating an elder's or deacon's fitness for office should be done thoughtfully, patiently, and biblically. The Scripture clearly states that no one is to be appointed to office in a hurried, thoughtless manner: "Do not lay hands upon anyone too hastily" (1 Tim. 5:22*a*).

Once a man is appointed to the pastors' council [eldership] he serves as long as he desires, functions in the work, and qualifies. It is unscriptural, harmful to the church, and demeaning to the elders to set limits on the time period a pastor elder can serve, or to limit the number of elders to a fixed number. If there are eight men in the church who love and desire to be pastor elders (1 Tim. 3:1), then there should be eight men functioning together as a pastoral council. Lawrence R. Eyres, a Presbyterian minister and author of *The Elders of the Church*, reasons biblically when he warns against term-eldership and arbitrary elder quotas:

> Then there is the matter of competition for office, as when there are more nominees than there are offices to be filled. This is an inherent danger where sessions [elderships] are organized with term-eldership and a fixed number of places to be filled in each class. To set a fixed number of elders is a dangerous precedent...if a man is ready to serve Christ's church as an elder, by what arbitrary rule is he to be kept back because another man is also ready? If the Holy Spirit makes men elders, then the church ought to be ruled by those men the Spirit has prepared.[10]

Chapter 15

Elders and the Congregation

"Live in peace with one another."

1 Thessalonians 5:13*b*

For the local Christian congregation that sincerely desires to follow the New Testament church model, Jesus Christ is Chief Shepherd, Scripture is the final and sufficient guide, and the elders are Christ's undershepherds. Using a different but compatible imagery, Paul refers to the elders as "God's stewards" (Titus 1:7). According to this model, the authority to govern and teach the local church resides in the plurality of elders—Christ's undershepherds, God's household managers.

As Christ's undershepherds and God's stewards, the elders are under the strict authority of Jesus Christ and His Holy Word. They are not a ruling oligarchy. They cannot do or say whatever they want. The church does not belong to the elders; it is Christ's church and God's flock. Thus the elders' leadership is to be exercised in a way that models Christlike, humble, loving leadership.

In the local church, there are no rulers who sit above or subjects who stand below. The same biblical writer who commanded the elders to shepherd and oversee God's flock also warned against lordly, controlling leadership practices (1 Peter 5:3). All are equally brothers and sisters in the church family, although some function as Spirit-placed overseers to authoritatively guide and protect the church family.

Because the elders bear greater responsibility for the spiritual care of the entire congregation than other members, Scripture teaches that the congregation is to highly esteem, love, and honor its pastor elders (1 Thess. 5:12,13; 1 Tim. 5:17). Scripture also expressly commands the congregation to obey and submit to its spiritual leaders (Heb. 13:17; cf. James 5:5).

Submission is always difficult. Our hearts are stubborn, prideful, and rebellious. Yet we are called to submit, even in trying and disagreeable situations. Children must submit to imperfect parents, wives to difficult husbands, and employees to demanding employers. Likewise, the congregation is required to submit to and obey its elders, even if the elders have weaknesses and faults. Indeed, most elders are quite imperfect, so those who are disobedient can always find reason to revolt. Of course the things we consider to be the elders' misjudgments or errors may well be our own errors, so we should not be too hasty to disregard the judgment of those God has chosen to provide for our spiritual care.

The requirement to submit, however, is not meant to suggest blind, mindless submission. Nor does it suggest that elders are above questioning or immune from public discipline (1 Tim. 5:19 ff.). The elders are most assuredly answerable to the congregation, and the congregation is responsible to hold its spiritual leaders accountable to faithful adherence to the truth of the Word. As we saw in chapter 14, the congregation is to be directly involved in the public examination and approval of prospective elders and deacons (1 Tim. 3:10). All members have a voice in assuring that what is done in the church family is done according to Scripture. So there is a tightly knit, delicate, and reciprocal relationship between elders and congregation.

Through the power of the gospel, every redeemed child of God is indwelt by the Holy Spirit of God, is placed in living union with Christ and made an heir with Christ, is gifted for ministry in the body of Christ, is constituted a priest to God and holy saint of God, and is a blood-bought son or daughter of God. Thus every member has a unique, high standing and must share in the responsibilities, privileges, ownership, obligations, and building up of the local church. This is why the New Testament authors always address the whole church—not just the elders—when they write to a local church. Neil Summerton's insightful comments on "the high position accorded in scripture to the congregation itself" deserve repeating:[1]

> Despite the existence of priestly and Levitical castes, and later of kings, that position can already be perceived in shadow in the Old Testament. The old covenant was with people rather than simply with leaders and under it a certain egalitarianism can be perceived in the relation between people and their covenant God: the superior status, as distinct from authority, later accorded to the monarch in Israel obviously derived from the hardness of the people's heart rather than the primitive purpose of God (see 1 *Samuel* 8:10-18; *Hosea* 8:4, 13-14). The promise is comprehensively fulfilled in the New Testament. There we see a new covenant with a new people which embraces the youngest to the oldest. All receive the sign and guarantee of the covenant—the Holy Spirit; from that Spirit all have knowledge of God and all have the heart of flesh to obey God; all are kings and priests to God; and each receives (from young to old) spiritual gifts, severally according to the will of God, for the mutual upbuilding of the church. The old Israel was dependent usually on a few leaders; in the new, spiritual insight, spiritual power, spiritual character and spiritual standing are now much more widely disseminated through the whole body.
>
> Consistent with this teaching, the New Testament accords a much higher status and role to the congregation at large than has often been accepted and practised in the experience of the church—though it should be noted that in times of revival and renewal there has been a constant tendency to rectify matters.[2]

Christ's presence is with the whole congregation, not just the elders. Christ ministers through all the members because all are Spirit-indwelt, but all members do not function as shepherds to the whole community—the council of elders does that. The congregation governs itself through the congregational elders. It is not governed by any external person or group.

The New Testament does not indicate that the congregation governs itself by majority vote, and there is no evidence that God has granted every member one equal vote with every other member. Rather, the New Testament congregation is governed by its own congregational elders. The elders, according to the express instruction of the New Testament, have the authority to shepherd the congregation.

Of course there are matters of congregational business and debate that require the involvement and decision of the whole congregation. Jesus taught that the discipline of an unrepentant, sinning member (after individual efforts to correct the sin had failed) requires the collective wisdom, action, and discipline of the whole congregation (Matt. 18:17-20; 1 Cor. 5:4,11; 2 Cor. 2:6). Paul also instructs the whole church to examine prospective elders or deacons (1 Tim. 3:10). When issues are brought to the congregation, the elders, as Spirit-placed shepherds, take the lead in guiding the congregation in orderly and prayerful decision making. As the congregation looks to its elders for wise leadership, the elders also look to the congregation—their brothers and sisters—for wisdom, counsel, inspiration, creative ideas, help, and prayer. Elders who understand the sacred nature and dynamic energy of the Spirit-empowered congregation know the necessity of congregational participation in all major decisions.

The goal of the elders and congregation should always be to speak and act as a united community. Both the leaders and the led should take the time and make the effort needed to work and pray together to achieve this oneness of mind. This means that elders must inoculate themselves against aloofness, secrecy, or independently seeking their own direction. Godly elders desire to involve every member of the body in the joy of living together as the family of God. This requires a great deal of free and open communication between the elders and congregation.

The first Christian congregation provides us with some examples of a leadership council and congregation working together in decision making and problem solving. In Acts 6, when conflict broke out between the Hebrew and Hellenistic widows in the congregation over the fair distribution of funds, the Twelve (the leadership council) immediately devised a plan for resolving the problem. They called the congregation together and presented their plan. The congregation approved the plan, which called for their participation in choosing seven men to take responsibility for the care of all the church widows. After the seven were chosen by the congregation, the apostles officially placed the seven men in charge of the poor by the laying on of hands and prayer (see chapter 14, page 282).

In Acts 15, the congregation in Jerusalem was confronted with serious doctrinal controversy. The account shows that the whole church was involved in resolving the controversy but that the apostles and elders took the lead in all the proceedings (Acts 15:4,6). The apostles and elders permitted public debate, including the presentation of the opposing view (Acts 15:5,7). The chief leaders within the leadership council brought the matters to a conclusion so that all the leaders could "become of one mind" (15:25). The final decision was the decision of the apostles, the elders, the whole church, and the Holy Spirit: "Then it seemed good to the apostles and the elders, with the whole church, to choose men from among them to send to Antioch....'For it seemed good to the Holy Spirit and to us to lay upon you no greater burden than these essentials'" (15:22,28).

From these two examples, it is clear that the leadership body takes the lead for the congregation, and that the congregation participates. Depending on the circumstances, the leaders wisely use different procedures and strategies to help the congregation solve problems and make decisions.

The New Testament does not prescribe detailed rules and regulations regarding the elder-congregation relationship or decision making process. The New Testament is absolutely clear, however, that Christlike love, humility, and prayer are to guide all our relationships and all our deliberations. As the Scripture says:

> But we [church leaders] will devote ourselves to prayer (Acts 6:4*a*).

> These all [the first congregation] with one mind were continually devoting themselves to prayer (Acts 1:14*a*).

> Make my joy complete by being of the same mind, maintaining the same love, united in spirit, intent on one purpose. Do nothing from selfishness or empty conceit, but with humility of mind let each of you regard one another as more important than himself; do not merely look out for your own personal interests, but also for the interests of others. Have this attitude in yourselves which was also in Christ Jesus, who, although He existed in the form of God, did not regard equality with God a thing to be grasped, but emptied Himself, taking the form of a bond-servant, and being made in the likeness of men. And being found in appearance as a man, He humbled Himself by becoming obedient to the point of death, even death on a cross (Phil. 2:2-8).

Notes

Why This Book Is Needed

1. Presbyterian churches, Reformed churches, Churches of Christ, Christian Churches, Brethren churches, numerous Baptist, charismatic, and independent churches.
2. Quoted by Alfred Kuen in *I Will Build My Church*, trans. Ruby Lindblad (Chicago: Moody, 1971), p. 27.
3. Calvin was one of the first to write about the demise of church eldership. Remonstrating the loss of the eldership, Calvin, quoting a Roman author named Ambrosiaster (ca. A.D. 375) who also decried the loss of the church elders, writes:

   > Gradually this institution degenerated from its original condition, so that already in the time of Ambrose the clergy alone sat in ecclesiastical judgment. He complained about this in the following words: "The old synagogue, and afterward the church, had elders, without whose counsel nothing was done. It has fallen out of use, by what negligence I do not know, unless perhaps through the sloth, or rather, pride of the learned, wishing to appear to be important by themselves alone" (*Institutes of the Christian Religion*, ed. J.T. Mc Neill, trans. F.L. Battles [Philadelphia: Westminster, 1960], 2:107).

4. See Emil Brunner, *The Misunderstanding of the Church*, trans. Harold Knight (Philadelphia: Westminster, 1953), pp. 103, 104.
5. See George Müller, *A Narrative of Some of the Lord's Dealings with George Müller* (London: James Nisbet, 1881), vol.1, pp. 206, 207, 276-281; Henry Craik, *New Testament Church Order* (Bristol: W. Mack, 1863), pp. 57, 58; H. Groves, *Memoir of the Late Anthony Norris Groves*, 2nd ed. (London: James Nisbet, 1857), p. 385.
6. See Alexander Campbell, *The Christian System* (1835; repr. Nashville: Gospel Advocate, 1964), pp. 60-67.

Chapter 1

1. Victor A. Constien, *The Caring Elder: A Training Manual for Serving* (St. Louis: Concordia, 1986), p. 10.
2. D.J. Tidball, *Skillful Shepherds: An Introduction to Pastoral Theology* (Grand Rapids: Zondervan, 1986), pp. 46,48.

3. Phillip W. Keller, *A Shepherd Looks at the Great Shepherd and His Sheep* (Grand Rapids: Eerdmans, 1981), p. 25.
4. Charles Edward Jefferson, *The Minister as Shepherd* (1912; repr. Fincastle: Scripture Truth, n.d.), p. 43.
5. James Orr, *The Christian View of God and the World* (Grand Rapids: Eerdmans, 1948), p. 20.
6. Jefferson, *The Minister as Shepherd*, pp. 59,60.
7. Neil Summerton, *A Noble Task: Eldership and Ministry in the Local Church,* 2nd ed. (Carlisle: Paternoster, 1994), pp. 26,27.
8. Jefferson, *The Minister as Shepherd*, p. 47.
9. For a good discussion of the differences between leaders and managers, see Kenneth O. Gangel, *Feeding and Leading* (Wheaton: Victor, 1989), pp. 13-46.
10. A. J. Broomhall, *Hudson Taylor and China's Open Century*, 7 vols., vol. 5: Refiner's Fire (London: Hodder and Stoughton, 1985), p. 350.
11. R. Paul Stevens, *Liberating the Laity* (Downers Grove: InterVarsity, 1985), p. 147.
12. Jefferson, *The Minister as Shepherd*, p. 65.
13. John J. Davis, *The Perfect Shepherd: Studies in the Twenty-Third Psalm* (Grand Rapids: Eerdmans, 1979), p. 39.
14. Phillip W. Keller, *A Shepherd Looks at Psalm 23* (Grand Rapids: Zondervan, 1970), p. 130.
15. D. A. Carson, *A Call to Spiritual Reformation: Priorities from Paul and His Prayers* (Grand Rapids: Baker, 1992), p. 81.
16. See Pauline G. Hamilton, *To a Different Drum* (Littleton: OMF Books, 1984), p. 38.
17. **The noun, *episkopos*:**

"Be on guard for yourselves and for all the flock, among which the Holy Spirit has made you *overseers*, to shepherd the church of God" (Acts 20:28; italics added).

"Paul and Timothy, bond-servants of Christ Jesus, to all the saints in Christ Jesus who are in Philippi, including the *overseers* and deacons" (Phil. 1:1; italics added).

"An *overseer*, then, must be above reproach, the husband of one wife, temperate, prudent, respectable, hospitable, able to teach" (1 Tim. 3:2; italics added).

"For the *overseer* must be above reproach as God's steward, not self-willed, not quick-tempered, not addicted to wine, not pugnacious, not fond of sordid gain" (Titus 1:7; italics added).

The related noun, *episkopē*:

"It is a trustworthy statement; if any man aspires to the *office of overseer*, it is a fine work he desires to do" (1 Tim. 3:1; italics added).

The related verb form, *episkopeō:*
"Shepherd the flock of God among you, *exercising oversight* not under compulsion, but voluntarily, according to the will of God" (1 Peter 5:2*a*; italics added).

18. Nigel Turner, *Christian Words* (Nashville: Thomas Nelson, 1981), p. viii.

Chapter 2

1. See Alexander Strauch, *The New Testament Deacon: The Church's Minister of Mercy* (Littleton: Lewis and Roth, 1992), pp. 44-54.
2. Bruce Stabbert, *The Team Concept: Paul's Church Leadership Patterns or Ours?* (Tacoma: Hegg, 1982), pp. 25,26.
3. C. S. Lewis, "How to Get Along with Difficult People," *Eternity* 16 (August, 1965): 14.
4. Robert Greenleaf, *Servant Leadership* (New York: Paulist, 1977), p. 63.
5. Erroll Hulse, "The Authority of Elders," *Reformation Today* 44 (July-August, 1978): 5.
6. Stabbert, *The Team Concept*, p. 51.
7. Earl D. Radmacher, *The Question of Elders* (Portland: Western Baptist, 1977), p. 7.
8. Ibid., p. 11.
9. Phyllis Thompson, *D. E. Hoste "A Prince with God*" (London: China Inland Mission, 1947), p. 119.
10. Neil Summerton, *A Noble Task: Eldership and Ministry in the Local Church,* 2nd ed. (Carlisle: Paternoster, 1994), p. 85.

Chapter 3

1. John Piper, "A Vision of Biblical Complementarity," in *Recovering Biblical Manhood and Womanhood* (Wheaton: Crossway, 1991), p. 32.
2. Cullen Murphy, "Women and the Bible," *The Atlantic Monthly*, (August, 1993): 41-43.
3. See Wayne Grudem's excellent article, "The Meaning of *Kephalē* ('Head'): A Response to Recent Studies," in *Recovering Biblical Manhood and Womanhood*, pp. 425-468.
4. George W. Knight III, "Husbands and Wives as Analogues of Christ and the Church," in *Recovering Biblical Manhood and Womanhood*, p. 168.
5. Ibid., p. 174.
6. Biblical feminists are notorious for equating the doctrine of male headship with the oppression of women. Certainly men misuse this doctrine to excuse their abusive behavior toward their wives, but that is not the biblical model, nor is it the pattern of most Christian marriages. Godly, Christian headship is marked by love—the kind of self-sacrificing love that Christ displayed on behalf of His bride. Ephesians 5:25 states: "Hus-

bands, love your wives, just as Christ also loved the church and gave Himself up for her." The Christian husband's leadership authority, then, is to be characterized by Christlike love and sacrifice on behalf of his wife's physical, emotional, and spiritual well-being.

7. Knight III, *Recovering Biblical Manhood and Womanhood*, p. 176.
8. Stephen B. Clark, *Man and Woman in Christ* (Ann Arbor: Servant, 1980), p. 630.
9. Many sound Bible commentators believe that 1 Timothy 3:11 refers to women deacons who serve women: "Women, must likewise be dignified, not malicious gossips, but temperate, faithful in all things." This is a highly debatable text. I understand these "women" to be wives who assist their deacon husbands. But even if they are women deacons, they hold an office of mercy ministries, not one of governance and teaching. Thus women deacons would not violate Paul's restriction against women teaching and leading men.
10. George W. Knight III, *The Pastoral Epistles*, The New International Greek Testament Commentary (Grand Rapids: Eerdmans, 1992), p. 141,142.
11. Ibid., p. 139.
12. S. Lewis Johnson, Jr., "Role Distinctions in the Church: Galatians 3:28," in *Recovering Biblical Manhood and Womanhood*, p. 164.
13. David Gooding, "Symbols of Headship and of Glory," in *Bible Topics*, 3 (Belfast: Operation O.F.F.E.R., n.d.), pp. 3,4.
14. For many twentieth-century people, the word *subordination* (or submission) has become a repulsive term that connotes inferiority, weakness, inequality, slavery, and oppression. This is unfortunate because subordination is actually a positive term. It primarily describes the way a relationship is ordered. Stephen B. Clark clarifies this point:

> Neither "inferiority" nor "equality" have any conceptually necessary link to "subordination" unless the terms are defined with such a link. The head and subordinate can both be of equal worth and value. In fact, they can be equal in many other ways, and still be in a relationship involving subordination. The subordinate can even be of greater rank and dignity, as Jesus was in relationship to his parents. To equate subordination with inferiority or inequality is either a confusion, or an attempt to win an argument by defining the terms in a way that is advantageous to one's own side (*Man and Woman in Christ*, p. 44).

Clark expands this definition of subordination in the following ways:

> The English word "subordination" means literally "ordered under," and its Greek counterpart means almost the same. The word does not carry with it a notion of inferior value. A subordinate could be more valuable in many ways than the person over him or her. Nor does the

word carry with it a notion of oppression or the use of force for domination. The word can be used to describe an oppressive relationship, but its normal use is for relationships in which the subordination involved is either neutral or good (*Man and Woman in Christ*, p. 23).

"Subordination" simply refers to the order of a relationship in which one person, the subordinate, depends upon another person for direction. The purpose of this order is to allow those in the relationship to function together in unity. Subordination is a broader concept than obedience and command. As will be seen, subordination usually implies a form of obedience. A person can give some commands to a subordinate and expect obedience, but to place the emphasis on obedience is to narrow the meaning of "subordination." A person could be subordinate without ever having to obey a command. People can subordinate their lives or actions to another in many ways: by serving another, by observing and cooperating with the other's purposes and desires, by dedicating their lives to the cause the other is upholding, or by following the other's teaching. The more that love and personal commitment are part of subordination, the more these other elements will be present along with whatever obedience is asked (*Man and Woman in Christ*, pp. 23,24).

Although "subordination" primarily describes a way of relating to another person, it also involves a character trait, a disposition to respond in a certain way. Subordination extends beyond obedience to commands to also include respectfulness and receptiveness to direction. "Submissiveness" is probably the best English term in such contexts. "Submissiveness," in this sense, is an overall character trait related to humility which all Christians should possess. The Christian character is portrayed in scripture as respectful of authority, not rebellious. Men as well as women should be submissive in their subordinate relationships (*Man and Woman in Christ*, p. 92).

15. F.F. Bruce, *The Epistle to the Galatians*, The New International Greek Testament Commentary (Grand Rapids: Eerdmans, 1982), p. 190.
16. Bruce Waltke, "The Relationship of the Sexes in the Bible," *Crux* 19 (September, 1983): 14.

Chapter 4

1. Jerome, "Letters 52," in *The Nicene and Post-Nicene Fathers,* 14 vols., Second Series, eds. Philip Schaff and Henry Wace (repr. Grand Rapids: Eerdmans, n.d.), 6: 94. (Hereafter cited as *The Nicene and Post-Nicene Fathers.*)
2. "A Biblical Style of Leadership?" *Leadership* 2 (Fall, 1981): 119-129.

3. John MacArthur, Jr., *Different By Design: Discovering God's Will for Today's Man and Woman* (Wheaton: Victor, 1994), p. 114.
4. Francis A. Schaeffer, *The Church at the End of the 20th Century* (Downers Grove: InterVarsity, 1970), p. 65.
5. Roland Allen, *Missionary Methods: St Paul's or Ours?* (1912; repr. Grand Rapids: Eerdmans, 1962), pp. 83,84.
6. Robertson McQuilkin, *An Introduction to Biblical Ethics* (Wheaton: Tyndale, 1989), p. 191.
7. For recent statistics see John H. Armstrong, *Can Fallen Pastors Be Restored? The Church's Response to Sexual Misconduct* (Chicago: Moody, 1995), pp. 17-27.
8. Richard N. Ostling, "The Second Reformation," *Time* (November 23, 1992), p. 54.
9. Armstrong, *Can Fallen Pastors Be Restored? The Church's Response to Sexual Misconduct*, pp. 78,79.
10. Ibid., p. 78.
11. J. Oswald Sanders, *Spiritual Leadership* (Chicago: Moody, 1980), p. 20.
12. Philip H. Towner, *1-2 Timothy & Titus*, The IVP New Testament Commentary Series (Downers Grove: InterVarsity, 1994), p. 228.
13. P. T. Forsyth, *The Church and the Sacraments* (1917; repr. London: Independent, 1955), p. 9.
14. J. Gresham Machen, "Faith and Knowledge," in *Education, Christianity, and the State*, ed. John W. Robbins (Jefferson: Trinity Foundation, 1987), p. 8.
15. Jon Zens, "The Major Concepts of Eldership in the New Testament," *Baptist Reformation Review* 7 (Summer, 1978): 29.

Chapter 5

1. Kenneth Scott Latourette, *History of Christianity*, 2 vols., 2nd ed. (New York: Harper & Row, 1975), 1: 269.
2. Ibid., 261.
3. Charles Colson, *Kingdoms in Conflict* (Grand Rapids: Zondervan, 1987), p. 274.
4. Ibid., p. 272.
5. John R. W. Stott, *The Cross of Christ* (Downers Grove: InterVarsity, 1986), p. 288.
6. Ibid., pp. 286,287.
7. The modern array of ecclesiastical titles accompanying the names of Christian leaders—reverend, archbishop, cardinal, pope, primate, metropolitan, canon, curate—is completely missing from the New Testament and would have appalled the apostles and early believers. Although both the Greeks and Jews employed a wealth of titles for their political

and religious leaders in order to express their power and authority, the early Christians avoided such titles. The early Christians used common and functional terms to describe themselves and their relationships. Some of these terms are "brother," "beloved," "fellow-worker," "laborer," "slave," "servant," "prisoner," "fellow-soldier," and "steward."

Of course there were prophets, teachers, apostles, evangelists, leaders, elders, and deacons within the first churches, but these terms were not used as formal titles for individuals. All Christians are saints, but there was no "Saint John." All are priests, but there was no "Priest Philip." Some are elders, but there was no "Elder Paul." Some are overseers, but there was no "Overseer John." Some are pastors, but there was no "Pastor James." Some are deacons, but there was no "Deacon Peter." Some are apostles, but there was no "Apostle Andrew."

Rather than gaining honor through titles and position, New Testament believers received honor primarily for their service and work (Acts 15:26; Rom. 16:1,2,4,12; 1 Cor. 16:15,16,18; 2 Cor. 8:18; Phil. 2:29,30; Col. 1:7; 4:12,13; 1 Thess. 5:12; 1 Tim. 3:1). The early Christians referred to each other by personal names (Timothy, Paul, Titus), the terms "brother" or "sister," or by describing an individual's spiritual character or work:

- Stephen, a man full of faith and of the Holy Spirit (Acts 6:5);
- Barnabas, a good man, and full of the Holy Spirit and of faith (Acts 11:24);
- Philip the evangelist (Acts 21:8);
- Greet Prisca and Aquila, my fellow workers in Christ Jesus (Rom. 16:3);
- Greet Mary, who has worked hard for you (Rom. 16:6).

8. Andrew Murray, *Humility* (Springdale: Whitaker, 1982), p. 7.
9. David Prior, *Jesus and Power* (Downers Grove: InterVarsity Press, 1987), p. 82.
10. John R. W. Stott, *Between Two Worlds: The Art of Preaching in the Twentieth Century* (Grand Rapids: Eerdmans, 1982), p. 320.
11. J. I. Packer, *Freedom and Authority* (Oakland: International Council on Biblical Inerrancy, 1981), p. 8.

Chapter 6

1. R. Paul Stevens, *Liberating the Laity* (Downers Grove: InterVarsity, 1985), p. 17.
2. George Eldon Ladd, *A Theology of the New Testament* (Grand Rapids: Eerdmans, 1974), p. 534.
3. J.A. Motyer, *The Message of James*, The Bible Speaks Today (Downers Grove: InterVarsity, 1985), p. 189.

4. Jon Zens, "The Major Concepts of Eldership in the New Testament," *Baptist Reformation Review* 7 (Summer, 1978): 28.
5. J.B. Lightfoot, *Saint Paul's Epistles to the Colossians and to Philemon* (London: MacMillan, 1892), p. 29,31.
6. Bruce Stabbert, *The Team Concept: Paul's Church Leadership Patterns or Ours?* (Tacoma: Hegg, 1982), p. 43.
7. Gerhard Kittel, "*aggelos*," in *Theological Dictionary of the New Testament*, eds. G. Kittel, and G. Friedrich, trans. and ed. G. W. Bromiley, 10 vols. (Grand Rapids: Eerdmans, 1964-76), 1 (1964): 86,87. (Hereafter cited as *Theological Dictionary of the New Testament.*)
8. Robert S. Rayburn, "Ministers, Elders, and Deacons," in *Order in the Offices: Essays Defining the Roles of Church Officers*, ed. Mark R. Brown (Duncansville: Classic Presbyterian Government Resources, 1993), pp. 223-227.
9. Robert Banks, *Paul's Idea of Community* (Grand Rapids: Eerdmans, 1980), p. 53.
10. Ibid., pp. 53,54.
11. Marjorie Warkentin, *Ordination* (Grand Rapids: Eerdmans, 1982), p. 100.
12. Dave and Vera Mace, *What's Happening to Clergy Marriages?* (Nashville: Abingdon, 1980), pp. 57,58.
13. John E. Johnson, "The Old Testament Offices as Paradigm for Pastoral Identity," *Bibliotheca Sacra* 152 (April-June, 1995): 194.
14. Ibid., 195.
15. Ibid., 199.
16. Ladd, *A Theology of the New Testament*, p. 534.
17. Alfred Kuen, *I Will Build My Church*, trans. Ruby Linbald (Chicago: Moody, 1971), p. 17.
18. Ibid., p. 253.

Chapter 7

1. F.F. Bruce, *The Book of the Acts*, The New International Commentary on the New Testament, rev. ed. (Grand Rapids: Eerdmans, 1988), p. 3.
2. Some scholars challenge the popular idea that Christians borrowed the eldership concept from the synagogue. See A.E. Harvey, "Elders," *The Journal of Theological Studies* 25 (October, 1974): 319; R. Alastair Campbell, *The Elders: Seniority Within Earliest Christianity* (Edinburgh: T&T Clark, 1994), p. 119.
3. Bruce, *The Book of the Acts*, p. 287.
4. William Kelly, *An Exposition of the Acts of the Apostles,* 3rd ed. (1890; repr. Denver: Wilson Foundation, 1952), p. 209.
5. The phrase in Acts 15:23, "the apostles and the brethren who are elders," is a bit unusual in Greek. It literally reads, "The apostles and the elders

brethren." The *Revised Version* (1881-85) translates this Greek phrase as, "The apostles and the elder brethren." According to this translation, "elders" is an adjective. If "elder brethren" is the correct translation, this is a definite identification of who the Jerusalem elders were. They were, indeed, the older men. However, Greek grammar does not require the translation "the elder brethren." Greek usage of the article in such appositional constructions is too imprecise to be certain. (See H. Hyman, *The Classical Review* 3[1889]: 73.) Following the norm in most modern English translations, then, it is better to understand the word "brethren" as a noun without an article—apposed to both "the apostles" and "the elders." Both the apostles and elders are brethren writing to fellow brethren. This rendering better fits the context. (See also F.F. Bruce *The Book of Acts*, p. 298.)

6. James Bannerman, *The Church of Christ*, 2 vols. (1869; repr. Cherry Hill: Mack, 1972), 2: 326. See also, William Cunningham, *Historical Theology*, 2 vols. (London: The Banner of Truth, 1969), 1: 59 ff.
7. Edwin Hatch, *The Organization of the Early Christian Churches* (London: Longmans, Green, and Co., 1901), pp. 170-172,175.
8. Ibid., p. 195.
9. For an excellent explanation of the elders' counsel and Paul's response, see David Gooding, *True to the Faith: A Fresh Approach to the Acts of the Apostles* (London: Hodder & Stoughton, 1990), pp. 366-372.
10. William Mitchell Ramsay, *St. Paul the Traveller and the Roman Citizen*, 3rd ed. (Grand Rapids: Baker, 1951), p. 121.
11. J. B. Lightfoot, *Saint Paul's Epistle to the Philippians* (New York: Macmillan, 1894), p. 193.
12. Roland Allen, *Missionary Methods: St. Paul's or Ours?* 6th ed. (1912; repr. Grand Rapids: Eerdmans, 1962), pp. 83,87,3.
13. Walter Bauer, *A Greek-English Lexicon of the New Testament and Other Early Christian Literature,* 2nd ed., trans. William F. Arndt and F. Wilbur Gingrich, rev. F. Wilbur Gingrich and Frederick W. Danker (Chicago: University of Chicago, 1979), s.v. "*ekklēsia*," p. 241. (Hereafter cited as Bauer, *A Greek-English Lexicon of the New Testament.*)
14. John Chrysostom, "A Commentary on the Acts of the Apostles," in *The Nicene and Post-Nicene Fathers*, 14 vols., First Series, ed. Philip Schaff (repr. Grand Rapids: Eerdmans, 1956), 11: 90. (Hereafter cited as *The Nicene and Post-Nicene Fathers*, First Series.)
15. Lawrence O. Richards, *Expository Dictionary of Bible Words* (Grand Rapids: Zondervan, 1985), s.v. "*appoint*," p. 68. John Calvin, *Institutes of the Christian Religion*, 2 vols., ed. John T. McNeill, trans. F.L. Battles (Philadelphia: Westminster, 1960), 2: 1066.
16. "This does not involve a choice by the group; here the word means

appoint, install, with the apostles as subject" (Bauer, *A Greek-English Lexicon of the New Testament*, s.v. "*cheirotoneō*," p. 881). "In Acts 14:23 the reference is not to election by the congregation. The presbyters are nominated by Paul and Barnabas and then with prayer and fasting they are instituted into their offices..." (E. Lohse, "*cheirotoneō*," in *Theological Dictionary of the New Testament*, 9 (1974): 437.

17. F.F. Bruce, *Answers to Questions* (Grand Rapids: Zondervan, 1972), pp. 29,30.
18. William Kelly, *Lectures on the Gospel of Matthew* (1868; repr. Denver: Wilson Foundation, 1971), p. 166.
19. Ignatius, *Ephesians*, 1. Unless otherwise stated, all quotes from the early Apostolic Fathers are taken from *The Apostolic Fathers*, ed. J.B. Lightfoot and R.J. Harmer (1891; repr. ed. Grand Rapids: Baker, 1984).
20. Thomas D. Lea and Hayne P. Griffin Jr., *1,2 Timothy, Titus*, The New American Commentary (Nashville: Broadman, 1992), p. 109; see also Campbell, *The Elders: Seniority Within Earliest Christianity*, p. 172.
21. Campbell, *The Elders: Seniority Within Earliest Christianity*, p. 172.
22. F.F. Bruce, "Lessons from the Early Church," in *In God's Community: Essays on the Church and Its Ministry*, eds. David J. Ellis and W. Ward Gasque (Wheaton: Shaw, 1978), p. 155. William L. Lane, *Hebrews 1-8*, Word Biblical Commentary (Dallas: Word, 1991), pp. liii, lv; Paul Ellingworth, *Commentary on Hebrews*, New International Greek Testament Commentary (Grand Rapids: Eerdmans, 1993), p. 26; Thomas Hewitt, *The Epistle to the Hebrews*, Tyndale Bible Commentaries (Grand Rapids: Eerdmans, 1960), p. 34.
23. *To the Ephesians*, 1.
24. A growing trend in biblical studies today explains the structure of the local church in terms of the Graeco-Roman household structure, which was the original social context. According to this line of thought, the senior head of the family and owner of the house in which the church met would naturally be the leader of the house church. In order to own a house large enough for a congregation to meet, the household head would most likely be a well-to-do, educated person. By society's standards and customs, he or she would serve as patron of the group, leading the household in prayer and worship and administering the group's finances for its needy members. The leadership of such a house church was then based on seniority and social status as was the case in all Graeco-Roman and Jewish households. R. Alastair Campbell writes:

    > So long as the local church was confined to one household, the household provided the leadership of the church. The church in the house came with its leadership so to speak 'built in'. The church that met in someone's house met under that person's presidency. The householder

was *ex hypothesi* a person of standing, a patron of others, and the space where the church met was his space, in which he was accustomed to the obedience of slaves and the deference of his wife and children. Those who came into it will have been to a large extent constrained by the norms of hospitality to treat the host as master of ceremonies, especially if he was a person of greater social standing or age than themselves. The table moreover was his table, and if any prayers were to be said, or bread or wine offered, the part was naturally his to play (*The Elders: Seniority Within Earliest Christianity*, p. 126.).

There is, of course, some truth to Campbell's theory. However, the New Testament Christian community and the apostles were not slaves to Graeco-Roman household patterns or Jewish synagogues. When writing to the church in Ephesus, Paul quotes a popular saying that the first Christians had developed, "if any man aspires to the office of overseer, it is a fine work he desires to do" (1 Tim. 3:1). Paul certainly concurs with this saying, but adds that a church overseer must be properly qualified before he can serve as a church overseer (1 Tim. 3:1-7). It is important to note that the apostolic qualifications for Christian eldership (overseership) do not list wealth, social status, seniority, or ownership of property as a requirement. Any mature, godly male could serve as a church elder (overseer) (1 Tim. 3:1-7). If a person opened his or her house for the church to meet, that did not, at least by apostolic standards, automatically make that person the spiritual leader of the group.

The newly founded Christian congregations were governed by God's Spirit and Christ's apostles. The apostles set the standards for these newly formed congregations by their distinctive, Spirit-inspired teachings (Acts 2:42; 1 Cor. 4:17; 11:34; 14:37,38; 1 Tim. 3:14,15). Thus the first churches were not simply reorganized synagogues or standard Roman or Jewish households. They were the Spirit-indwelt households of God that followed new standards for worship and community relationships. By trying to explain eldership in terms of the Roman household pattern or the Jewish community elder, of which we know very little, Campbell distorts the apostolic, New Testament eldership, *which is distinctly Christian.*

25. Gooding, *True to the Faith: A Fresh Approach to the Acts of the Apostles*, p. 360.
26. *The NIV Matthew Henry Commentary* (Grand Rapids: Zondervan, 1992), p. 529.
27. Richard Baxter, *The Reformed Pastor* (repr. Grand Rapids: Sovereign Grace, 1971), p. 7.
28. Michael Green, *The Second Epistle General of Peter and the General Epistle of Jude*, Tyndale Bible Commentaries (Grand Rapids: Eerdmans, 1968), p. 149.

29. Commenting on the verb *tithēmi* and its use in the middle voice, J.I. Packer writes: "In the middle voice (which insofar as it differs from the active accentuates the thought of action for the agent's own benefit).... The thought of God settling what shall be by sovereign decision runs through all these passages" (J.I. Packer, "*tithēmi*," in *The New International Dictionary of New Testament Theology*, ed. Colin Brown, 3 vols. (Grand Rapids: Zondervan, 1 (1975): 477).
30. H. W. Beyer, "*episkopos*," in *Theological Dictionary of the New Testament*, 2 (1964): 612.
31. Ibid., p. 614.
32. The best rendering seems to be, "the church of God, which He obtained by means of the blood of His own One." For an alternate translation, *The Revised English Bible* reads, "the church of the Lord, which he won for himself by his own blood."
33. Gooding, *True to the Faith: A Fresh Approach to the Acts of the Apostles*, p. 360.
34. Baxter, *The Reformed Pastor*, p. 55.
35. Gooding, *True to the Faith: A Fresh Approach to the Acts of the Apostles*, pp. 356,357.
36. J. Behm, "*noutheteō*," in *Theological Dictionary of the New Testament*, 4 (1967): 1019.
37. Gooding, *True to the Faith: A Fresh Approach to the Acts of the Apostles*, p. 362.
38. Kelly, *An Exposition of the Acts of the Apostles*, pp. 314,315.
39. C. H. Mackintosh, *Genesis to Deuteronomy: Notes on the Pentateuch* (1881, repr., ed. Neptune: Loizeaux , 1972), pp. 760-762.

Chapter 8

1. Ernst Käsemann, "Ministry and Community in the New Testament," in *Essays on New Testament Themes* (Naperville: Alec R. Allenson, 1964), p. 86.
2. Hans Küng, *The Church* (New York: Sheed and Ward, 1967), p. 405; also Hans Conzelmann, *History of Primitive Christianity*, trans. John E. Steely (New York: Abingdon, 1973), p. 106.
3. As to the presence of elders in the church at Corinth at this time (A.D. 50), we are not informed. We do know from the letter of *1 Clement* (ca. A.D. 96), which is a noninspired letter from the church in Rome to the church in Corinth, that there was a well-established eldership in Corinth forty years later. The letter of *1 Clement* indicates that the apostles themselves had appointed elders in Corinth, but we don't know exactly when (see pages 266, 267).
4. John Calvin, *The Epistles of Paul the Apostle to the Romans and to the*

Thessalonians, Calvin's Commentaries, trans. Ross Mackenzie, ed. D.W. and T.F. Torrance (Grand Rapids: Eerdmans, 1973), p. 371.

5. There are three present tense participles (labor, lead, and admonish) preceded by one definite article (*tous*) and joined by the repetition of the conjunction "and" (*kai*).
6. James Denney, *The Epistles to the Thessalonians*, The Expositors' Bible (Cincinnati: Jennings & Graham, n.d.), p. 205.
7. Bo Reicke, "*prohistēmi*," in *Theological Dictionary of the New Testament*, 6 (1968): 701,702.
8. E. K. Simpson, *Pastoral Epistles* (Grand Rapids: Eerdmans, 1954), p. 77.
9. John R.W. Stott, *The Gospel and the End of Time: The Message of 1 & 2 Thessalonians* (Downers Grove: InterVarsity, 1991), pp. 120,121.
10. Denney, *The Epistles to the Thessalonians*, pp. 207, 208.
11. George G. Findlay, *The Epistles to the Thessalonians*, The Cambridge Bible for Schools and Colleges (Cambridge: Cambridge University, 1908), p. 117.
12. William Hendriksen, *Exposition of I and II Thessalonians,* New Testament Commentary (Grand Rapids: Baker, 1955), p. 135.
13. E.J. Bricknell, *The First and Second Epistles to the Thessalonians*, Westminster Commentaries (London: Methuen, 1932), p. 59.
14. Paul E. Billheimer, *Love Covers* (Fort Washington: Christian Literature Crusade, 1981), p. 34.
15. Francis Schaeffer, *The Mark of the Christian* (Downers Grove: InterVarsity, 1970), p. 22.
16. Leon Morris, *Testaments of Love* (Grand Rapids: Eerdmans, 1981), p. 205.
17. Leon Morris, *The First and Second Epistles to the Thessalonians*, The New International Commentary of the New Testament (Grand Rapids: Eerdmans, 1959), p. 167.
18. Fenton John Anthony Hort, *The Christian Ecclesia* (1897; repr. ed. London: Macmillan, 1914), p. 123.
19. John Eadie, *A Commentary on the Greek Text of the Epistles of Paul to the Thessalonians*, ed. William Young (1877; repr. ed. Minneapolis: James Publications, 1976), p. 196.
20. Ernest Best, "Bishops and Deacons: Philippians 1:1," in *Studia Evangelica*, ed. F.L. Cross (Berlin: Akademia Verlag, 1968), 4: 371.
21. Polycarp, *Philippians*, 5,6.
22. Ignatius, *Polycarp*, 1,1;5,2;6,1.
23. Polycarp, *Philippians*, 1,1.
24. Polycarp, *Philippians*, 5.
25. John Eadie, *A Commentary on the Greek Text of the Epistles of Paul to the Philippians* (1894; repr. ed. Minneapolis: James and Klock, 1977), p. 4.

26. At the beginning of the second century, many churches developed three separate offices or leadership ministries. That was the start of episcopally structured churches:

    The overseer (bishop)
    A council of elders
    A body of deacons

    At the start of the second century, the overseer (bishop) presided over one local church, not a group of churches. Thus he is called the monarchical bishop. Through the centuries, inordinate authority became concentrated in the bishop. Unchecked by the New Testament Scriptures, his role continued to expand. The bishop became ruler over a group of churches. Some bishops emerged as supreme over other bishops. Eventually they formed councils of bishops. Finally, in the West, one bishop emerged as head over every Christian and every church.

    But in the churches of the New Testament period, there was no clearly defined, three-office system. Instead, there were only two offices as found in Philippians 1:1.

    The council of overseer elders
    The body of deacons

27. Quoted in *The Faith of the Early Fathers,* ed. and trans. W.A. Jurgens, 3 vols. (Collegeville: The Liturgical Press, 1979), 2: 194.
28. J.B. Lightfoot, *Saint Paul's Epistle to the Philippians* (London: Macmillan, 1894), p. 99.
29. Ibid., p. 95.

Chapter 9

1. Philip H. Towner, *1-2 Timothy & Titus*, The IVP New Testament Commentary Series (Downers Grove: InterVarsity, 1994), p. 123.
2. J.N.D. Kelly, *The Pastoral Epistles* (London: Adam and Charles Black, 1972), p. 115.
3. Patrick Fairbairn, *Pastoral Epistles* (1874; repr. Minneapolis: James and Klock, 1976), p. 70.
4. Bauer, *A Greek-English Lexicon of the New Testament*, s.v. "*anastrephō*," p. 61.
5. Kelly, *The Pastoral Epistles*, p. 86.
6. George W. Knight III, *The Pastoral Epistles*, The New International Greek Testament Commentary (Grand Rapids: Eerdmans, 1992), p. 156.
7. Kelly, *The Pastoral Epistles*, p. 75.
8. Although this view seems to have the literalness of the phrase in its favor,

and so must be taken seriously, it is in disharmony with the overall biblical teaching regarding marriage for several reasons:

(1) The Bible unequivocally teaches that death dissolves the marriage bond and frees the living spouse to remarry without sinning (1 Cor. 7:39; Rom. 7:2,3).

(2) From the biblical perspective, remarriage after the death of a spouse is not reproachful. Those who hold the married-only-once view cannot identify the shame or defect in remarriage that disqualifies a man from eldership or deaconship. This is especially true of deacons. Since deacons are not the spiritual overseers of the church, it is close to impossible to understand the reproach a deacon would face if he remarried following the death of his spouse. In fact, those who try to show the reproach of a second marriage do little more than raise serious questions about the first marriage as well.

This interpretation smacks of false asceticism, the very thing Paul condemns in 1 Timothy 4:3. Of the false teachers at Ephesus, Paul says they are "men who forbid marriage and advocate abstaining from foods." Yet this interpretation portrays Paul as forbidding church leaders and needy widows to remarry.

(3) This interpretation creates two standards for two grades of saints. For some bewildering reason, elders, deacons, and needy widows cannot remarry following the death of a spouse, but other saints can. Such division in the family of God is incongruous with the rest of the New Testament. "To postulate grades of official sanctity," E.K. Simpson writes, "among members of the same spiritual body may be orthodox clericalism, but it is heterodox Christianity" (*The Pastoral Epistles* [Grand Rapids: Eerdmans, 1954], p. 50).

(4) In the context of instruction on marriage, singleness, and remarriage, Paul says to the Corinthians, "And this I say for your own benefit; not to put a restraint upon you" (1 Cor. 7:35). This interpretation of the phrase "the husband of one wife," however, restrains an innocent man, penalizing him for not having the gift of singleness.

(5) First Timothy 5:9 lists the qualifications for widows whom the local church is obligated to support: "Let a widow be put on the list only if she is not less than sixty years old, having been the wife of one man." If the phrase "the wife of one man" means having only one husband in a lifetime, then Paul's later counsel to younger widows to remarry is very

confusing. For verse 14, Paul specifically urges younger widows to marry: "Therefore, I want younger widows to get married, bear children, keep house, and give the enemy no occasion for reproach." What if a widow's second husband were to die? Would she then no longer be eligible for the widows' roll because she followed the apostle's advice to remarry when she was young and, therefore, had been the wife of two men? This would be confusing counsel indeed. If the phrase "the wife of one man" doesn't limit a woman to having but one husband in a lifetime, then there is no conflict in Paul's counsel.

(6) It is almost unthinkable that Paul, who is so sensitive to marital issues (1 Cor. 7:2-5,7,8,15,32-36,39), would use an ambiguous, three-word phrase to teach something so vital to widows and widowers. It is particularly unusual that he would offer no further explanation for a teaching that is in apparent disharmony with the rest of Scripture. In 1 Corinthians, for example, where Paul counsels unmarried Christians to consider singleness, he is quick to qualify his words. He knew the propensity to asceticism. He knew that people could take his words to mean he was speaking disparagingly of marriage. But he is in no way discrediting marriage. Marriage is the norm, but singleness, which Paul wants his readers to consider, can be effectively used to further the work of God. So he writes, "Yet I wish that all men were even as I myself am. However, each man has his own gift from God, one in this manner, and another in that. But I say to the unmarried and to widows that it is good for them if they remain even as I. But if they do not have self-control, let them marry, for it is better to marry than to burn" (1 Cor. 7:7-9). This counsel is for elders and deacons, as well as for every other member of the congregation. If an elder is a widower and decides to remain single for greater undivided service to God, that is good. But if he must marry, that is also good.

(7) Finally, if this phrase means married only once, it is an extremely frightening and potentially harmful restriction. During the time that Paul wrote, and for the next eighteen hundred years, it was not uncommon for a person to lose a spouse through death at a relatively young age. So if a good elder or deacon lost his wife and remarried, he also lost his place of leadership in the church. That would hurt the whole church. Good elders and deacons are hard to find, so to disqualify an elder or deacon because he remarried is a terrible loss. We know that God loves the church. Thus it is hard to believe that He would place a requirement upon its leaders that would bring harm to them or to the church.

9. J.E. Huther, *Critical and Exegetical Hand-book to the Epistles to*

Timothy and Titus, Meyer's Commentary on the New Testament (New York: Funk and Wagnalls, 1890), p. 118.

10. Philip H. Towner, *The Goal of Our Instruction: The Structure of Theology and Ethics in the Pastoral Epistles*, Journal for the Study of the New Testament Supplement Series 34 (Sheffield: JOST Press, 1989), p. 232.
11. The Greek word *nēphalios* means "wineless" or sobriety in the use of wine. A few interpreters think that in this context the word should be understood in its literal sense, but that is doubtful. In verse 3, Paul writes that overseers must not be "addicted to wine." Paul is not warning overseers twice about the use of wine. Instead, he is using the word "temperate," both in verse 2 and in verse 11, in a figurative sense to mean mental sobriety.
12. Knight, *The Pastoral Epistles*, p. 159.
13. Lewis J. Lord, "Coming To Grips with Alcoholism," *U. S. News & World Report* (November 30, 1987): 56-62.
14. J.A. Motyer, *The Message of James*, The Bible Speaks Today (Downers Grove: InterVarsity, 1985), p. 136.
15. Knight, *The Pastoral Epistles*, p. 160.
16. Donald Guthrie, *The Pastoral Epistles*, The Tyndale New Testament Commentaries (Grand Rapids: Eerdmans, 1957), p. 81.
17. Bauer, *A Greek-English Lexicon of the New Testament*, s.v. "*echō*," p. 332.
18. Knight, *The Pastoral Epistles*, p. 165.
19. Some commentators deny that the "and...also" (Greek, *kai...de*) construction refers back to overseers. They contend that these words add only a further precaution about deacons. For example, Alford writes, "the *de* introduces a caution—the slight contrast of a necessary addition to their mere present character" (Henry Alford, *The Greek New Testament,* 4 vols., 5th ed.[London: Rivingtons, 1871], 3: 327).

    It is difficult to be certain, but the Greek construction, *kai* ("also") before *houtoi* ("these"), seems best served by understanding that deacons are compared to overseers in the testing process. It creates no problem, however, if the text does not refer back to the overseers. First Timothy 5:24,25 shows that an examination of elders was necessary, (by inference, if overseers needed to be examined as to their qualifications, so do deacons). As long as character qualifications are demanded, examination will also be demanded.
20. Richard C. Trench, *Synonyms of the New Testament* (1880; repr. Grand Rapids: Eerdmans, 1969), p. 278.
21. Walter Grundmann, "*dokimazō*," *in Theological Dictionary of the New Testament*, 2 (1964): 256.
22. Bauer, *A Greek-English Lexicon of the New Testament*, s.v. "*dokimazō*," p. 202.

23. *Presbyteros* in 1 Timothy 5:1 is correctly translated by the NASB as "older man." The context refers to age and gender, not to the office of elder. The comparison is between older men and younger men and older women and younger women. Paul is not referring to elders and elderesses. In verse 17 of this same chapter, however, *presbyteroi* must be translated as "elders" in the official sense of community leaders. The word *presbyteros* bears both meanings. The context alone determines the difference.

    John the apostle, refers to himself as *ho presbyteros*, "the elder," but it is not clear exactly what he means by this self-designation. The Second Epistle of John begins with the words, "The elder [*ho presbyteros*] to the chosen lady and her children." The Third Epistle also begins, "The elder to the beloved Gaius." John could mean that he was "the elder," *par excellence*, that is, the distinguished Christian teacher and leader of the Church because of his unique status as the only living original apostle. Or *ho presbyteros* may be simply an honorable title John acquired in his old age, meaning "the ancient one," "the senior man," or "the patriarch." Either view is possible, and the last is perhaps best. At the time John wrote these epistles, he was an exceptionally old man, "a veritable patriarch in age" writes John Stott (John R.W. Stott, *The Epistle of John*, Tyndale Bible Commentaries [Grand Rapids: Eerdmans, 1964], p. 40). By using *ho presbyteros*, in the sense of age, John is referring to himself as "the aged one," "the ancient one," "the senior man." It is, therefore, a well-known, special designation of honor bestowed on him by the Christian community.

    According to many Bible translations, Paul also refers to himself as "the old man" or "the aged one." In Philemon 9 we read, "Paul, the aged [*presbytes*], and now also the prisoner of Christ Jesus." Many commentators, however, understand *presbytēs* here to mean "ambassador," not "old man." The meaning of *presbytēs* in this passage is a debatable point.
24. T.C. Skeat (1907-1992), former Keeper of Manuscripts of the British Museum, documents from Greek literature examples of *malista* used as a defining term. He argues quite effectively that Paul uses *malista* as a defining term in 1 Timothy 4:10; 2 Timothy 4:13 and Titus 1:10; see "'Especially the Parchments:' A Note on 2 Timothy 4:13," in *The Journal of Theological Studies* 30 (April, 1979):173-177.
25. Knight, *The Pastoral Epistles*, p. 232.
26. R.C. Sproul, "The Whole Man," in *The Preacher and Preaching*, ed. S. T. Logan (Phillipsburg: Presbyterian and Reformed, 1986), pp. 107,108.
27. Most commentators think that the two terms "shepherds" and "teachers" refer to one group: shepherd-teachers. Others think that "shepherds" and "teachers" are two entirely distinct groups. Daniel B. Wallace argues quite effectively for the view that the two terms are distinct, yet related. He

argues that the first term "pastor" is a subset of the second, "teacher," since similar formations are well attested in many other adjective and noun constructions. ("The Semantic Range of the Article-Noun-Kai-Noun Plural Construction in the New Testament," *Grace Theological Journal* 4 [Spring, 1983]: 59-84).

28. For a thorough defense of the three-office view see, *Order in the Offices: Essays Defining the Roles of Church Officers*, ed. Mark R. Brown (Duncansville: Classic Presbyterian Government Resources, 1993).
29. Huther, *Critical and Exegetical Hand-book to the Epistles to Timothy and Titus*, p. 181.
30. William Hendriksen, *Exposition of the Pastoral Epistles*, New Testament Commentary (Grand Rapids: Baker, 1957), pp. 179,180.
31. R.C.H. Lenski, *The Interpretation of St. Paul's Epistles to the Colossians, to the Thessalonians, to Timothy, to Titus and to Philemon* (Minneapolis: Augsburg, 1964), p. 680.
32. John Calvin, *The Second Epistle of Paul to the Corinthians, and the Epistles to Timothy, Titus and Philemon*, trans. T.A. Smail, ed. D.W. and T.F. Torrance (Grand Rapids: Eerdmans, 1964), p. 261.
33. A.J. Broomhall, *Hudson Taylor and China's Open Century*, 6 vols., vol. 4: *Survivors' Pact* (London: Hodder and Stoughton, 1984), p. 289.
34. Knight, *The Pastoral Epistles*, p. 235.
35. Knight, *The Pastoral Epistles*, p. 236.
36. See Elinor Burkett and Frank Bruni, *A Gospel of Shame: Children, Sexual Abuse and the Catholic Church* (New York: Viking, 1993).
37. J. Carl Laney, *A Guide to Church Discipline* (Minneapolis: Bethany, 1985), p. 124.
38. Lenski, *The Interpretation of St. Paul's Epistles to the Colossians, to the Thessalonians, to Timothy, to Titus, and to Philemon*, p. 691.
39. Simpson, *Pastoral Epistles*, p. 80.
40. Lenski, *The Interpretation of St. Paul's Epistles to the Colossians, to the Thessalonians, to Timothy, to Titus, and to Philemon*, p. 691,692.

Chapter 10

1. R.J. Knowling, "Acts of the Apostles," in *The Expositor's Greek Testaments*, ed. W. Robertson Nicoll, 5 vols. (1900-10; repr. Grand Rapids: Eerdmans, 1976), 2: 169.
2. F.J.A. Hort, *The Christian Ecclesia* (1897; repr. ed. London: Macmillan, 1914), p. 176.
3. F.F. Bruce, *The Letters of Paul: An Expanded Paraphrase* (Grand Rapids: Eerdmans, 1965), p. 291.
4. John Calvin, *The Second Epistle of Paul to the Corinthians, and the*

Epistles to Timothy, Titus and Philemon, trans. T.A. Smail, ed. D.W. and T.F. Torrance (Grand Rapids: Eerdmans, 1964), p. 358.

5. A.E. Harvey, "Elders," *The Journal of Theological Studies* 25 (October, 1974): 330,331.
6. E.F. Scott, *The Pastoral Epistles*, The Moffatt New Testament Commentary (London: Hodder and Stoughton, 1936), p. 155.
7. John C. Pollock, *Hudson Taylor and Maria* (Grand Rapids: Zondervan, 1962), p. 33.
8. Hermann Cremer, *Biblico-Theological Lexicon of New Testament Greek*, trans. W. Urwick (Edinburgh: T. & T. Clark, 1895), s.v. "*philagathos*," p. 9.
9. William Hendriksen, *Pastoral Epistles*, New Testament Commentary (Grand Rapids: Baker, 1957), p. 348.
10. Walter Grundmann, "*philagathos*," in *Theological Dictionary of the New Testament*, 1 (1964): 18.
11. George W. Knight III, *The Pastoral Epistles*, The New International Greek Testament Commentary (Grand Rapids: Eerdmans, 1992), p. 293.
12. Newport J.D. White, "The First and Second Epistles to Timothy and the Epistles to Titus," in T*he Expositor's Greek Testament*, ed. W. Robertson Nicoll, 5 vols. (1900-10; repr. ed., Grand Rapids: Eerdmans, 1976), 4: 188.
13. Calvin, *The Second Epistle of Paul to the Corinthians, and the Epistles to Timothy, Titus and Philemon*, p. 361.

Chapter 11

1. J. Ramsey Michaels, *1 Peter*, Word Biblical Commentary (Waco: Word, 1988), p. 262.
2. R.C.H. Lenski, *The Interpretation of the Epistles of St. Peter, St. John and St. Jude* (Minneapolis: Augsburg, 1966), p. 217.
3. C.E.B. Cranfield, *The First Epistle of Peter* (London: SCM, 1950), p. 110.
4. Ibid., p. 110.
5. The mid-fourth century Greek manuscript, Codex Vaticanus (B) omits the participle, *overseeing*, as does Codex Sinaiticus (Aleph), the eleventh century Codex Colbertinus (33), and Coptic Sahidac (the oldest Egyptian version). But *oversight* is included in the oldest, and perhaps best, manuscript (P^{72}) as well as in the Codex Sinaiticus by a later corrector, Codex Alexandrinus (A), Codex Leicestrensis (69), Codex Athous Laure (1739), the Latin Vulgate, the Coptic Bohairic, and all later manuscripts.

   The overall evidence favors the inclusion of the participle for the following reasons: (1) the participle, *overseeing,* is superfluous. The text makes perfectly good sense without it, so it is difficult to see why a scribe would add it to the text. It is not a characteristic interpolation. (2) The widespread belief among ancient scholars that bishops and elders are two separate offices with bishops being superior to elders (priests) stands against the addition of the participle by later scribes. Elders (priests), many ancient churchmen believed, did not do the work of a bishop. (3) The word *overseer* is a participle, and this agrees with Peter's frequent use of it. (4) Peter has already used the combination of shepherd and overseer in 2:25.

6. Num. 27:16,17; Jer. 23:2; Ezek. 34:11,12; Zech. 11:16; Acts 20:28; 1 Pet. 2:25; 5:2.
7. Lenski, *The Interpretation of the Epistles of St. Peter, St. John and St. Jude*, pp. 218,219.
8. J.H. Jowett, *The Redeemed Family of God, Studies in the Epistles of Peter* (New York: Hodder and Stoughton, n.d.), p. 186.
9. Cranfield, *The First Epistle of Peter*, p. 112.
10. Jowett, *The Redeemed Family of God*, p. 189.
11. Cranfield, *The First Epistle of Peter*, p. 113.
12. Lenski, *The Interpretation of the Epistles of St. Peter, St. John and St. Jude*, p. 219.
13. W. Foerster, "*klēros*," in *Theological Dictionary of the New Testament*, 3 (1965): 763.
14. Peter H. Davids, *The First Epistle of Peter*, The New International Commentary on the New Testament (Grand Rapids: Eerdmans, 1990), p. 181.
15. John Brown, *Expository Discourses on 1 Peter*, 2 vols. (1848; repr. Carlisle: The Banner of Truth, 1975), 2: 453.
16. I. Howard Marshall, *1 Peter*, The IVP New Testament Commentary Series (Downers Grove: InterVarsity, 1991), p. 164.
17. Robert Leighton, *Commentary on First Peter* (1853; repr. Grand Rapids: Kregel, 1972), p. 473.
18. Polycarp, *Philippians* 5.
19. Davids, *The First Epistle of Peter*, p. 184.

Chapter 12

1. For arguments for this early date, read Douglas J. Moo, *James*, Tyndale New Testament Commentaries (Grand Rapids: Eerdmans, 1985), pp. 30-34.
2. James B. Adamson, *The Epistle of James*, The New International Commentary on the New Testament (Grand Rapids: Eerdmans, 1976), p. 210.
3. Thomas Manton, *An Exposition of the Epistle of James* (Grand Rapids: Associated Publishers and Authors, n.d.), p. 450.
4. S.J. Kistemaker, *Exposition of the Epistle of James and the Epistles of John*, New Testament Commentary (Grand Rapids: Baker, 1986), p. 177.
5. Manton, *An Exposition of the Epistle of James*, p. 452.

6. R.V.G. Tasker, *The General Epistle of James*, Tyndale Bible Commentaries (Grand Rapids: Eerdmans, 1956), p. 129.
7. C.L. Mitton, *The Epistle of James* (Grand Rapids: Eerdmans, 1966), p. 198.
8. The aorist participle "anointing" can be understood as contemporaneous with the main verb "let them pray," or as preceding prayer. The former—at the same time as prayer—seems most likely, but we cannot be certain.
9. Matt. 5:13,29,30,39-41; 6:3,24,25; Lk. 14:26,33.
10. J.A. Motyer, *The Message of James*, The Bible Speaks Today (Downers Grove: InterVarsity, 1985), p. 66.

Chapter 13

1. *Shepherd of Hermas*, Visions 2,4.
2. Ibid., Visions 3,5; Similitudes 9,27.
3. *1 Clement*, 42.
4. Ibid., 44.
5. John Chrysostom, "Homilies on Hebrews," in *The Nicene and Post-Nicene Fathers*, First Series, 14: 518.
6. William Kelly, *An Exposition of the Epistle to the Hebrews* (1905; repr. ed. Charlotte: Books for Christians, n.d.), p. 267.
7. In Hebrews 11:2 the writer speaks of "the elders," [*hoi presbyteroi*], or as the NASB translation expresses it, "the men of old." Here *hoi presbyteroi* does not mean church officers or older men, but "the ones of old," "the ancients," "the ancestors," "the earlier generations." It includes both men and women, verses 11,31.
8. R.C.H. Lenski, *The Interpretation of the Epistle to the Hebrews and the Epistle of James* (Minneapolis: Augburg, 1966), p. 491.
9. William L. Lane, *Hebrews*, Word Biblical Commentary, 2 vols. (Waco: Word, 1982), 2: 555.
10. Lenski, *The Interpretation of the Epistle to the Hebrews and the Epistle of James*, p. 491.
11. Lane, *Hebrews*, 2: 556.

Chapter 14

1. Kenneth O. Gangel, *Feeding and Leading* (Wheaton: Victor, 1989), p. 313.
2. Ibid., p. 309.
3. Bruce Stabbert, *The Team Concept: Paul's Church Leadership Patterns or Ours?* (Tacoma: Heggs, 1982), p. 120.
4. Neil Summerton, *A Noble Task: Eldership and Ministry in the Local Church*, 2nd ed. (Carlisle: Paternoster, 1994), p. 33.

5. John Nelson Darby (1800-1882), father of modern dispensational theology and dominant leader in the exclusive branch of the Brethren Movement, taught that churches or missionaries today cannot lawfully appoint elders because there is no one with God-given authority to officially appoint elders. Darby defends this teaching with two arguments:

(1) He interprets the fact that the only New Testament examples of elder appointment are by apostles or their delegates to mean that only apostles can appoint elders (see "Reply to Two Fresh Letters from Count De Gasparin," in *The Collected Writings of J.N. Darby*, ed. William Kelly [repr. ed., Sunbury: Believers Bookshelf, n.d.], 4:339-373). Apostolic appointment is thus a requirement for New Testament elders. Since there are no living apostles or delegates today, there can be no office of eldership.

(2) Darby also argues that the churches in Paul's day were beginning to fall into spiritual ruin, thus God, in judgment, did not allow the office of eldership or any external structure of the church to continue. Elders, therefore, were limited to the first century churches, and are irrecoverably lost to churches today (see R.A. Huebner, *The Ruin of the Church, Eldership, and Ministry of the Word and Gift* [Morganville: Present Truth, n.d.], pp. 33-35).

It is true that the only New Testament examples of elder appointment are by Paul or one of his delegates (Acts 14:23; Titus 1:5), but to conclude from these examples, as Darby does, that the biblical writers intended to teach that only apostles can or did appoint elders is an interpretation of the historical facts that cannot be substantiated by the facts themselves or by the rest of the New Testament's teaching on eldership. Darby's conclusion goes beyond the expressed teaching of Scripture. He is arguing from silence. The New Testament doesn't say that only apostles appointed elders. So it is important to be able to differentiate between what the Bible states historically and what Darby infers doctrinally from these historical examples and then teaches as biblical principle.

To illustrate, one can take the same historical facts that Darby has taken and propose a completely different theory. One can say that Paul's example of appointing elders is meant to be a biblical model for all church planters, missionaries and their helpers, elders, or evangelists. It can also be asserted that Paul's authority to appoint elders rested not only on the fact that he was an apostle but that he was, at least in the case of the Galatian churches, the original church planter, evangelist, spiritual father, and proven servant of God (Acts 14:23). Since the historical examples Darby uses don't expressly confirm or negate his theory that only apostles have the authority to appoint elders, we must test his theory by the whole of Scripture's teaching on eldership.

Starting with the Old Testament, government by elders was a fundamental institution in Israel. Yet nowhere in the Old Testament are we informed about the qualifications for elders or who had the authority to appoint elders. We can only assume that such matters were left to the people of God and their leaders. Since, according to Scripture, men and women were made to rule over the earth, organizing society in a righteous and fair way is a God-given duty (Gen. 1:28).

In the New Testament, the overriding concern regarding eldership is not who can lawfully appoint elders, but who is properly qualified to be an elder? In the lists of elder qualifications, apostolic appointment is never mentioned. The New Testament, in agreement with the Old Testament, does not make the appointment of elders the exclusive duty of a special class of people. The issue of who has the rightful authority to appoint elders is not discussed in the New Testament. The central issue focuses on qualifications and examination.

The apostles fully expected the churches to be self-perpetuating, self-governing, and dependent on God for their future progress and needs. Paul's written instructions to Timothy and Titus concerning the qualifications and examination of elders were meant to remain with the churches after the departure of Timothy and Titus in order to guide the churches in their absence. These letters, which are not strictly private letters, provide sufficient authority and guidance for the local church, the elders, or missionaries to appoint church elders (1 Tim. 3:15).

Furthermore, the fact that Paul's instructions concerning the qualifications and examination of elders were written toward the end of his life suggests that he was arranging for the perpetuation of the office, not its demise. Thus we can say today with the same spirit of encouragement and approval, "if any man aspires to the office of overseer, it is a fine work he desires to do." But we must add, in accordance with Scripture, that such a person "must be above reproach."

From the divine side, the Scripture states that the Holy Spirit places men in the church as overseers to shepherd the flock (Acts 20:28). Surely the Holy Spirit hasn't departed, so as long as the Holy Spirit motivates and equips men to be pastor elders, the office of eldership must continue. But in order for the local assembly to be able to distinguish between those the Spirit has separated to this work and those who are self-willed and unqualified, the local church and its leaders must examine the candidates according to the apostolic qualifications (1 Tim. 3:10).

Finally, the elders, as the official overseers of the church, have the authority, as implied in their office, to develop and appoint others as elders. Overseeing a church, or any organization, includes the duty of assuring future, ongoing leadership. The apostles established the offices of elder and deacon and provided written directives so that churches and their leaders would know the proper qualifications for future elders and deacons. These offices should be established, maintained, and upheld by all local churches and church planters today. Darby is drawing an unwarranted, indefensible conclusion that in the end eliminates the very thing Paul sought to establish by appointing elders—a qualified, recognized, official leadership body for each local church.

Regarding Darby's other theory, which states that because the Church is in ruin there can be no outward structure of the original apostolic order, we again must point out that this is another gratuitous assumption. Even if Darby is right about the ruin of the Church, he has not demonstrated why faithful believers cannot still gather together and organize themselves on the basis of apostolic instruction and example as provided by the New Testament. This is just another example of a personal assumption and pronouncement that must not be confused with biblical truth.

6. *New Bible Dictionary*, 2nd ed., s.v. "Ordination," by Leon Morris, p. 861.
7. Alfred Plummer, "The Pastoral Epistles," in *The Expositor's Bible*, ed. W. Robertson Nicoll, 25 vols. (New York: Armstrong, 1903), 23: 219-221.
8. Marjorie Warkentin, *Ordination* (Grand Rapids: Eerdmans, 1982), p. 33.
9. Acts 6 is the first recorded example of the laying on of hands in the Christian community. The imposition of hands is used for various reasons in the Bible, but as James Orr writes, "The primary idea seems to be that of conveyance or transference (cf. Lev. 16:21) but, conjoined with this, in certain instances are the ideas of identification and of devotion to God."

   Looking first at Old Testament examples, we note that the laying on of hands was used to:

   - convey blessing (Gen. 48:14)
   - identify with a sacrifice to God (Lev. 1:4)
   - transfer sin (Lev. 16:21)
   - transfer defilement (Lev. 24:14)
   - identify man's actions with God's (2 Kings 13:16)
   - set people apart, such as in conveying a special commission, responsibility, or authority (Num. 8:10,14; 27:15-23; Deut. 34:9)

   In the New Testament, the laying on of hands was used to:

   - convey blessing (Matt. 19:15; Mark 10:16)
   - convey the Holy Spirit's healing power (Mark 6:5; 8:23,25; 16:18; Luke 4:40; 13:13; Acts 9:12; 19:11; 28:8)
   - convey the Holy Spirit to certain believers through the apostles' hands (Acts 8:17-19; 19:6)

• convey healing and the Holy Spirit to Paul through Ananias's hands (Acts 9:17)
• convey a spiritual gift to Timothy through Paul's hands (2 Tim. 1:6)
• set apart or place in office (Acts 6:6; 13:3; 1 Tim. 4:14; 5:22)

In light of this background, it seems reasonable to assume that the imposition of hands in Acts 6 visually expressed the apostles' blessing, commissioned the Seven to a special task (Num. 27:22,23), and transferred the authority to do the job. Because of the Seven's responsible task of handling large sums of money (Acts 4:34-37) and the growing tensions between the Hellenistic Jews and Hebrews, the apostles knew that the situation demanded an official, public act of appointment.

The laying on of hands in Acts 6, however, did not install the Seven to higher ministerial positions (priest or minister), nor did it make the Seven successors to the apostles. It was not ordination that authorized them to preach and administer the sacraments. The laying on of hands did not convey grace or the Holy Spirit, for the Seven were already filled with the Holy Spirit. Rather, the laying on of hands commissioned the Seven to serve the poor and needy.

At the beginning of the first missionary journey, the church at Antioch laid hands on Paul and Barnabas: "Then, when they had fasted and prayed and laid their hands on them, they sent them away" (Acts 13:3). Despite what leading commentators say, this passage has nothing to do with ordination in the modern sense. It is another example of how tradition blinds the eyes of even the best expositors. J.B. Lightfoot, for instance, wrongly refers to this account as Paul's ordination to apostleship: "It does not follow that the actual call to the apostleship should come from an outward personal communication with our Lord... But the actual investiture, the completion of his call, as may be gathered from St. Luke's narrative, took place some years later at Antioch (Acts 13:2)" (*Saint Paul's Epistle to the Galatians* [1865; repr. London: Macmillan, 1892], p. 98). This passage cannot refer to ordination as we know it for the following reasons:

Barnabas and Paul were already eminently gifted men in the church (Acts 13:1). The Jerusalem church had sent Barnabas to investigate and encourage the new work at Antioch (Acts 11:22-26). Both Paul and Barnabas were the leading teachers in the church and were veteran laborers for Christ. Paul was already an apostle—appointed directly by Jesus Christ. No man or group could claim to have ordained him as an apostle (Acts 26:16-19; Gal. 1:1). Thus, this act was not ordination to the ministry, for Paul and Barnabas were already in the ministry. Instead, the Spirit selected Paul and Barnabas for a special task in spreading the gospel, not for a higher office or gift.

According to the record, Paul and Barnabas did not receive the Holy Spirit, spiritual gifts, or any other power for service on this occasion. They already possessed the Holy Spirit and His gifts (Acts 13:1).

Higher officials did not lay hands on Paul and Barnabas. It appears that the church and its leaders placed their hands on their two brethren (Acts 14:26; 15:40) who were leaving the church to minister, not coming to the church to minister.

What, then, is the significance of the imposition of hands in this situation? The context indicates that the church, by prayer and the laying on of hands, set Paul and Barnabas apart to a special mission in the gospel. Jesus had said, "The harvest is plentiful, but the laborers are few; therefore beseech the Lord of the harvest to send out laborers into His harvest" (Luke 10:2). So, led by the prophets and teachers, the church was fasting (Acts 13:2) and offering special prayer concerning laborers for the harvest in obedience to Jesus' instruction. Thus, this is the first organized church missionary outreach recorded in Acts. It is a critical turning point in Christian church history. Until this time, missionary expansion was due to persecution or individual desire. But here, for the first time, a local assembly sought to be involved in praying for laborers for the harvest while ministering to the Lord and fasting.

Both the divine and human involvement in sending out Paul and Barnabas are beautifully woven together in these few verses. The Holy Spirit responded by means of a prophetic utterance: "Set apart for Me Barnabas and Saul for the work to which I have called them" (Acts 13:2). So, the Holy Spirit called and sent out the two men—the divine initiative. By ministering to the Lord and fasting, the local Christians became an active and intimate part of Paul and Barnabas's sending out by the Holy Spirit—the human initiative.

In obedience to the Holy Spirit's command to set Paul and Barnabas apart, the church prayed, fasted, and laid hands on them. They then released them to the new work of evangelizing the Gentiles (Acts 14:27; 15:3,12). The text suggests that the prophets and teachers (Simeon, Lucius, and Manaen), took the lead throughout this event. But from Acts 14:26, where it says, "they sailed to Antioch from which they had been commended," it is evident that the whole church commended Paul and Barnabas to God for the work. Later, Paul and Barnabas reported their success to the whole church: "And when they had arrived and gathered the church together, they began to report all things that God had done with them" (Acts 14:27). The farewell ceremony for the two departing messengers of the gospel (cf. Acts 14:23) involved fasting, praying, and the laying on of hands.

Luke does not explain the significance of the laying on of hands in this instance. But as in Acts 6:1-6, the context involves setting apart select men in the church for a special task (in v. 2, the Greek word *aphorizō* is used, meaning to set apart). So, by the laying on of hands (probably the hands of the other prophets and teachers) the church set Paul and Barnabas apart, bestowed its blessing, and commissioned them for the special work that the Holy Spirit called them to in response to their prayers.

According to 1 Timothy 5:22, the laying on of hands in appointment establishes a partnership between two parties. There is a sense in which the one (or ones) who appoints shares in the failure or success of the one appointed. Also, the one set apart has some accountability toward those who placed their hands on him. Thus, the laying on of hands creates a deeper sense of responsibility, accountability, and fellowship between the parties involved.

10. Lawrence R. Eyres, *The Elders of the Church* (Philadelphia: Presbyterian and Reformed, 1975), p. 51.

Chapter 15

1. Neil Summerton, *A Noble Task: Eldership and Ministry in the Local Church,* 2nd ed. (Carlisle: Paternoster, 1994), p. 102.
2. Ibid., pp. 102,103.

Scripture Index

Old Testament

Romans

1 Corinthians

2 Corinthians

2 Timothy

Titus

Philemon

Hebrews

Author Index

General Index